"There is no doubt that the fall of Jerusalem and the exile in the sixth century BCE were of pivotal importance for the history, literature, and theology of biblical Israel. In *Jerusalem Burning*, Robert Canfield brings the events, stories, and personages of the time to life for interested readers. In an informed and highly readable overview, he provides a view of and beyond the disaster that is as timely as it is engaging."

—**Jill Middlemas**
Associate professor of biblical theology and Abrahamic religions, University of Copenhagen

"In this daring and erudite study of the Babylonian destruction of Jerusalem in 587 BCE, Robert Canfield brings clarity to the process of meaning-making and moral imagination in biblical texts grappling with individual and community suffering."

—**Louis Stulman**
Professor of religious studies, University of Findlay

"Robert Canfield develops a rich and absorbing cultural-historical narrative of the fall of Jerusalem that is meant to help us explore how such a trauma inspired—required?—a distinctively new religious understanding. While the proximate causes were clear enough—one king betrayed another—Canfield has a deeper interest: making sense of God's love in light of tragedy. This is still important today. So, alas, is the great cost of ignoring warnings of impending disaster."

—**Paul K. Wason**
Senior director, Culture and Global Perspectives, John Templeton Foundation

"By carefully navigating through historical criticism of biblical texts, uncertainty of dates, and divergent interpretations of archeological evidence, this book skillfully analyses a watershed moment in the biblical history: the destruction of Jerusalem in 587 BC carried out by Nebuchadnezzar, the king of Babylon. *Jerusalem Burning* is an indispensable book for students and scholars of biblical studies, archeology of religion, and religious studies broadly construed."

—**Ashok Kumar Mocherla**
Yang Visiting Scholar, Harvard Divinity School

"*Jerusalem Burning* tells the story of how the Israelites made sense of their plight following the Babylonian attack on Jerusalem and how they came to understand their demise as an act of God's love. With a detailed presentation of events, this brilliant book will leave the readers to ponder its relevance to the world that we live in today."

—**Lihong Shi**
Associate professor of anthropology, Case Western Reserve University

"*Jerusalem Burning* is an elegantly written and expertly constructed analysis of the meaning and significance of a most terrifying event, the destruction of Jerusalem in the year 587 BCE by the armies of Nebuchadnezzar. This book should interest general readers and those interested in the history of religions, and it is a valuable resource for adoption to the courses on comparative religion and the anthropology of religion in colleges and universities."

—**M. Nazif Shahrani**
Professor emeritus of anthropology, Middle Eastern, and Central Asian studies, Indiana University

"Infused with knowledge and wisdom gained from a lifetime spent in the study of the biblical text, combined with years of anthropological research and university instruction, *Jerusalem Burning* is an invitation to look deeply into the impact of the destruction of Jerusalem in 587 BC and the exile of its people to Babylon. I highly recommend this refreshing look at how a people came to make sense of their circumstances and find hope in the midst of great loss."

—**Katherine M. Johnson**
Author of *Lectio Divina Catholic Prayer Journal Series*

"Robert Canfield's gift for storytelling and meticulous research brings this history to life, and his use of textual, linguistic, and cultural sources illuminates this history. His explanations of these source materials are crucial, especially for the non-specialist reader. It places a society's experiences and ideologies in their historical reality: what they shared with their neighbors, what made them distinctive, how they interpreted society-altering events, and the lessons they took from the violence and upheaval they experienced."

—**Laura Cochran**
Professor of anthropology, Central Michigan University

# JERUSALEM BURNING

OTHER BOOKS BY ROBERT L CANFIELD

*Walking Blind and Other Essays on Biblical Texts*

*Faction and Conversion in a Plural Society: Religious Alignments in the Hindu Kush*

EDITED BOOKS

*Ethnicity, Authority, and Power in Central Asia: New Games Great and Small* (Co-edited with Gabriele Paleczek)

*Turko-Persia in Historical Perspective* (Editor)

*Afghanistan and the Soviet Union: Collision and Transformation* (Co-edited with Milan Hauner)

*Revolutions and Rebellions in Afghanistan* (Co-edited with Nazif Shahrani)

# JERUSALEM BURNING

The Terror and Promise of the "Wrath of Love"

ROBERT L. CANFIELD

Foreword by Darrell Whiteman

CASCADE *Books* · Eugene, Oregon

JERUSALEM BURNING
The Terror and Promise of the "Wrath of Love"

Copyright © 2024 Robert L. Canfield. All rights reserved. Except for brief quotations in critical publications or reviews, no part of this book may be reproduced in any manner without prior written permission from the publisher. Write: Permissions, Wipf and Stock Publishers, 199 W. 8th Ave., Suite 3, Eugene, OR 97401.

Cascade Books
An Imprint of Wipf and Stock Publishers
199 W. 8th Ave., Suite 3
Eugene, OR 97401

www.wipfandstock.com

PAPERBACK ISBN: 978-1-6667-7443-6
HARDCOVER ISBN: 978-1-6667-7444-3
EBOOK ISBN: 978-1-6667-7445-0

*Cataloguing-in-Publication data:*

Names: Canfield, Robert L. (Robert Leroy) [author]. | Whiteman, Darrell L. [foreword writer].

Title: Jerusalem burning : the terror and promise of the "wrath of love" / Robert L. Canfield ; with a foreword by Darrell Whiteman.

Description: Eugene, OR: Cascade Books, 2024 | Includes bibliographical references and index.

Identifiers: ISBN 978-1-6667-7443-6 (paperback) | ISBN 978-1-6667-7444-3 (hardcover) | ISBN 978-1-6667-7445-0 (ebook)

Subjects: LCSH: Jews—History—Babylonian captivity, 598–515 B.C. | Bible.—Old Testament—Criticism, interpretation, etc. | Exile (Punishment)—Biblical teaching. | Jews—Restoration. | Sociology, Biblical. | Ethnology in the Bible.

Classification: BS410 C36 2024 (paperback) | BS410 (ebook)

VERSION NUMBER 010224

Unmarked scripture quotations are taken from the HOLY BIBLE, NEW INTERNATIONAL VERSION®. THE HOLY BIBLE, NEW INTERNATIONAL VERSION®, NIV® Copyright © 1973, 1978, 1984, 2011 by Biblica, Inc.™ Used by permission. All rights reserved worldwide.

Quotations indicating NET come from the NEW ENGLISH TRANSLATION. Scripture quoted by permission. Copyright © 2005 by Biblical Studies Press, L.L.C. www.netbible.com. All rights reserved.

Quotations indicated NRSV are taken from the NEW REVISED STANDARD VERSION of the Bible, copyright 1989 by the Division of Christian Education by the National Council of the Churches of Christ in the USA and are used by permission. All rights reserved.

To the one who shared the journey with me for sixty-two years

What is remarkable about human beings, in distinction from other animals, is what we have done with our illusions—with our free imaginations.

MARSHALL HODGSON, *THE VENTURE OF ISLAM*, I, 159

The world is not given to us "on a plate," it is given to us as a creative task. It is impossible to banish morality from this picture. We work, using or failing to use our honesty, our courage, our truthful imagination, at the interpretation of what is present to us, as we of necessity shape it and "make something of it." We help it be. We work at the meeting point where we deal with a world which is other than ourselves.

IRIS MURDOCH, *THE SOVEREIGNTY OF GOOD*, 215

# Contents

*Illustrations* | ix
*Chronology of Events* | xi
*Foreword by Darrell Whiteman* | xix
*Preface* | xxiii
*Acknowledgments* | xxv

1. Event and Challenge | 1
2. Syria-Palestine in the Eighth Century BCE | 10
3. Hezekiah and Josiah | 22
4. The Deuteronomist Movement | 34
5. Throes of Change | 44
6. Jehoiakim's Nemesis | 53
7. The Prophet's Warnings | 60
8. Prophet in Babylon: Ezekiel | 70
9. Zedekiah | 85
10. On the Verge | 99
11. Collapse | 106
12. Chaotic Aftermath | 116
13. Struggle to Comprehend: The Problem of Understanding | 122
14. Cyrus and a New Prophet: Two New Actors | 135
15. New Community: Community in Formation | 147

**16** Learned Authorities | 156

**17** Moral Imagination in Social Practice | 164

*Appendix: Topics for Discussion* | 175
*Bibliography* | 181
*Biblical Citations Index* | 189
*General Index* | 195

# Illustrations

Trade Routes of Syria-Palestine | 11
Ancient Orient around 700 BCE | 13

# Chronology of Events

| DATES BCE | EVENTS IN NEAR EAST SIGNIFICANT FOR JUDAH AND ISRAEL | DATABLE EVENTS IN ISRAEL AND JUDAH | APPROXIMATE TIMES OF UNDATABLE EVENTS IN JUDAH |
|---|---|---|---|
| 732 | A new Neo-Assyrian king, Tiglath-Pileser III (r. 745–727 BC), arrives in Syria-Palestine. Subjects Damascus, all of Syria to Assyrian control. | | |
| 732 | | Hoshea appointed king of Israel by the Assyrians. | |
| ~732+ | | Prophets Hosea and Amos preach in Israel. | |
| 725 | | Hoshea broke from Assyria, tried to ally with Egypt. | |
| 724? | | Shalmaneser V king of Assyria (r. 726–722) attacked Israel. | |
| 722 | | Samaria falls; Sargon II (721–705 BC) dislocates the population of Israel. | Disciples of Hosea and Amos (if not the prophets themselves) flee to Judah. |
| 716 | | Hezekiah (r. 716–697) becomes king of Judah. | |

# Chronology of Events

| DATES BCE | EVENTS IN NEAR EAST SIGNIFICANT FOR JUDAH AND ISRAEL | DATABLE EVENTS IN ISRAEL AND JUDAH | APPROXIMATE TIMES OF UNDATABLE EVENTS IN JUDAH |
|---|---|---|---|
| ~740–700 | | Prophets Isaiah and Micah prophesy in Judah. | |
| 701 | | Sennacherib threatens Jerusalem; suddenly leaves. | The belief develops in Judah that Jerusalem will never be overtaken by alien armies. |
| 687–643 | | Manasseh is king of Judah. | |
| | | | |
| 640–609 | | Josiah is king of Judah. | Scroll that may have been an early edition of Deuteronomy was found in the temple. During Josiah's reign the historical works, Joshua, Judges, Samuel, Kings were drafted or possibly revised from earlier editions. |
| 627 | Ashurbanipal dies. Nabopolassar initiates a rebellion against Assyria. | Jeremiah is called to prophesy in Judah. | Early declarations of Jer (3:6—4:4). |
| ~615 | | Nahum prophesies against Assyria. | |
| ~640–609 | | Zephaniah and Habakkuk prophesy in Judah. | |
| 626–605 | Nabopolassar is king of Babylon, leads rebellion against the Assyrians. | | |
| 612 | Babylonians and Medes attack Nineveh, drive Assyrian army out; they flee to Haran in Syria. | | |

# Chronology of Events

| DATES BCE | EVENTS IN NEAR EAST SIGNIFICANT FOR JUDAH AND ISRAEL | DATABLE EVENTS IN ISRAEL AND JUDAH | APPROXIMATE TIMES OF UNDATABLE EVENTS IN JUDAH |
|---|---|---|---|
| 609 | Necho II brings army toward Syria to protect against Babylonian advance; in battle of Megiddo kills Josiah. | Josiah objects to Egyptian march through his territories and challenges Necho's army, is killed. | |
| 609b | Necho II proceeds up to Carchemish to place a force on west bank of Euphrates. | Jehoahaz (Shallum) is appointed Josiah's replacement by the elders in Jerusalem. | Jeremiah's message to Shallum 22:1–12. |
| 609 | Necho II returns to Judah, places a different king in Jerusalem: Jehoiakim. | Jehoiakim is made king of Judah, vassal of Necho. He at once uses his new status to aggrandize himself at the expense of his subjects. | Jeremiah challenges Jehoiakim openly for his selfishness. Jer 22:13–23. |
| 605 | Battle of Carchemish. Babylonians crush Egyptians. | | Jeremiah challenges the belief that Jerusalem will never be destroyed. Jer 26:1–24; 7:1—8:3. (Cf. 2 Kgs 18:17—19:27) Elders try to execute him. He may have been banished from the temple at this time. |
| July 605 | Nabopolassar dies; Nebuchadnezzar races to Babylon to claim the throne. | | |
| 604–601 | 604 Nebuchadnezzar destroys Ashkelon, which refused to pay dues to him. | 604 Jehoiakim, after a pause, pays dues to Nebuchadnezzar. In fear of Nebuchadnezzar Jehoiakim proclaims a fast. | Jeremiah denounces the fast and has a scroll of his critique of Judah read in the temple. Jer 36. |
| Dec 601– Jan 600 | Nebuchadnezzar's army attacks Egypt but is severely rebuffed. | | |

# Chronology of Events

| DATES BCE | EVENTS IN NEAR EAST SIGNIFICANT FOR JUDAH AND ISRAEL | DATABLE EVENTS IN ISRAEL AND JUDAH | APPROXIMATE TIMES OF UNDATABLE EVENTS IN JUDAH |
|---|---|---|---|
| 600 | | Jehoiakim breaks with Babylon, proposes alliance with Egypt. 2 Kgs 24:1. | |
| Nov 598– Mar 597 | | Nebuchadnezzar besieges Jerusalem. Jehoiakim disappears during the siege; Jehoiachin and his mother negotiate a surrender; Nebuchadnezzar replaces Jehoiachin with Zedekiah. | 2 Kgs 24:10–13; 2 Chr 36:6; Jer 22:24–30 speaks to Jehoiachin; predicts the future for those in Babylon vs those in Jerusalem. Statement on Good/bad figs is prediction of what will happen in Judah vs Babylon 24:10. He also sends a letter to the exiles. 29:1–32. |
| ?597 | | Zedekiah is king of Judah. | Plot against Jeremiah; threats to kill him if he does not stop prophesying against Judah. |
| ~596 | | Zedekiah convenes a conference to plan a region-wide rebellion against the Babylonians. Jeremiah pickets the convention, has an intense public debate with Hananiah. Jeremiah chapters 27 and 28. Also Jeremiah sends a letter to the exiles and Shemaiah sends a request that Jeremiah be punished in the stocks. Jer 29. | |

## Chronology of Events

| DATES BCE | EVENTS IN NEAR EAST SIGNIFICANT FOR JUDAH AND ISRAEL | DATABLE EVENTS IN ISRAEL AND JUDAH | APPROXIMATE TIMES OF UNDATABLE EVENTS IN JUDAH |
|---|---|---|---|
| July 31, 593 | Ezekiel, captive in Babylon, is called to be a prophet. Begins to tell his countrymen in captivity that there is no use hoping to return to Jerusalem. | | |
| 595–592 | Babylonians have to quell a rebellion among their own ranks; are distracted from Syria-Palestine. In 592 Pharaoh Psammitic II (r. 595–589 BC) takes a naval force up the coast of Syria-Palestine, beginning to extend his influence northward. | | |
| 589 | Pharaoh Psammitic II dies. | Upon the accession of a new Pharaoh Zedekiah sends delegation to Egypt to propose alliance, breaks with Babylonians. | 2 Kgs 25. Ezekiel predicts Zedekiah's gamble won't work. 17:15. |
| 589 | Nebuchadnezzar besieges Jerusalem. | Jerusalem is under siege for 18 [or 30?] months. | Zedekiah consults Jeremiah, is advised to capitulate. Jer 21. |
| ~598a | Egyptians feign a readiness to attack the Babylonians; Babylonians briefly leave off the siege; but soon return after Egyptians leave. | | The rich betray their slaves; set them free during the siege but when Babylonians leave, they demand they return. Jeremiah objects (Jer 34). |
| ~?598b | | Zedekiah consults Jeremiah for advice. Jer 37:1–3. | |
| 598c | | | Jeremiah tries to leave the city; is arrested, imprisoned. Jer 37:4–22. |

xv

## Chronology of Events

| DATES BCE | EVENTS IN NEAR EAST SIGNIFICANT FOR JUDAH AND ISRAEL | DATABLE EVENTS IN ISRAEL AND JUDAH | APPROXIMATE TIMES OF UNDATABLE EVENTS IN JUDAH |
|---|---|---|---|
| 598d | | | Jeremiah dropped into a cistern, saved by a eunuch in the court. Jer 38:1–13. |
| 598e | | Zedekiah consults Jeremiah a third time, gets the same answer. Jer 38:14–20. | |
| 598f | | | Jeremiah purchases land and promises that Judah will again be inhabited, a flourishing country. Jer 39:16b–18. |
| 598g | Ezekiel's wife dies in Babylon; he is required not to lament or grieve, as an object-lesson to his fellow exiles in Babylon of what the inhabitants of Jerusalem will experience. | | |
| July 587 | | Jerusalem collapses: army flees, is caught. | |
| Aug 587 | | Nebuzaradan comes to Jerusalem, organizes the pillaging of the city, Burns it. Takes many of the notables of the city to Nebuchadnezzar in Riblah (300 miles from Jerusalem), where they are all slaughtered. Then he organized the movement of many of the survivors of the attack into Babylon where they became servants of the empire. | |

## Chronology of Events

| DATES BCE | EVENTS IN NEAR EAST SIGNIFICANT FOR JUDAH AND ISRAEL | DATABLE EVENTS IN ISRAEL AND JUDAH | APPROXIMATE TIMES OF UNDATABLE EVENTS IN JUDAH |
|---|---|---|---|
| 586–539 | | Poetic laments are produced by the survivors of the attack, preserved in the book of Lamentations. | |
| 586–539 | | Period of Exile in Babylon; many people from Judah were living far from home in Babylonian lands where they reflected on all that had happened. | |
| 562 | King Jehoiachin is released from prison in Babylon. | | |
| 539–538 | Persian army of Cyrus possesses Babylon and takes over the reins of the Babylonian empire. | | |
| 516 | | Second temple is finished in Jerusalem. | |
| 458 | | Ezra arrives in Jerusalem. | |
| 445 | | Nehemiah arrives in Jerusalem. During the time he and Ezra are in the city they organize a general confession of the community to Yahweh. | |

# Foreword

As I began to leaf through the pages of Robert Canfield's manuscript of *Jerusalem Burning*, I wondered, "What can a socio-cultural anthropologist, with vast experience in Afghanistan, bring to ancient biblical texts dealing with the collapse and total destruction of the Holy City of Jerusalem at the hands of the Babylonians, led by King Nebuchadnezzar in 587 BCE?" I quickly discovered there was plenty to learn from this historic event, and many insights to apply to our broken world today.

Canfield, a preeminent scholar on social affairs in Afghanistan, sees anthropology as the science of history and has applied that lens to examine biblical texts and to piece together a fascinating story of how the Israelites made sense of their own history following the devastation of their beloved Jerusalem. He probes the Old Testament story with an eye for detail and the ethnographic skill of a good anthropologist by asking penetrating questions of the text. Like a good ethnographer, he gives us the social, political, and cultural context in which the total devastation of Jerusalem occurred in 587 BCE. In the aftermath for the next several hundred years the Israelites attempted to make sense out of this tragedy. How could Yahweh both love them and punish them at the same time? At first blush this seems like an oxymoron, but as you read through the following pages of Canfield's interpretation of the biblical text and discover how the story unfolds, you'll see that it was completely consistent.

All human beings in every culture, at every period of history have been created in the image of God, and yet we suffer from our own brokenness and the consequences of sin. As cultural creatures we must make meaning out of our existence; as social animals we desperately need to belong and to find a place in the world where we can feel at home. How do we explain and make sense out of so much in life that seems to go wrong?

# Foreword

The perennial question of why do bad things happen to good people is on the tongue of human beings in every culture.

As part of being created in the image of God, we have a social imagination that enables us to make sense out of events that seem inexplicable. We can't survive for long without meaning and purpose. Yuval Noah Harari notes that "humans think in stories, and we try to make sense of the world by telling stories." Every culture needs a narrative in order to make sense out of their history and this one for the Jews was developed at a low point in their history, following the burning of Jerusalem, and demonstrates the power of a metanarrative to bring hope that a better day is ahead.

This book reads like a good historical novel, but the difference is that it is not fiction. It draws on familiar Old Testament passages, especially the major and minor prophets, and weaves together a compelling story of how the Israelites made sense out of what they imagined could never happen—the total devastation of their Holy City, Jerusalem. Canfield's elegant prose on page after page will at times take your literary breath away. The depth of his insights and applications to our troubled world today made me wish that I had used my training as an anthropologist to make such insightful discoveries from the biblical text.

American anthropologist Clifford Geertz defines religion as a "system of symbols which acts to establish powerful, pervasive, and long-lasting moods in men by formulating conceptions of a general order of existence and clothing those conceptions with such an aura of factuality that the moods and motivations seem uniquely realistic." This seems to describe rather accurately what the Jews made of their devastating history by recognizing the presence of a personal God in human affairs. They came to understand that God's wrath was because of Yahweh's covenantal love for them. What God demanded of them, and of us today, is to act justly, to love mercy, and to walk humbly with our God (Mic 6:8).

The big story here is not that the Israelites tried to convince God to love them, but that God relentlessly pursued them even though, for their part, they had refused to give him the respect and reverence that he claimed as a right. What relevance does this story have for us in the twenty-first century, other than an interesting Bible story? Canfield warns us that, "beyond its interest as an example of the moral imagination in social practice, it should be instructive on how costly it can be for a community to ignore impending disaster until there is no escape. In fact, the closer

## Foreword

we get to some foreseeable events in our own time the more relevant this story becomes" (p. xxiv).

Darrell Whiteman<br>
Gig Harbor, WA<br>
May 10, 2023

# Preface

This work was inspired by the recent interest among anthropologists in the meanings of events and their consequences. Following the work of Marshall Sahlins and William Sewell, I take every event to have "a distinctive cultural signature"[1] and some events to be climactic, with radical consequences for societal relations and communal understanding.[2] This is a study of an event whose consequences induced a community to construct a distinctly novel religious understanding of themselves and their affairs.

I had intended this to be an article on how events influence human moral understandings and vice versa. I thought the article could be completed within a reasonable time span. Little did I know what I was in for. It turned out that the empirical material on which my argument was to be based required a deep dive into a body of writings and a morass of discussion and dispute that was far beyond my competence. The questions and controversies about specifics were older and more convoluted than I had dreamed. There was so much more to learn, so much more to examine, so much more to sort out. This work thus reflects a long, hemmed-in period when I was trapped in an ever-rising pile of books, articles, and essays about details that were necessary for me to understand if they were ever to be used in my argument. The release of this book is a desperate act of emancipation from the bog of detail that has entrapped me, held me captive for many years.

Even so, for me the issues have seemed worth the project. For all of us in the twenty-first century there are multiple lessons to be learned from this story. Beyond its interest as an example of the moral imagination in social practice, it should be instructive on how costly it can be for a community

---

1. Sahlins, *Islands of History*, xiii.
2. Sahlins, *Historical Metaphors*; Sahlins, *Apologies*; Sewell, *Logics of History*.

to ignore impending disaster until there is no escape. In fact, the closer we get to some foreseeable events in our own time the more relevant this story becomes.

# Acknowledgments

To THE MANY SCHOLARS who have done the close, careful, disciplined examination of biblical texts that make it possible for this novice to undertake a project like this, I have to say, "I am in awe of what you have done; thank you. I hope you are not too disappointed with this." To Daniel Stulac and Robert Vasholz I am indebted for thoughtful and extensive critical comments on an earlier draft of this work, and for bibliographic direction. To Katherine Mills Johnson and Joshua Berndt I extend my gratitude for extended comments on earlier drafts of this work. Also to Michael Jindra and Paul Wason for helpful suggestions; to Morgan Liu and Craig Scandrett-Leatherman for early encouragement; to Robert Lowes for his wise counsel and encouragement; to James Canfield for guidance and assistance on technical issues; and to Kim Canfield-Kackely for finding the illustrations. The term "Wrath of Love" has been purloined from Louis Stulman's *Jeremiah*. Finally, thank you, Rita, for the grace, patience, and faithfulness that gave me courage.

# 1

# Event and Challenge

## The Attack

IN 587 BCE A Babylonian army led by its king, Nebuchadnezzar, after a siege of at least eighteen months, broke into the city of Jerusalem, pillaged it, slaughtered many of its leaders, set its great mansions on fire, broke down its defensive walls, and forced many of those who survived to set out on a journey of several weeks to Babylon, where they would become servants of the Chaldean Empire.[1] Along with the sacking of Jerusalem by the Romans in 70 CE and the Holocaust of World War II, the Babylonian attack on Jerusalem was among the most crushing moments in Jewish history.[2] For those who survived the attack it challenged their capacities to understand what happened, for despite numerous warnings, many of them were unprepared for what actually took place. For more than a year they had suffered starvation and thirst, and in the period of a few weeks witnessed the slaughter of their leaders, the wrecking and burning of their homes and their city, and

---

1. This was a Neo-Babylonian force. The Neo-Babylonian period extended from 612 to 539 BCE.

2. Dates of events in the Hebrew Bible can be referenced in two ways: according to the Hebrew calendar, which began in autumn, or the Babylonian calendar, which began in spring. Thus, the collapse of Jerusalem can be dated in either 587 or 586 BCE. I here follow dates as they are used by most experts (cf. Albertz, *Israel in Exile*, 78–81). However, recent geomagnetic studies seem to indicate that the attack took place in 586 (Vaknin et al., "Reconstructing"). The significance of this remains to be absorbed into the current literature.

their displacement into an alien land to serve a gentile nation. Traumatized, it was not easy at first for the survivors to make sense of what they had been through. The certainties they had lived by no longer applied. Many of them wondered how they had come to such a state.

Eventually many of these Israelites came to believe that the disaster they had suffered had been an act of their god Yahweh because they had been worshipping other gods and had persistently ignored Yahweh's commandments.[3] And moreover, they decided that Yahweh's violent disruption of their lives in this attack was an act of love. I suppose that they came to such a belief only after some discussion and debate. It is evident that there were among these folks some who had been respectful of Yahweh's claims all along, and no one could have missed the urgent appeals and remonstrations of certain prophets who had insisted on warning them and challenging their leaders, even down to the last minute before everything collapsed. And yet the preponderance of the survivors had commonly practiced forms of worship declaimed by the prophets of Yahweh. The prophet Jeremiah had been challenging their ways of life in Jerusalem for years, and in Babylon the prophet Ezekiel was declaring to his fellow refugees that Jerusalem would be destroyed; nothing worth coming back to would remain, he said. And these two prophets were but the most current of a long train of prophets who had been warning of a terrible moment of Yahweh's wrath for Judah's citizens if they continued their offensive practices.

The problem for me as I approach my question about the moral understanding of the Judahites is that the survivors of the attack actually had what would seem to be a clear-eyed understanding of why the Babylonians had attacked the city. Their king, Zedekiah, had sworn a promise of fealty to Nebuchadnezzar, the new hegemon of the Near East, but then Zedekiah secretly sought Pharaoh's help to escape the Babylonian conqueror's demands on his treasury. That brought down on himself and his country the full force of Nebuchadnezzar's fury. This was clearly the reason their society had come to such a complete and humiliating demise. But the Judahites also believed in malign spirits and other deities that might have brought about this disaster. So they had reason to wonder what spiritual forces could have also been operative in this affair. The belief that Yahweh had brought about the demise of their society was not the only possible way they might have attributed the cause to spiritual forces. The Israelites had for generations

---

3. I use the term "Israelite" to refer to the people in both the kingdoms, Israel and Judah.

## Event and Challenge

been worshipping various gods as well as using magical devices in their attempts to cope with the challenges of living in the world. The gods they had worshipped included the deities they had learned about from their neighbors: Canaanite, Egyptian, and Assyrian gods. From among all the deities they had solicited the Israelites decided that it had been the ancient god of their ancestors, Yahweh, who had willed it. Why did the surviving community of Judahites come to believe that Yahweh—this god and no other—had been the source of the disaster?

They had two explanations for how their great city had come to ruin. Without sensing a contradiction, they knew that it had been brought down by Nebuchadnezzar's wrath for being betrayed, an earthly-materialistic explanation; and they also embraced a spiritual explanation: that Yahweh had wanted this to happen because they had persistently rejected his claims on their lives. Here is the way the writer of the book of Chronicles explained it.

> Zedekiah ... did evil in the eyes of the LORD his God and did not humble himself before Jeremiah the prophet. ... He also rebelled against King Nebuchadnezzar. ... He became stiff-necked and hardened his heart and would not turn to the LORD. ... Furthermore, all the leaders of the priests and the people became more and more unfaithful, following all the detestable practices of the nations and defiling the temple of the LORD, which he had consecrated in Jerusalem. The LORD, the God of their ancestors, sent word to them through his messengers again and again, because he had pity on his people and on his dwelling place. But they mocked God's messengers, despised his words, and scoffed at his prophets until the wrath of the LORD was aroused against his people and there was no remedy. He brought up against them the king of the Babylonians, who killed their young men with the sword in the sanctuary, and did not spare young men or young women, the elderly or the infirm. God gave them all into the hands of Nebuchadnezzar. He carried to Babylon all the articles from the temple of God, both large and small, and the treasures of the LORD's temple and the treasures of the king and his officials. They set fire to God's temple and broke down the wall of Jerusalem; they burned all the palaces and destroyed everything of value there. He carried into exile to Babylon the remnant, who escaped from the sword, and they became servants to him and his successors.[4]

---

4. 2 Chr 36:11–20. In quotations from the Bible, I retain the form the LORD (small caps) for the divine name (YHVH), now usually believed to have been pronounced "Yahveh" (though usually written as Yahweh).

From one viewpoint the destruction of Jerusalem was an act of God: "The LORD . . . sent word . . . ; God gave them all into the hands. . . ." From another viewpoint it was human beings acting in the world: "the Babylonians . . . killed . . . did not spare . . . carried [objects] to Babylon . . . destroyed . . . set fire . . . ; carried [people] into exile. . . ." It was simultaneously an act of God and an act of a worldly military force.[5]

In this work I examine the way the surviving community of Israelites came to the certainty that Yahweh had been the moral-spiritual cause of the demise of their society. The god who was mentioned in the stories and legends they had retained from the past had willed this cruel, terrifying, and ruinous attack on their community because he was angry that they had persisted, despite many warnings, in worshipping other gods and flouting his commandments.

## The Sources

The best sources from which to construct an account of how the Israelites came to believe this are in the Bible. However one regards Jerusalem, it is the primary source for any serious examination of the affairs of the Israelite peoples in the ancient past. Here is how Robert Bellah puts it in his masterful work, *Religion in Human Evolution*: "What we have to work with is essentially the Hebrew Bible . . . with some archaeological evidence and some appearance of Israel in the archives of neighboring societies, but, in the end, it is the Bible that is the primary source. The problem is that after 200 years of intensive scholarship there is still only weak and contested consensus on such elementary facts as the dating of various biblical texts. . . ."[6]

The texts we have to examine are, for most of us, religious documents, but for the people who composed them, revised them, and edited them they were not religious documents any more than they were political or

---

5. The difference between explanations of material process and explanations of enduring significance are sometimes confused in debates about religious explanations. Collins (*The Language of God*) believes that God authored morality in humans; Cunningham (*Decoding the Language of God*) believes that behavioral genetics provides a sufficiently naturalistic explanation for human morality, obviating, he says, any need for the concept of God. For him, if something can be explained in naturalistic terms, then God had nothing to do with it. For Collins, in contrast, God works *in* nature and history; for him, what science discovers is merely the mechanisms of God's creation work, as God stands outside of and apart from his creation. This, I understand, was presumed by Newton.

6. Bellah, *Religion*, 283.

economic writings. They wrote about the world as they knew it. The unseen forces in their lives were a "real" part of their experience. Their experiences were of one piece, giving form to their understanding of who they were and what happened to them. As Goodman puts it, "the concept of 'religion' as a separate sphere has been a product of Western Christian culture since the Enlightenment and had no precise equivalent in the ancient world, since the relation of humans to the divine was fully integrated into the rest of life."[7]

As I proceed with my story of how this particular interpretive turn occurred among the exiles living in Babylon, I will discuss the respective issues entailed in using each text as it comes up in my story. We are fortunate that a vast body of translation, commentary, and interpretation has been done by biblical scholars over many generations, and I draw as I best can from that rich body of knowledge. But much remains contested. Martin Goodman notes that "uncertainty about the dating and process of composition of key biblical texts and about the significance of archaeological evidence from the biblical period has sustained remarkably divergent interpretations of the historicity of these narratives."[8] I am obliged, in producing this story, to negotiate through the cloud of competing views and methods that have been deployed in the critical examination of the Bible. This story is my own best attempts to make sense of the texts and the critical writings that have been produced about them.[9] If I miss or gloss over certain insights important to the experts, I can only claim that, while I have sought to respect their work, my questions may be different from theirs, and my methods of inquiry and demonstration likewise different from theirs.

It is fair to say at the beginning that one approach to the Bible is by its nature inimical to my task, as it takes an essentially skeptical view of what the Bible declares. Historical criticism seeks to explain phenomena ascribed to Yahweh in biblical texts in naturalistic terms. It disallows at the outset the influence of a divine force in human affairs.[10] Walter Bruegge-

---

7. Goodman, *History of Judaism*, xxviii.

8. Goodman, *History of Judaism*, xxix.

9. The warning of one notable member of the biblical studies community reveals how much is open to speculation in the interpretation of the biblical texts: "Because of the paucity of external evidence and the high number and complexity of internal exegetical and historical data the discussions seem to be influenced by unconscious prejudices and ideological limits, which are difficult to clarify" (quoted in Albertz, "Open Mindedness," 2).

10. John J. Collins describes the principles of the historical critical approach to the

mann describes this viewpoint as "deeply wrongheaded." It seeks to find in the ancient texts "what they did not intend to deliver."[11] Jon Levenson accuses historical criticism of arrogating to itself greater insight into the lives of people in the ancient world than those folks had themselves. Historical critics, he says, claim to have

> a definitive insight, not empirically derived, into the meaning of things, even things that they have never directly experienced.... They assume that the observer's observation [i.e., their own] is truer than the practitioners' [ancient Israelite] practice.... [Their view] shifts the locus of truth from the practicing community to the non-practicing and unaffiliated individual.... [T]he real meaning of religious phenomena is available only to the outside observer.[12]

Historical criticism, that is, screens out of consideration the practical "reality" that the folks living in ancient times lived in. Brueggemann says, "The claim that 'God acts in history' is not compatible with our Enlightenment notions of control, reason, objectivity, and technique. Indeed, if one begins with the assumptions of modernity, history can only be thought of as a mere story of power, in which the god of the Bible can never make a significant appearance."[13] We cannot leave these folks without the humanity that must be recovered in the texts that they produced about themselves and their world.[14] When a psalmist sings to God, "You have made known to me the path of life; you will fill me with joy in your presence, with eternal

---

Bible to be: "(1) The principle of... methodological doubt... (2) The principle of analogy: historical knowledge is possible because all events are similar in principle... (the laws of nature in biblical times were the same as now). (3) The principle of correlations: the phenomena of history are inter-related and inter dependent and no event can be isolated from the sequence of historical cause and effect" (taken from Levenson, *The Hebrew Bible*, 119). The second and third principles in this list are indistinguishable from the central principles of modern geology.

11. Brueggemann, *Introduction*, 8.

12. Levenson, *Hebrew Bible*, 115. Levenson and Baruch Halpern (*The First Historians*, 4) both regard historical criticism as a kind of fundamentalism. Halpern (16) calls it a "delusion" for biblical scholars to believe that they could know history "just as one could know chemistry."

13. Brueggemann, "Like Fire," 74.

14. Sociologist Irving Zeitlin (*Ancient Judaism*, 120, 146) objects to the "traditio-historical" or "form-critical" (essentially positivist-empiricist) analyses of biblical texts, which he accuses of being "highly subjective and they tend to obliterate the factual materials contained in the narratives."

pleasures at your right hand," he is reacting to a compelling Presence in his experience, a presence that historical criticism essentially denies.[15] Transcendent values of the sort that historical critics would discount are the reality of life for this psalmist, and for the people I want to understand.[16] In the end, suggests Brueggemann, the writings of the ancient Israelites must be read as testimony whose validity has to be received, like the voices that come from the holocaust; it "requires a wholesale break with all positivistic epistemology." It begins "at a different place, and so ends up with a different sort of certitude."[17]

If we are to understand the people who composed these texts we must grant them the transcendent "realities" that they experienced. As Clifford Geertz points out, all of us look at "the lives of others through lenses of our own grinding" so that we are biased by perceptions that seem "natural" to us, leaving us liable to viewing the opinions of others as biased.[18] Walter Brueggemann notes that the "skepticism about the text in some scholarly circles is also an act of interpretive imagination."[19]

In a brilliant essay on the importance of understanding the moral worlds of others Professor Wendy James recommends that the task is to understand their "moral knowledge," a term that blends the emotional and the conceptual aspects of experience. If we are to know people as they are, we must see ourselves in them. We want, as philosopher Iris Murdoch puts it, to "inhabit" their lives. In fact, Murdoch avers, we human beings all live in a common moral world. If we can see courage, generosity, humility, and pride in others—even if they practice customs radically unlike our own—we are acknowledging that they and we live in comparable moral worlds.[20]

---

15. Ps 16:11.

16. It seems crucial to me to grant the salience, even the reality, of what we are used to calling transcendent "values" in shaping the affairs of human beings. Even an avowed atheist, Ronald Dworkin, argues that for human beings "inherent, objective value permeates everything." "The universe and its creatures are awe-inspiring." And human life "has purpose and the universe order" so that people can have a "commitment to the independent reality of value" and respect a "force" in the universe that is "greater than we are." That reality, he believes, imbues human affairs with moral significance. None of us is free from a tendency to ascribe meanings to our lives that assume values too sublime to be examined critically. All of us approach situations with premises taken for granted as "natural," fundamental, unassailable. We are creatures of our own imaginative creativity.

17. Brueggemann, *Theology*, 119.

18. Geertz, "Anti Anti-Relativism."

19. Brueggemann, *Introduction*, 8.

20. Murdoch, *Sovereignty of Good*.

Mary Midgley puts the point succinctly: "Morally as well as physically, there is only one world. . . ."[21]

My task in this critical enterprise is to examine the moral knowledge of the Israelites in captivity so as to see people like myself and others in my world.[22] I want to appreciate the way transcendent values influenced their lives lest I flatten their essential humanity. Isaiah Berlin urges that this "inhabiting" of others' worlds is in any case crucial to historical understanding. "History . . . seeks to provide as complete an account as it can of what men do and suffer; to call them men [sic] is to ascribe to them values that we must be able to recognize as such. Otherwise, they are not men for us."[23]

If we understand religion as "an existential encounter with holy reality and as a responsive action of the human being existentially determined by the holy," then we seek to treat with respect the accounts of those who believed they had encountered "holy reality."[24] We want to listen to their ancient texts for what they say about their lives and affairs as they lived them. This is why it is fair, as sociologist Irving Zeitlin proposes, to practice the methodological rule that, "where biblical criticism is concerned . . . one ought not reject any statement in the scriptures which is not inherently impossible, nor contradicted by a more reliable source."[25] Baruch Halpern similarly argues for appreciating biblical texts in their own terms.[26] When people write down their experiences and opinions, he says, they are trying to communicate something about what is real to them. "History is referential," he says. "[H]istorians try to communicate information about phenomena extrinsic to the text." Accordingly, we as readers should search the materials before us for the "data its author meant the reader to extract."[27] We want to know "what they mean to say," he says.[28] He believes that the writers of these texts intended their work to be taken seriously by their readers. They knew, he says, that their task entailed a certain discipline in

---

21. Midgley, *Heart and Mind*, 74.
22. James, *Listening Ebony*, 152, 155.
23. Quoted in James, *Listening Ebony*, 148.
24. Quotation is by Gustav Mensching, cited in Albertz, *History of Israelite Religion*, 246n48.
25. Zeitlin, *A History*, 43.
26. Halpern, *First Historians*, xvii.
27. Halpern, *First Historians*, 11.
28. Halpern, *First Historians*, xvii, emphasis original.

what they were doing. They were writing "true" reports of their affairs as they knew them.[29]

What makes these texts worth the consideration of later generations is what they purport to reveal, something about the deity and the world of values that informed their experience. The theologian Otto Eissfeldt was "[w]eary of historicism and psychologism and relativism of the history-of-religions method, [because] people are longing for revelation and calling for a scientific treatment of the Bible which does justice to its claim to be the revelation of absolute values."[30] Rainer Albertz says, "Historians must be content with the statement that they are dealing with an entity which claims to be the revelation of the Word of God."[31]

So as to enter the worlds of the ancient Judahites I quote liberally from the texts they produced, to retain their vivid and earthy way of expressing their ideas in writing.

I take this whole affair as an example of the way human beings make sense of their lives, sometimes even to impute a historical moment with iconic significance.

---

29. Halpern, *First Historians*, 3.
30. Quoted in Albertz, *A History*, 8.
31. Albertz, *A History*, 12–17.

# 2

# Syria-Palestine in the Eighth Century BCE

## *The Age*

THE EVENTS OF INTEREST to my project took place between roughly 700 and 300 BCE, that is, a period that almost perfectly corresponds to what the German philosopher Karl Jaspers called the Axial Age (800–200 BCE).[1] It also fits a narrower timeframe that John Stuart Stuart-Glennie called a period of Moral Evolution, centering around 600–500 BCE. It was a time when important intellectual and religious traditions of thought were being expressed in the writings of people in several parts of the world. It seems to be the period in which the technology for recording thoughts in writing was becoming conventional among elites in many societies, enabling ideas to be discussed and promoted in a group of literate individuals in written form. The writings they were producing addressed issues of the sort that humans ponder: the problem of evil, the meaning and purpose of life, the problem of suffering, questions that have been discussed by human beings, I suppose, from time immemorial. In China the teachings of Confucius and Mencius were being circulated in a small community of literate experts engrossed in philosophical argumentation about the great questions. In India, Sanskritic texts, the Upanishads, were discussing the problems of consciousness, thought, and knowledge in reaction against the

---

1. Jaspers, *The Future of Mankind*.

preoccupation of religious specialists with the most efficacious mantras to be recited. In Iran Zoroaster was breaking with traditional Iranian beliefs by teaching that people should struggle for good against evil, maintain a positive-constructive mind, use a vocabulary of good words, and practice good deeds. In Greece Homer was writing epic poetry, and Plato was recording his dialogues with Socrates as a grand tradition of philosophical enquiry was taking form. And in Israel, the locus of my project, significant transformations in thought were taking place.[2]

## Geopolitical Context of Israelite Affairs

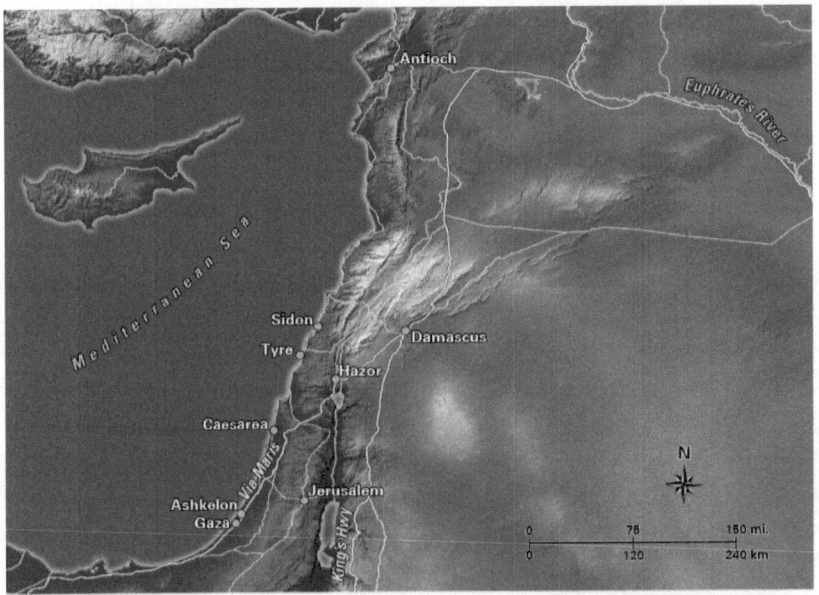

The region of "Hatti-Land" [Syria-Palestine] lies west and south of the Euphrates River to the Nile Valley. Source: Bible Odyssey. Used by permission.

In the period of the eighth and seventh centuries BCE the Israelite peoples were divided into two countries, the Northern Kingdom of Israel ("Ephraim," "Samaria") and the southern kingdom of Judah.[3] These

---

2. The most ambitious recent examination of the Axial Age is by Bellah (*Religion in Human Evolution*). Another recent re-examination of the topic is Baumard et al., "What Changed?"

3. To refer to the Northern Kingdom as Israel introduces an ambiguity, as the term can also mean "all Israel," that is, including Judah, so at points I will indicate which region or people the term refers to.

countries lay astride a fertile plateau running north and south whose spine, the Judean mountains, reach in the north over 1,200 meters. On the western side of these mountains the waters drain into the Mediterranean Sea and on the east side drain into the Jordan River which disgorges into the Dead Sea. Beyond the Jordan lay the marginally watered steppes of Transjordan, which gradually dry up toward the east until the land becomes desert.[4] The mountainous topography allows for three corridors of north-south traffic through the Israelite lands. The ancient Via Maris highway runs along the coastlands of the Mediterranean sea while the Kings Highway on the east side of the Jordan tracks along the margins of the rising topography. A less traveled pathway known as the Ridge Road stays on the high ground and passes near the mountain city of Jerusalem. These roadways connect in the north at Damascus with the east-west highway from Mesopotamia, and in the south they link into the pathways of the Nile Delta. It is along these corridors that a system of social, political, and economic interaction has pulsed for millennia, linking the more densely populated regions of Egypt in the south with the "lands between the rivers," Mesopotamia, in the northeast. Together these lands, from the Tigris to the Nile, have long constituted a single geopolitical region, deflected into a crescent shape by the necessity to avoid the parched lands of the Arabian desert. The region that connects the great population centers in Egypt with those of Mesopotamia was known to the Babylonians as "Hatti-land," a term that recalled an earlier time when a Hittite empire had dominated the region.[5] I call it Syria-Palestine.[6] In this intermediate zone, the great imperial forces that congealed in the ancient past in the populous regions of Mesopotamia and Egypt at opposite ends of this zone have jostled for dominance, each from its respective heartland. Sometimes Egypt arose in the west to advance its claims over the lessor principalities of Syria-Palestine—but rarely as far as Mesopotamia. More often, it was a Mesopotamian power that arose from the other end of the region to dominate the local peoples of Syria-Palestine, and even, sometimes, Egypt. The local chiefs ("kings") of the intermediate communities of Syria-Palestine were forced to adjust to the geopolitical currents of their times, sometimes to play off the

---

4. Called the Syrian Desert on some maps.

5. Technically the land of Canaan as such was never under the Hittites, whose control never extended south of Byblos, the lands to the south during Hittite times being dominated by Egypt until roughly 1200 BCE.

6. The region includes Phoenicia, the Levant, and Syria (i.e., west of the Euphrates).

opposing powers against each other. In any case, the informal ways of life of the dominant powers over Syria-Palestine at any one time, whether Egyptian or Mesopotamian, tended to influence the styles of dress, forms of courtesy and etiquette, and religious practices of the subject communities in the region.

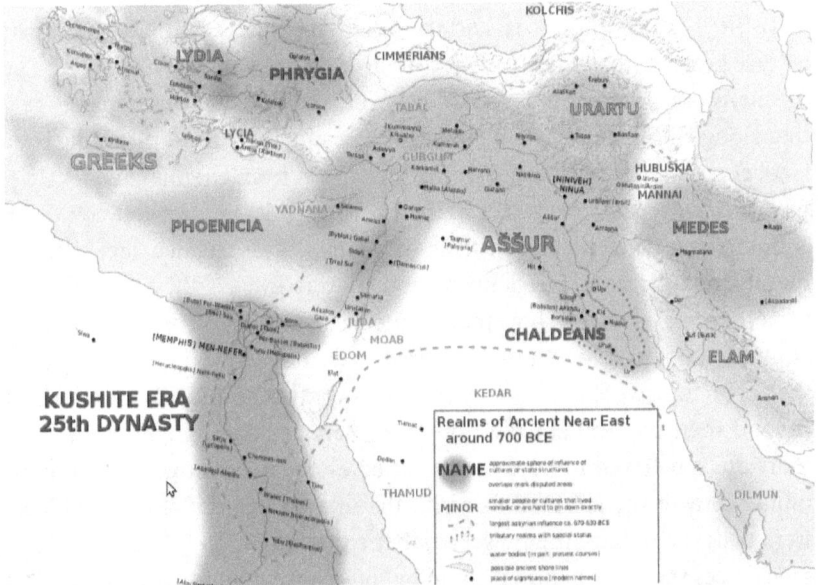

The Fertile Crescent

In the sixth century BCE a Neo-Assyrian empire based in Mesopotamia was dominant in this region through "a combination of horsemanship, of cruel terror, of moral earnestness, and of administrative efficiency."[7] Accordingly, the subject peoples tended to acquire the beliefs and rituals, patterns of dress, and conventions of courtesy and etiquette of the Assyrians, as well as their administrative language, Aramaic—not Accadian, the Assyrian language—which turned out to be the most lasting legacy of the Assyrian Empire, possibly because the alphabetic orthography of Aramaic, adapted from the Phoenicians, was easy for the subject peoples to learn. Aramaic continued to be the lingua franca of the Middle East for centuries; it was even spoken among some Assyrian Christians into the twenty-first century.

---

7. Hodgson, *Venture*, 111. This was the Neo-Assyrian empire that dominated the region from 911 to 609 BCE.

# JERUSALEM BURNING

## *The Tools of Efficacy*

Most of the peoples of Syria-Palestine lived by farming and shepherding animal stock. But typically they also sought the help of spirits and deities in their attempts to manage the urgent problems of their lives. For these people as well as for people everywhere, says Robert Bellah, "the world of daily life is never all there is, and the other [spiritual] realities that human culture give rise to cannot fail but overlap with the world of daily life."[8] For the many practical and inter-relational problems of living with others—getting along within a household, managing personal quarrels, disputing over land, competing for brides, ensuring protection from enemies and rivals—people deployed the resources of the unseen world as they best could. As circumstances and turns of events in peoples' lives seemed inexplicable, they turned to those mechanisms and powers even if they were unsure what those powers were, how they worked, or how they were best accessed.[9] No one could be sure that malign forces were not actively working against them, for they were buffeted in various ways that seemed capricious and beyond their control. For their physical maladies they sought cures from individuals believed to have secret remedies or special powers, or to have influence with the spiritual forces in the unseen world. Some individuals were believed to have the power to divine the future. To influence the unseen forces that they believed could be interrupting their lives they recited incantations at sacred places, sewed capsules of amulets consisting of "holy" words or images on their clothes or attached them to doorposts, wept ritually at holy gravesites, prayed to their ancestors, shaved and slashed their bodies to awaken the attention of the gods.[10] And they sacrificed objects of value, such as agricultural produce, animals, or, in situations of extreme distress, their own children.[11]

---

8. Bellah, *Religion*, xv.

9. Schniedewind (*How the Bible Became a Book*, 27) cites a spell published by R. K. Ritner (*Mechanics*, 100) that instructs the supplicant to "write the name Inmar, Inc on two male eggs. Regarding one, you are to cleanse yourself thoroughly; Then lick off the name, break it, and throw it away. Hold the other in your partially open right hand and show it to the sun at dawn. . . . Then speak the formula 7 times, crack the egg open, and swallow its contents." For examples of an incantation, see Canfield *Efficacy and Hierarchy*.

10. Cf. Isa 15:2–3.

11. The precise nature of the child sacrifice ritual is unclear.

# Syria-Palestine in the Eighth Century BCE

## *The Yahwist Heritage of the Israelites*

Some communities gave special attention and veneration to a particular deity among a panoply of deities believed able to help with their worldly problems.[12] A twelfth-century BCE amulet from the archaeological site Arslan Tash referred to the god Marduk as one who had a special relationship with a certain prince: "I alone, all you gods, have a covenant with him," it says.[13] A text in the Hurrian language at Ugarit dating even earlier refers to the Canaanite god "El of the Covenant."[14]

The name of the god that was given special importance among the ancient Israelites was written as YHWH, a name so sacred that in later generations the Israelites avoided pronouncing it; it is generally believed to have been pronounced "Yahweh."[15] Yahweh as a god essentially appears in the ancient writings of the Israelites, but there is no uncontested etymology, other than its connection with the ancient Semites.[16] Early Bronze Age records have Yahweh as one among several Canaanite gods along with, notably, El, Asherah, and Baal. Asherah was believed to be the consort of El, but she was also venerated by some Semites as the wife of Yahweh.[17]

---

12. For further examples see Rollston, *The Rise of Monotheism*.
13. Sperling, *An Arslan Tash Incantation*.
14. Mentioned in Cook, *Social Roots*, 27.
15. Many Jews to this day will not use the term.
16. Kaiser, *Exodus*; Hoffman, *In the Beginning*, 236.
17. Much of what we know about the mythology of the ancient Near East comes from the archaeological discovery of the ancient city of Ugarit in a mound at Ras Shamra (Syria). Ugarit flourished in the period 1400–1200 BCE as a nexus of trade and cultural interaction among the peoples of Mesopotamia, Syria-Canaan, and Egypt. Its library housed a busy correspondence with many other rulership of the Near East. The tales those materials tell provide much of what is known about the mythology of the times. Note that it was in this period that the Israelite exodus from Egypt may have been taking place. An archaeological discovery on Mount Ebal seems to indicate the Israelites, at least some of them, were able to write at about the time they entered Canaan, which would be roughly 1200 BCE. A folded lead tablet on which the name YHWH has been written was found among the debris from an excavation from a cultic site on Mount Ebal, the hill on which the Israelites are told to recite the curses they will experience if they disobey the commandments given by Yahweh. (Borschel-Dan, "Archaeologist Claims to Find Oldest Hebrew Text"; Zertal *The Altar on Mount Ebal*).

# Jerusalem Burning

## *Writing among the Early Israelites*

The problem of when the Israelites first began to write out their treaties and national stories and agreements has been much discussed. Obviously, the earliest forms of Israelite "literature," including the terms of the ancient covenant with Yahweh, were originally expressed verbally and retained in a community by repetition and memorization. Most of what people knew about was expressed in communal sayings, proverbs, poetry, ballads, songs, narratives—devices, that is, that enhanced memory. The earliest Israelite stories recorded in the Bible must have been told over many generations, and like the epics of Homer, in poetic form.

It is hard to know when the cherished sayings, poetry, and stories of the ancient past were first put down in writing. The earliest writing in the ancient Near East appeared after about 3400 BCE. Hammurabi's code was in use some time after 1800 BCE, indicating that by that time conventional ways of recording the spoken language were in existence. In that period, of course, reading and writing would have been skills acquired mainly by experts. Writing in that time was a specialty of the courts of kings. Scribes who worked in the service of kings would have recorded matters of interest to the court, such as debts, treaties, official agreements. The accidental discovery in 1928 of the Ugaritic texts at Ras Shamra in northwestern Syria revealed that writing was a useful tool of kings in the region after about 1400 BCE. In that community written messages were being exchanged among kings, documented in letters, agreements, treaties, formal transactions, and other matters of importance. They were stored on clay tablets and collected in the king's library at Ras Shamra. It was a century or two after this time that the events described in the book of Exodus would have taken place. Moses as a member of the upper class in Egypt would have been literate even if the Israelite people as a whole would not have been. Schniedewind states that writing in the early period of the monarchy was "the property of either the state or the temple, which guarded the secrets of writing."[18] There would have been scribal schools but the schools were not initially open to, or even desired by, the commoners. The skill would gradually become more common and broadly adopted among ordinary folks as middle classes developed. In that setting alternate grounds of influence and leverage were developing besides that of the kingship, enabling information and opinions to be more widely shared among the elite. This kind of transformation took

---

18. Schniedewind, *How the Bible Became*, 93.

place in the cities of the Near East in the eighth century BCE, each of them developing archives of records of interest to them, sometimes by wealthy individuals quite apart from the interest of the court.

Evidence that many ordinary people in the Israelite countries began to read and write appears in the proverbs attributed to Solomon at about this time.[19] Later, in the time of King Hezekiah (r. 716/15–687/86 or 697–642) scribes recorded affairs of interest to the court as a "projection of royal power and ideology, particularly as it related to the fall of the northern country of Israel and the survival of the House of David in Judah." Schniedewind believes that Hezekiah's literary projects "included historical work, the collections of mosaic and priestly traditions, and the writing down of the prophetic traditions, including those of Isaiah of Jerusalem, Micah, Amos, and Hosea."[20]

## *The Patriarchs*

The book of Genesis tells the story of how Yahweh interacted with the patriarchs, Abraham, Isaac, and Jacob, whose heirs would become known as the Israelites.[21] Abraham first appears in Genesis as Abram in the city of Ur of the Chaldees. He is directed by Yahweh to "[g]o out from your country, your relatives, and your father's household to the land that I will show you. Then I will make you into a great nation, and I will bless you, . . . and I will make your name great, . . . so that all the families of the earth may receive blessing through you."[22] In Yahweh's relationship to Abraham and his descendants there were obligations on both sides. Yahweh would be their god, to protect and guide them, and they were to honor him and obey him.

The story of the early formation of the Israelites as a people is told in the books of the Pentateuch. The book of Genesis tells the story of how the family of Jacob ("Israel"), grandson of Abraham, moved into Egypt to escape a famine and because they had discovered, to their surprise, that a long-lost son of Jacob, Joseph, was ruling Egypt on behalf of Pharaoh.

---

19. Some scholars believe the earliest text that preserves the features of Hebrew as of the twelfth century BCE is the Song of Deborah (Judg 5). https://biblicalhistoricalcontext.com/israelite-origins/israelite-origins-the-song-of-deborah/, accessed 03/13/2023.

20. Schniedewind, *How the Bible Became*, 76.

21. I am going to tell the biblical story as the authors of the texts understood it. I will not be overly concerned with issues such as historical reliability.

22. Gen 12:2–3. See also Gen 13:14–18; 14:17–24; 15:1–20.

The book of Exodus tells the story of how the Children of Israel became slaves in Egypt under a different pharaoh, and how under the leadership of Moses they were led out of Egypt into the Sinai desert. It was there that the Israelites had a decisive encounter with Yahweh. On the mountain of Sinai Yahweh gave Moses and the Israelites a code for living, which directed how he was to be honored and how they were to live in relationship with each other. This "law" was fundamental to the formation of the Israelite nation and is still critical to Jewish identity. Professor Jon Levenson says that "there is . . . no voice more central to Judaism than the voice heard on Mount Sinai."[23] That voice established for the Israelites the singular importance of Yahweh as their king, and obedience to the commandments of Yahweh as essential to pleasing him. He would be their god, their only god, and they were to be fully committed to him, and to him only: "You shall not bow down to [other gods] or serve them, for I, the Lord, your God, am a jealous God, responding to the transgression of fathers by dealing with children to the third and fourth generations of those who reject me, and showing covenant faithfulness to a thousand generations of those who love me and keep my commandments."[24] Yahweh could be a terrifying force for those who dismissed him, but he would also be a friend of those who feared him. Moses's directive to the Israelites was critical to their relationship to Yahweh: "The Lord is our God, the Lord is one! You must love the Lord your God with your whole mind, your whole being, and all your strength."[25]

After many years of wandering in the deserts of Sinai the Israelites were directed to move into the land of Canaan, for which Yahweh said to them, "I am going to send an angel before you to protect you as you journey and to bring you into the place that I have prepared. Take heed because of him, and obey his voice; do not rebel against him, for he will not pardon your transgressions, for my Name is in him. But if you diligently obey him and do all that I command, then I will be an enemy to your enemies, and . . . an adversary to your adversaries."[26]

These were the terms of Israel's special relationship to Yahweh. In the book of Exodus Yahweh refers to them as "my treasured possession out of

---

23. This statement appears in Bellah, *Religion*, 232.
24. Exod 20:4–6.
25. Deut 6:4–5.
26. Exod 23:20.

## Syria-Palestine in the Eighth Century BCE

all the peoples."[27] "Patriarchal religion" continued to be a kind of "substratum" among the Yahwist believers throughout Israelite history.[28]

The Israelites' relationship to Yahweh was marked in later generations by the oaths they pronounced in his name, and, especially after the monarchy was instituted, their incorporation of references to him in the names of their children: *Jeho*shaphat ("Yahweh has judged"), *Jeho*ram ("Yahweh is exalted"), *Jeho*ash ("Yahweh has given"). In such ways the Israelites acknowledged their official tie to Yahweh. In practice, however, they were not particularly committed to his commandments. In practice the Israelites, as they interacted with their neighbors, proved unreliable in fulfilling their obligations to Yahweh. From their neighbors they acquired other customs, including religious practices contrary to their obligations to Yahweh, namely the veneration of other gods and use of soothsayers and necromancy. The biblical texts indicate that the Children of Israel were worshipping a number of gods and deploying magical techniques such as necromancy. The tradition of Yahweh-worship became merely one of several ritual traditions that the Israelites practiced. Few worshipped him exclusively. We see this plurality of gods being worshipped in the Israelite community in the time of Joshua. In his farewell address he urged them,

> Now fear the LORD and serve him with all faithfulness. Throw away the gods your ancestors worshiped beyond the Euphrates River and in Egypt, and serve the LORD. But if serving the LORD seems undesirable to you, then choose for yourselves this day whom you will serve, whether the gods your ancestors served beyond the Euphrates, or the gods of the Amorites, in whose land you are living. But as for me and my household, we will serve the LORD.[29]

Much later when Jeroboam led a rebellion from Rehoboam, king of Judah, he deliberately turned his followers away from the worship of Yahweh. He wanted to keep his followers from journeying to Jerusalem to worship at the temple of Yahweh, so he set up idols, golden calves, for them to worship at two places in the lands of the northern tribes, Bethel and Dan, and said to them, "It is too much trouble for you to go up to Jerusalem. Look, Israel, here are your gods who brought you up from the land of Egypt."[30]

27. Exod 19:5.
28. Albertz, *History*, 29.
29. Josh 24:14–15 NET.
30. 1 Kgs 12:26–29 NET. See also 2 Kgs 22:17; 23:4–16; Mic 1:7; 5:13; 6:16; 2 Chr 13:9; Ps 78:58–62. Also Hosea and Amos, in many places.

## Jerusalem Burning

This was the setting in which the prophets of Yahweh arose among the Israelites after the time of Moses. They warned them that if Israel did not repent of their worship of other gods they would be liable to the wrath of Yahweh. In fact, many of these prophets were not well accepted by the people. Some of them were abused, some killed; even if they were respected, their advice and criticisms were rarely taken seriously.[31]

A few kings loyal to Yahweh, however, did arise at various times in Judah, and they were often aggressive in purging their communities of their acts of apostasy against Yahweh.[32] For instance, when King Hezekiah came to power he "eliminated the high places, smashed the sacred pillars to bits, and cut down the Asherah pole. He also demolished the bronze serpent that Moses had made, for up to that time the Israelites had been offering incense to it; it was called Nehushtan."[33] And the prophets who arose in the name of Yahweh after the formation of the monarchy typically spoke out against the worship of other gods. Micah, living in roughly the time of Hezekiah, prophesied against the idols being venerated during his time.[34]

> In that day, declares the LORD, "I will destroy your horses from among you and demolish your chariots. I will destroy the cities of your land and tear down all your strongholds. I will destroy your witchcraft and you will no longer cast spells. I will destroy your idols and your sacred stones from among you; you will no longer bow down to the work of your hands. I will uproot from among you your Asherah poles when I demolish your cities. I will take vengeance in anger and wrath on the nations that have not obeyed me."[35]

---

31. The persistence of the worship of other gods, for instance, throughout the history of the Israelites can be traced throughout their Scriptures. Cf. Judg 17:5; 18:14, 24, 30; 1 Sam 7:3; 19:13; 2 Sam 5:21; 7:5; 1 Kgs 9:8–9; 11:4–6; 12:26–33; 14:22–23; 18:20–40; 22:44–47; 2 Kgs 11:17–18; 12:4; 13:6; 15:24; 16:3, 10–19; 17:7–17, 30–41; 18:4; 21:18, 21; 23:4–24.

32. Stephen L. Cook (*Social Roots*) argues that the books of Hosea, Deuteronomy, Jeremiah, and Micah, and the Psalms of Asaph share a "family resemblance" to an "archaic Israelite religion" which he calls "Sinai theology." That moral perspective predated Hezekiah's reign (722–687 BCE), but throughout most of Israel's history [the worship of Yahweh] was a minority perspective, with a few exceptions, notably during the reigns of Hezekiah and Josiah (640–609 BCE). Sinai theological viewpoints, he says, eventually acquired a "dominant role in the final shaping of the Hebrew Bible" (267).

33. 2 Kgs 18:4.

34. Mic 1:7; 5:13; 6:16.

35. Mic 5:10–15.

Zephaniah said, "I will stretch out my hand against Judah and against all who live in Jerusalem. I will destroy every remnant of Baal worship in this place, the very names of the idolatrous priests—those who bow down on the roofs to worship the starry host, those who bow down and swear by the LORD and who also swear by Molek...."[36]

The prophetess Huldah, speaking to King Josiah almost a century later, warned that Yahweh was "about to bring disaster on this place and its residents, all the things in the scroll that the king of Judah has read... because they have abandoned me and offered sacrifices to other gods, angering me with all the idols they have made."[37]

It was from the cultural resources in the collective memory of the Israelites—their language, aphorisms, proverbs, historical memories, stories, and heroic tales of past events—that the survivors of the attack on their city drew in finding explanations for what they were experiencing. The critiques and warnings of the prophets of Yahweh now became useful in explaining how the refugees from the destroyed city had come to their debased condition far from home. Despite their initial confusion and disarray during and after the attack, they could not fail to recognize it as an act of Yahweh. The warnings and urgings of the Yahwistic prophets seemed to them the compelling explanation for what had happened to them. What Moses and the prophets had said—that Yahweh was a jealous god and could act against those who scorned his claims on their lives—provided the explanation they needed. Yahweh, they decided, had been the spiritual and moral force behind their calamity. The prophetic critique would "contribute substantially to a far-reaching reformulation of Yahweh religion" in later times.[38]

---

36. Zeph 1:4–6.
37. 2 Kgs 22:16–17 NET.
38. Albertz, *History*, 159.

# 3

# Hezekiah and Josiah

## *The Neo-Assyrian Invasion*

IN 732 BCE A Neo-Assyrian force invaded Syria-Palestine. The leader of this force, King Tiglath-Pileser III (r. 745–727 BCE) was coming to collect dues from the several kings of the region. At the border of the Northern Kingdom of Israel, he sent emissaries to demand that the king, Pekah, pay him the necessary tribute. Pekah immediately sought help from the king of Damascus, Rezin, who recognized that he would be next, so the two kings together invited Ahaz, king of Judah, to join them in resisting the Assyrian invader. Ahaz refused. Pekah and Rezin then decided to attack Ahaz, possibly to commandeer his wealth in order to pay off Tiglath-Pileser. But Ahaz appealed directly to Tiglath-Pileser for help.[1] In response, the Assyrian commander moved quickly to seize the lands on the Mediterranean coast, shutting off access to the sea for both Damascus and Israel. Then he took on each of them in turn. He attacked and crushed the army of Israel first, killing Pekah, and replacing him with a man named Hoshea who promised to be his vassal and pay the necessary annual tribute. He then turned north, seized Damascus, and executed its king, Rezin. Virtually all of the lands of Syria-Palestine, essentially down to the borderlands of Egypt, were now open to Assyrian claims.

---

1. 2 Kgs 16.

# Hezekiah and Josiah

## Assyria in Israelite Lands

The Assyrian grip on Syria-Palestine, however, was not secure for long. Seven years later (725 BCE) Hoshea, the appointed king of Israel, proved to be an unreliable vassal. He ceased paying his yearly tribute and privately solicited protection from the Egyptian pharaoh.[2] In response the Assyrian successor of Tiglath-Pileser, Shalmaneser V, invaded Israel and besieged its capital city, Samaria. The siege lasted for three years, and when all resistance in the starving city collapsed in 722 BCE, Shalmaneser set about to obliterate every sign that the kingdom of Israel had ever existed. He destroyed Samaria and then moved its citizens out of the area and distributed them into various places near his homeland in northern Mesopotamia. To replace them he imported peoples from various other parts of his empire.[3] This was the ignominious end of the northern Israelite country of Israel.[4]

Hoshea's perfidy was not the only rebellion in Syria-Palestine that Shalmaneser and his successors would have to deal with. In 720 BCE several cities along the Mediterranean coast refused to pay and were brutally forced to submit. And in 712 there was another rebellion; and again the Assyrians invaded the region to secure their writ on the area.

## Hezekiah

Throughout this period, ever since the time of Tiglath-Pileser, the southern kingdom of Judah was dutifully paying tribute. But shortly after the collapse of Israel a newly enthroned king in Judah, Hezekiah (r. 716–697 BCE)[5] determined to free himself of this onerous draw on his treasury and began to build a defensive infrastructure for the time when he could repel the Assyrian dues-collectors.[6] The moment came in 705 when the Assyrian king at the time, Sargon II, died. Urged by the Egyptians who aspired to a larger position in Syria-Palestine, Hezekiah, joined several other

---

2. Bloch-Smith, *Assyrians*; 2 Kgs 17:1–6.

3. This may have been accomplished by his successor Sargon II, as he seems to have died during the siege.

4. 2 Kgs 17:23–24.

5. He was coregent with his father 729–716, and again coregent with his son Manasseh 697–687.

6. Keimer, *Socioeconomic*.

principalities in Syria-Palestine in refusing to pay dues to the Assyrians.[7] In response, Sennacherib, successor of Sargon II, brought an army again into Syria-Palestine. He moved first against Lebanon and then against the coastal principalities of Sidon, Ashkelon, and Ekron.

Judah was next. When Sennacherib reached Jerusalem in 701 BCE, with his army stationed just outside the city gates he sent his field commander to formally and publicly demand tribute from Hezekiah. This was a test of the king's resolve.[8] Of course, he and his advisers were alarmed, for his position resembled that of the king of Israel when confronted by the Assyrian army two decades earlier. Could Jerusalem be besieged and eventually destroyed like Samaria? Could the people of Judah, like those of Israel, be dispersed into far-flung places also? Under the influence of the prophet Isaiah Hezekiah did nothing and prayed to Yahweh for protection.

The demise of Israel had an impact on the social consciousness of the citizens of Judah, as some of the refugees from that attack had fled to Judah to escape the conflict. Among those new immigrants were two prophets of Yahweh—or more likely the disciples of these prophets.[9] Hosea and Amos had warned the Israelites that they were breaking the commandments of Yahweh and were subject to his wrath, for the Israelites were tolerating the abuse of the weak in their communities. Hosea said that there was "neither faithfulness nor loyalty in the land, nor do they acknowledge God. There is only cursing, lying, murder, stealing, and adultery. They resort to violence and bloodshed."[10] The prophet Amos had objected that the rich in Israel "trample on the dirt-covered heads of the poor; they push the destitute away. A man and his father go to the same girl" and "[t]hey stretch out on clothing seized as collateral. . . ."[11] The prophets' criticisms of the people in Israel, as it happened, applied well to the similar practices among the people of Judah. So the warnings of Hosea and Amos to Israel, applied to the Judahites as well, reason for the people of Judah, faced with extinction, to wonder if Yahweh might allow their country to be destroyed also. Moreover, other prophets had been speaking out in Judah, denouncing

---

7. He apparently hoped that the relative inaccessibility of Judah and his newly built fortifications around Jerusalem would suffice to restrain the Assyrians from taking the costly venture of invading his mountainous perch, but he prepared for an assault, in case they would venture an invasion anyway.

8. Isa 36–37.

9. Albertz, *History*, 181–86.

10. Hos 4:1b–2.

11. Amos 2:7–8a NET.

their religious and social practices in the name of Yahweh. Micah had challenged the rich in Judah, who he said, "devise calamity as they lie in bed. As soon as morning dawns they carry out their plans, because they have the power to do so. They confiscate the fields they desire and seize the houses they want. They defraud people of their homes and deprive people of the land they have inherited."[12] Isaiah, friend of King Hezekiah, had also been predicting disaster for those in power because they were abusing the weak: "Woe [to] those who decree evil decrees; those who are always instituting unfair regulations, to keep the poor from getting fair treatment, and to deprive the oppressed among my people of justice, so they can steal what widows own, and loot what belongs to orphans."[13] These critiques of the common social practices in Judah would have seemed eminently relevant to the situation of Sennacherib's invasion of their country. Judah was at risk of being obliterated like its sister kingdom, Israel.

Sennacherib, for his part, had no doubts about what was going to happen. Fresh from victories elsewhere he reminded the city of what he could do, and pointedly challenged Hezekiah's hope that somehow his god Yahweh would save them. None of the gods of the other nations had successfully resisted him, he declared, and Hezekiah's god would be no different.

> In whom are you trusting, that you would dare to rebel against me? Look, you must be trusting in Egypt, that splintered reed staff. If someone leans on it for support, it punctures his hand and wounds him. That is what Pharaoh king of Egypt does to all who trust in him! Perhaps you will tell me, "We are trusting in the LORD our God." But Hezekiah is the one who eliminated his high places and altars and then told the people of Judah and Jerusalem, "You must worship at this altar." Now make a deal with my master the king of Assyria, and I will give you 2,000 horses, provided you can find enough riders for them. Certainly you will not refuse one of my master's minor officials and trust in Egypt for chariots and horsemen. Furthermore it was by the command of the LORD that I marched up against this land to destroy it. The LORD told me, "March up against this land and destroy it!"[14]

According to the book of Isaiah, Hezekiah held back from responding, encouraged by the prophet. Shortly after the moment when the Assyrian was pronouncing his challenge, something happened that no one

---

12. Mic 2:1–2 NET.
13. Isa 10:1–2 NET, note *a*.
14. Isa 36:5–10 NET.

could have foreseen. For reasons that seemed unclear, the threat collapsed. According to the text, his army began to fight among themselves, so that Sennacherib was forced to bring them home. The book of Isaiah says that he was later assassinated by his own sons. Judah was saved.[15]

Many people in Judah believed that their deliverance had been due to Yahweh's commitment to his holy city, a place that Yahweh himself had chosen and where Solomon had built the splendid temple to Yahweh. Yahweh was credited with saving Judah because of his temple. Together with the influence of the prophets who had warned against the worship of other gods, the deliverance of the city from Sennacherib provided impetus for Hezekiah to continue his project to purge Judah of all images associated with the veneration of other gods. But his program of purging from Judah the objects of worship outside of Jerusalem ended with his death, for his successor Manasseh immediately embraced the customs of the Assyrians, even to bring in more alien practices than before.[16] He had determined that cooperation with the Assyrians was wiser than opposing them.

After the passing of Hezekiah the prophecies of Hosea, Amos, Isaiah of Jerusalem, and Micah, which had seemed so relevant when the threat of destruction had been so real when the Assyrian army was at the gates of the city, made an enduring impression on the collective memory of the city.

## After Hezekiah

But the Assyrian invasion of Judah in 701 BCE weakened Judah politically and economically so that Manasseh's embrace of Assyrian cultural practices might have seemed necessary, at least wise. In any case, during the reign of Manasseh (r. 687–643 BCE) Assyrian customs were introduced into the court and even the temple.[17] He brought in "astronomical omens" associated with the sun-god Shamash, represented by images of horses and chariots. He fostered the worship of the female god Ishtar by the women, "to whom they turned in the minor distresses of everyday life...."[18] "Idolatrous priests" served a star cult, and the "Moloch cult" of child sacrifice

---

15. 2 Kgs 18:13–16.

16. Albertz (*History*, 180–186) believes that Hezekiah's reforms were influenced by the so-called "Book of the Covenant" (Exod 20:23—23:19).

17. He had shared the regency with his father 697–687.

18. Albertz, *History*, 194.

was resumed.[19] Manasseh also brought male and female prostitutes into the temple to provide sexual services as part of a fertility cult.[20] These cultic innovations were accepted mostly by the upper classes.

## *The Prophet Nahum*

In was in this period that a unique prophetic voice began to speak out in the name of Yahweh against the Assyrians. In the face of the new excitement about Assyrian customs and rituals, the prophet Nahum arose to consign the empire, even when it was at its zenith, to extinction.[21] The capital city Nineveh, the most impressive city of its day, would suffer the same fate as the Egyptian city of Thebes, he declared, which the Assyrians had only recently overrun and destroyed (663 BCE). "Your destruction is like an incurable wound; your demise is like a fatal injury. All who hear what has happened to you will clap their hands for joy, for no one ever escaped your endless cruelty!"[22]

Perhaps one reason Nahum's prophecies were written down and preserved, as they must have been soon after his time, was that they were demonstrably fulfilled. Assyria collapsed only a few years after it had reached its prime, validating Nahum's assertions that Yahweh was the god of history, the judge of kings and empires.[23] For the people of Judah bearing the oppressions of their masters, Nahum was declaring that Yahweh had the power to control the affairs of nations, and by implication those of their own country. He could be fierce, Nahum said. He was not easily aroused, but when angered he was capable of terrifying acts, for he controls the storms, the clouds, the dust, and the sea. He causes the mountains to shake. Also, he holds the wicked accountable. At the same time he cares for his own; he avenges them when they are oppressed. Nahum's preaching also offered hope to those in Judah who lamented the hardships of serving the Assyrians. He declared, "Never again will the wicked Assyrians invade you." And Yahweh will restore "the majesty of Jacob."[24] Nahum's vision of

---

19. Zeph 1:4; 2 Kgs 23:5.
20. Albertz, *History*, 189–95.
21. He specifically mentions the capture of Thebes in 664 BCE.
22. Nah 3:19 NET.
23. Some scholars believe Nahum was preaching even as Nineveh was being overrun by the Babylonians in 612 BCE.
24. Nah 1:1; 2:2.

Yahweh reinforced the ancient tradition of Yahweh-veneration among the people of Judah. And he predicted the eventual renewal of their country.

## *Problems in Assyria*

It was after a few decades that the Assyrian economy in Syria-Palestine began to falter. Problems were arising close to home which sapped their military strength. In 755 BCE the governor of the province of Babylon, Nabopolassar, organized a rebellion against his Assyrian masters. Essentially it was a quarrel with the governor of Nineveh (who happened to be his own brother), but he was joined by chiefs of some other subject peoples nearby—Elamites, Persians, Chaldeans, even immigrants from Canaan. His rebellion was put down through a huge effort by the Assyrian army, but the scale of the rebellion reflected a deep bitterness that had festered against the Assyrians from an earlier time when Sennacherib cruelly crushed the people of Babylon. The resentment remained, ready to burst out again on another day. And the Assyrian army was tired.

As the Assyrians were distracted by their problems close by, the Egyptians in the far west were taking advantage of their absence in Syria-Palestine to reach out to several cities along the Mediterranean coast, to offer them protection but also to collect tribute from them.[25] The lessor principalities of Syria-Palestine at this time also realized that, as no one from the empire was coming around to collect dues, they could ignore them.

## *Josiah*

It was during this time that changes were taking place in Judah that would prove momentous. For King Amon, son and successor of Manasseh, was assassinated after he had ruled for only two years. His death provided an opportunity for a group of Yahwists in the court to gain control of the administration of Judah. They placed Amon's son, Josiah (r. 640–609 BCE), a child only eight years old, on the throne. They protected, mentored, and tutored this young king in the Yahwist tradition until he reached adulthood.[26]

---

25. Albertz, *History*, 198.

26. As will become evident in the way I refer to affairs among the Israelite peoples, I assume that as in other societies the members of the community don't always agree on current issues, many of which entailed religious practices. There are, I assume, variations in the religious attitudes and practices of the religious leaders and those of the ordinary

What that would mean for the country of Judah was the introduction of significant reforms.

What kind of education did this young king get? The text implies that the scribe Shaphan and the high priest Hilkiah were involved in the king's education. For Josiah turned out to have a formative influence on the country, once he came into his majority. So, it can be helpful to speculate regarding what this young man learned from his mentors during his minority. He would have learned about Moses and the exodus, and of course about the formation of the country under the early kings, Saul, David, and Solomon. He would have been taught that Yahweh had promised his ancestor David that his issue, a descendant like himself, would rule over Israel in perpetuity. He would have learned about Jeroboam's rebellion after the death of Solomon, and the formation of the kingdom of Israel, and the practice of the northern tribes of worshipping at two sites in which national shrines to Baal had been set up in Israel. Josiah would have become familiar with the Psalms sung by the Levites in the temple. He knew about his great-grandfather Hezekiah, who had instituted Yahwist reforms in Judah, and he may have heard something about the prophets of judgment who had spoken out in earlier times. The stories he heard from his tutors would have given him a sense of what to expect in his own life and enabled him to visualize ways of responding to the challenges that he himself would face.[27] In any case, whatever he learned about the history of his people and the influence of Yahweh on their affairs manifestly shaped the way he would behave as king of Judah, once he reached his majority.

## The Scroll

The writer of Chronicles states that when Josiah was sixteen he sought the god of his ancestor David, and that when he was twenty-six he ordered the temple of Yahweh to be cleansed and refurbished.[28] That decision, as it would happen, would be fateful, for in the refurbishing process the high priest, Hilkiah, found a scroll (this would have been about 622 BCE), which was brought to Josiah and read to him. Scholars have debated whether it

---

people. As it will become clear here, leaders such as Kings Hezekiah and Josiah could honor Yahweh in public rituals without the ordinary populations making a serious commitment to them.

27. Cf. Ortner, *High Religion*, 14.
28. 2 Kgs 22:3; 2 Chr 34:1–3, 8.

was the book of Deuteronomy and how it came to be in the temple. Josiah's reaction suggests that it might well have been the book of Deuteronomy, or at least some version of it, which some believe could have been extant as early as the time of Hezekiah, if not before.[29] The scroll in any case is referred to in the book of Kings as "the book of the law" and "the book of the covenant."[30] As John Bright puts it, the scroll "was no new law, still less a document piously concocted for the occasion, but rather a homiletical collection of ancient laws that stemmed ultimately from the legal tradition of Israel's earliest period." It reflected the central message of the Torah, and indeed this is how the book presents itself, as the last words of Moses.[31]

Whether this scroll was deliberately intended to be a revolutionary document, as some commentators have proposed, the scroll had a dramatic effect on Josiah. The text says that after hearing it read to him he tore his clothes—a public declaration of alarm. Manifestly, he understood from this scroll that Yahweh had reason to be displeased with his country, because the idolatrous practices that were conventional among the Judahites at the time were specifically condemned in the book of Deuteronomy.[32] And the consequences could be dire, at least as they are described in this book:

> Today the LORD your God is commanding you to keep these statutes and ordinances, something you must do with all your heart and soul. Today you have declared the LORD to be your God, and that you will walk in his ways, keep his statutes, commandments, and ordinances, and obey him. And today the LORD has declared you to be his special people (as he already promised you) so you may keep all his commandments.[33]

However,

> if you ignore the LORD your God and are not careful to keep all his commandments and statutes . . . then all these curses will come

---

29. Miller and Hayes, *History*, 394.

30. 2 Kgs 22:8; 23:2. Some scholars take Deuteronomy to have been produced in Josiah's time and specifically written to direct corrections to be made in religious practices of the time (Albertz, *History*, 198–206).

31. Bright, *Jeremiah*, xlii.

32. 2 Kgs 22:11–13. There is a Moabite inscription that describes how their god Kemosh was angry with them and thus allowed their country to be overrun by the forces of Ephraim, a story that is similar to the story of the Israelites whose countries were destroyed by Yahweh (Rollston, *Rise*, 100n12).

33. Deut 26:16–19 NET. These terms of the covenant are stated succinctly in 13:5 and elsewhere in Deuteronomy.

upon you in full force: You will be cursed in the city and cursed in the field. Your basket and your mixing bowl will be cursed. Your children will be cursed, as well as the produce of your soil, the calves of your herds, and the lambs of your flocks.[34]

The passage continues with a list of more curses relating to many aspects of their lives so that Josiah had good reason to be struck with terror; no one could read it without the sense that in every conceivable way Yahweh would punish disobedience. The English text of the curses comes almost to 1,500 words.

No wonder that Josiah tore his clothes. The people of Judah were eminently vulnerable to the curses described in the Deuteronomic text, for they had been worshipping other gods as a usual practice, and they had paid no attention to Yahweh's commandments.

## *Huldah's Predictions*

Josiah sent for someone who could help understand what the scroll meant for him and his country. Someone with prophetic gifts was found, a woman named Huldah. She came from the Second (or New) Quarter of Jerusalem, a part of the city where refugees from the north had emigrated when the Assyrians invaded Israel in 722 BCE; it was a place where the disciples of Hosea and Amos may have settled after they had fled the Assyrian attack on Samaria.[35] But Huldah could provide no encouragement for the king. She told him that the disasters that were foretold in the scroll were about to come upon Judah. However, because of Josiah's devotion to Yahweh, he himself would not see them.[36]

## *Josiah's Reforms*

According to the text, Josiah set about to correct the practices offensive to Yahweh. He himself read the scroll aloud to his courtiers, and publicly declared his commitment to carry out the reforms necessary to fulfill the

---

34. Deut 28:15–44 NET. A similar list appears in Lev 26:14–26.

35. Cook, *Social Roots*, 61; Carr, *Holy*.

36. 2 Kgs 22:16–19. This passage, as already noted, reached its final form many years after the event and so, some believe, was given this form in order to carry forward the great didactic theme of the Deuteronomic series.

covenant; he would remove many traces of idolatrous practices in Jerusalem and its environs.[37]

- He brought out of the temple all the items used in the worship of Baal, of the worship of the Ugaritic god Asherah, and of the deity associated with "stars-of-the-sky" worship, and he burned them outside the city, distributing the ashes on the site of a wrecked shrine to Baal erected by Jeroboam.
- He executed the pagan priests who were offering sacrifices to deities on the high places in the area around Jerusalem.
- He removed from the temple a pole dedicated to the god Asherah and burned it, distributing the ashes across a public graveyard.
- He tore down the quarters of the cultic prostitutes in the temple, male and female, and where women were making weavings to be donated to Asherah.
- He ruined the high places in the country where sacrifices were being offered to various gods.
- He destroyed the hearth [Topheth] on which children were being sacrificed to the Ammonite god Molech.[38]
- He removed from the entrance of the temple the statues of horses used in venerating the sun god.
- He burned the chariots devoted to the sun god that had been placed in the temple.
- He tore down and crushed the altars that the kings before him had set up for their own ritual practice in the palace and in the palace courtyard, dumping what was left of them into the Kidron valley.
- He even ventured into the lands of Israel and wrecked and burned some of the sites where sacrifices had been made to Baal and other gods.[39]
- Moreover, he tried to shut down the conjuring up of spirits from the dead and other magical practices. He found and destroyed the

---

37. 2 Chr 34:3–7. The biblical texts ascribe these reforms to King Josiah. Some scholars regard them, on the other hand, as animated by the tradents who educated Josiah, given his young age (Albertz, *History*, 201).

38. Cross, *Child Sacrifice*.

39. 2 Chr 34:6–7. Lipschits, *Fall and Rise*, 136–37.

"personal idols"—"disgusting images," "detestable idols"—kept by some families.[40]

- One of the most memorable of his reforms was the reinstitution of the Passover, a formal and collective ritual aimed at reminding the citizens of Judah of the escape of their ancestors from Egypt, and thus of their fundamental bond to Yahweh, who had led them out. Through this national ritual the whole country was engaged in the re-institution of practices honoring Yahweh.

Aggressive as he was in purging his country from idolatrous activities, Josiah could not have foreseen what lay ahead.

---

40. Deut 18:9 (and elsewhere in the book); Jer 32:32–35.

# 4

# The Deuteronomist Movement

BIBLICAL SCHOLARS SEE IN these reform activities indications that a new movement in Judahite society was being animated by a group of reformers whom they call "Deuteronomists," for they were promoting reforms that accorded with the teachings in the book of Deuteronomy.[1]

The book of Deuteronomy presents itself as the last words of Moses to the Children of Israel before they entered the land of Canaan. Moses says to them,

> These are the commands, decrees, and laws the LORD your God directed me to teach you to observe in the land that you are crossing the Jordan to possess, so that you, your children and their children after them may fear the LORD your God as long as you live by keeping all his decrees and commands that I give you, and so that you may enjoy long life. Hear, Israel, and be careful to obey so that it may go well with you and that you may increase greatly in a land flowing with milk and honey, just as the LORD, the God of your ancestors, promised you.[2]

Yahweh's favor, as defined in this covenant, was conditional on whether the Children of Israel would "keep all [Yahweh's] decrees and commands."

Who these "Deuteronomists" were, appearing in the time of Josiah, can only be guessed. It has been proposed that they came from "the people of the land," that is, the folks who arose to avenge the death of Josiah's

1. Knight, *Deuteronomy*.
2. Deut 6:1–3.

father. At least, the movement seems to have grown out of the wider community.³ An influential element might have come from "the middle class land-owning farmers" and the military leaders who were allied with the royal family.⁴ These were the social elements who encouraged the king and the country broadly to take advantage of the situation, while the Assyrians were distracted at home, to reshape the orientation of Judah to fit the parochial interests of the middle class.⁵

The Deuteronomists are believed by some scholars to have had something to do with the production of the "scroll" that was found in the temple. They are believed to have at least produced and promoted the ideas taught in the book of Deuteronomy, notably chapters 5–26. Other scholars believe that "the discovery" of the scroll in the temple was a fabrication introduced into the book of Kings in order to give importance to the reforms instituted by Josiah.⁶ There is little doubt that the scroll preserved at least some version of what we now know as Deuteronomy.

To emphasize the significance of the covenant for the Children of Israel the Deuteronomists instituted a project to produce a series of historical books that described the way the covenantal relationship to Yahweh had worked out in the affairs of the Israelites after the time they entered Canaan.⁷ The books Joshua, Judges, Samuel, and Kings—at least an early version of them—may have been produced in this period of Josiah's rule. In producing these books, "the Deuteronomic history," they made use of various sources: legal corpora, archival records, court records, tales, historical narratives, chronicles, prophetic narratives, etc.⁸ The central concern of these writings was to show why the Northern Kingdom, Israel, had been destroyed: the people and the leaders had refused to live by the terms of the

---

3. 2 Kgs 21:24.

4. Albertz, *History*, 201. Some scholars have proposed that the book of Deuteronomy was produced earlier, in the time of Hezekiah, but Albertz (200–201) rejects this idea: "The eighteen years of his reign before 622 under the tutelage of Shaphan and Hilkiah are sufficient 'prelude' to the composition of a first version of Deuteronomy."

5. Albertz, *History*, 199.

6. Albertz, *History*, 197–231; he specifically connects Josiah's reforms with Deuteronomy 12–26.

7. The original concept of the relationship between Deuteronomy and the historical works was proposed by Martin Noth (*Deuteronomistic; History*). His concept has been much revised and emended subsequently (cf. Lipshits, *Fall and Rise*). Albertz, *History*, is an extensive reconsideration of this issue.

8. Alberts, *Israel*, 274.

covenant with Yahweh.[9] The story as produced by these Deuteronomists proceeded as far as the destruction of the country of Israel (2 Kgs 17) and concluded with a forceful statement of the reason for it:

> All this took place because the Israelites had sinned against the LORD their God.... They worshiped other gods and followed the practices of the nations the LORD had driven out before them, as well as the practices that the kings of Israel had introduced.... The LORD warned Israel and Judah through all his prophets and seers: "Turn from your evil ways. Observe my commands and decrees, in accordance with the entire Law that I commanded your ancestors to obey and that I delivered to you through my servants the prophets." But they would not listen.... So the LORD was very angry with Israel and removed them from his presence.[10]

This statement would have been the conclusion of the book of Kings as of the time of Josiah. The term "Judah" in the statement above was added later when other learned authorities, those living in exile after the destruction of Jerusalem, were describing the ignominious end of Judah, which they believed had taken place for essentially the same reasons.

## Prophetic Voices in Josiah's Time

Besides the Deuteronomists, or at least among them, there were individuals who promoted the importance of obeying Yahweh's commandments. These were the Yahwist prophets of Josiah's time. They arose to challenge the religious practices and moral failures of the people of Judah, reminding them of their obligations to Yahweh and warning that their idolatrous behavior and their persistent disregard for Yahweh's laws could bring about his wrath. It is not clear when the sayings and teachings of these prophets were written down, but it seems clear that the following prophets were active roughly in the period of Josiah's rule.

---

9. The prophets also referred to the Northern Kingdom as "Ephraim," referring to one of most prominent of the northern tribes, or "Samaria," the city that would in later times be the capital of the kingdom.

10. 2 Kgs 17:7–13, 41.

# The Deuteronomist Movement

## *Zephaniah*

The prophet Zephaniah may have been a distant cousin of Josiah, and probably was younger.[11] His name, "Yahweh has hidden," may refer to his parents' feelings about the situation at the time of his birth, for he was born when Manasseh was fostering Assyrian idolatrous customs.[12] The text of Zephaniah may have been edited to emphasize themes promoted by the Deuteronomists.[13] His prophetic message was similar to that of Huldah. Because of the worship of other gods Yahweh would punish Judah: "I will cut off from this place every remnant of Baal and the name of the idolatrous priests; those who bow down . . . to the host of the heavens; . . . and swear to the Lord, but also swear by Milcom; and . . . turn their backs on the Lord. . . ."[14]

The elite of the city were targeted by Zephaniah because they took "wealth . . . by violence and deceit."[15] The princes were "roaring lions, hungry wolves who devour their prey by morning." The prophets were proud and deceitful. Even the priests "defile what is holy."[16] Yahweh was therefore frustrated, says the prophet. "I thought, Surely the city will fear me, it will accept correction." But the truth was otherwise: they had no interest in God's laws.[17] A "great day" is coming, says the prophet, a "day of wrath, . . . distress and anguish, . . . ruin and devastation" when Yahweh would act to force his people to remember to honor him when they worship, reciting his name only.[18] He would humble the arrogant, show mercy to the vulnerable, honor the humble and the meek who "do no wrong" and utter no lies.[19] However, Zephaniah looks ahead to a time when, he says, the Israelite

---

11. Zeph 1:1.

12. *New Bible Dictionary*, 1268.

13. Albertz (*Israel*, 204–37) sees this work as one of four prophets whose writings were brought together in the period after the 587 BCE Babylonian attack on Jerusalem, the others being Amos, Hosea, and Micah; these works were extensively edited and joined together, says Albertz, for the benefit of the survivors of the attack on Jerusalem during the Babylonian exile period. See also Hadjiev, *Zephaniah*.

14. Zeph 1:4–6 NRSV.
15. Zeph 1:9 NET.
16. Zeph 3:3–4.
17. Zeph 3:7.
18. Zeph 3:9.
19. Zeph 3:11–12.

peoples will rejoice and be safe from their enemies because Yahweh will be with them.[20]

Whatever his audience thought about his prophecies, Zephaniah's warnings, along with Huldah's, could have fostered a sense in Judah that Yahweh was about to act against them for flouting his commandments. We can wonder if any folks in Judah had a foreboding about things to come.

## *Habakkuk*

Another prophet who may have lived in Josiah's time or shortly afterward was Habakkuk. He likewise foresaw a dark future ahead for Judah.[21] It has been suggested that the book of Habakkuk was redacted during the exile period, possibly to make it correspond to social conditions at another time. But as it stands it seems fitting to Josiah's times, especially given how soon the king's influence would be lost.[22] The book consists of a dialogue between Habakkuk and Yahweh about the sinful practices of the Judahites. Habakkuk complains about injustice and violence in the society, the intimidation of the innocent by the strong, and the perversion of the law. Why, he says, does Yahweh allow all this?[23] Yahweh responds that he has a solution: he is empowering the Babylonians to bring destruction to the land.[24]

Habakkuk was stunned. For Yahweh to use a gentile army, especially one so revolting as the Babylonians, was unthinkable. How could Yahweh deploy such a brutal and repugnant army against his own people? No, the prophet insists, the Babylonians are wicked and idolatrous, and they are cruel. Surely Yahweh would not bring such a people upon Judah?[25] Yahweh assures the prophet that he is in command of history and he enjoins Habakkuk to be patient. Those who long for a just world, he says, will in due

---

20. These verses, Zeph 3:14–20, are believed by some to be a later addition to the text. Hadjiev (*Zephaniah*, 335) is, however, not so sure: "This passage is closely linked to the preceding material both thematically and lexically and so would have fulfilled very well its function of a conclusion to the book of Zephaniah."

21. I here follow Albertz (*Israel*, 240) who believes most of the book of Habakkuk was "produced" during the exile even though the prophet himself was active as early as 605 BCE. This is earlier than many scholars place Habakkuk. The consensus is that he lived perhaps as late as the time of Zedekiah (597–587).

22. Albertz, *Israel*, 237–45.

23. Hab 1:3–4.

24. Hab 1:5–10.

25. Hab 1:13–15.

time see the unjust punished and the righteous rewarded. In the end, the whole earth will be speechless before Yahweh.[26] Left with such a scenario Habakkuk commits himself to wait for the calamity that he knows is coming, believing that Yahweh would enable him to endure it, even with joy. "When the fig tree does not bud, and there are no grapes on the vines; when the olive trees do not produce and the fields yield no crops; when the sheep disappear from the pen and there are no cattle in the stalls—I will rejoice because of the Lord; I will be happy because of the God who delivers me! The Sovereign Lord is my source of strength."[27]

Habakkuk like Nahum sees Yahweh as the god of history. The Babylonians were mere tools of Yahweh to bring judgment upon his people because of their apostasy. And yet Yahweh was still committed to his people. The prophet, in whatever form his presentations appeared, even before the later redactions, must have conveyed a message of relevance for the Judahites in his time. In its present form believers in any age can see in Habakkuk's discourse with Yahweh how manifestly relevant his problem was, for it is a universal problem: How could evil exist in the world when God is supposed to be just? But Yahweh's answer reassures Habakkuk that he can look forward to the judgment that was to come. Habakkuk and Nahum revealed to the Children of Israel that God, even in the dark moments, is still at work in history.[28]

## Joel

No one is sure when Joel's elegant and powerful book was written. Joel wrote in order to use a terrible attack of locusts on the lands of Judah as reason to call the people to dedicate themselves to Yahweh. And he promises that Yahweh had a plan for them, to restore their lands and prosper them when they repent. "Even now," declares the Lord, "return to me with all your heart, with fasting and weeping and mourning. Rend your heart and not your garments. Return to the Lord your God, for he is gracious and compassionate, slow to anger and abounding in love, and he relents from sending calamity. Who knows? He may turn and relent and leave behind a blessing—grain offerings and drink offerings for the Lord your God."[29]

26. Hab:3:2.
27. Hab 3:17–19a NET.
28. Albertz, *Israel*, 238–45.
29. Joel 2:12–15.

Joel predicts an invasion of a terrible force into Judah:

> Let all who live in the land tremble, for the day of the LORD is coming. It is close at hand—a day of darkness and gloom, a day of clouds and blackness. Like dawn spreading across the mountains a large and mighty army comes, such as never was in ancient times nor ever will be in ages to come. Before them fire devours, behind them a flame blazes. Before them the land is like the garden of Eden, behind them, a desert waste—nothing escapes them. They have the appearance of horses; they gallop along like cavalry. With a noise like that of chariots they leap over the mountaintops, like a crackling fire consuming stubble, like a mighty army drawn up for battle. At the sight of them, nations are in anguish; every face turns pale. They charge like warriors; they scale walls like soldiers. They all march in line, not swerving from their course. They do not jostle each other; each marches straight ahead. They plunge through defenses without breaking ranks. They rush upon the city; they run along the wall. They climb into the houses; like thieves they enter through the windows. Before them the earth shakes, the heavens tremble, the sun and moon are darkened, and the stars no longer shine. The LORD thunders at the head of his army; his forces are beyond number, and mighty is the army that obeys his command. The day of the LORD is great; it is dreadful. Who can endure it?[30]

Joel's prophecy of a coming day of the LORD is so vivid that he surely would have impressed his hearers, but it is hard to know when he lived and to what attack he was referring. Scholars have speculated that he could have uttered this prophecy well before the time of the Babylonian attack, possibly in the time of Hezekiah or Josiah, but others believe Joel could have lived after the attack. In any case, he prophesied about a time of restoration for Judah after a time of judgment.

> The LORD replied to them: "I am sending you grain, new wine and olive oil, enough to satisfy you fully; never again will I make you an object of scorn to the nations. I will drive the northern horde far from you. . . . Do not be afraid, land of Judah; be glad and rejoice. . . . [T]he pastures in the wilderness are becoming green. The trees are bearing their fruit; the fig tree and the vine yield their riches. Be glad, people of Zion, rejoice in the LORD your God, for he has given you the autumn rains because he is faithful. . . . The threshing floors will be filled with grain; the vats will overflow

---

30. Joel 2:1b–11.

with new wine and oil. I will repay you for the years the locusts have eaten.... You will have plenty to eat, until you are full, and you will praise the name of the LORD your God, who has worked wonders for you; never again will my people be shamed.[31]

What Joel said about the day of the Lord was quoted by the apostle Peter when he preached his first sermon on the Day of Pentecost.[32]

Joel's prophecy, I believe, would have impressed his audience even if some of his prophetic statements must have seemed fanciful. We can only note here that this powerful prophetic word was not forgotten, and the reference to a powerful army coming upon Judah would seem eminently relevant to what a later generation of the citizens of Judah would experience in 587 BCE.

The prophets who lived in Josiah's time, Huldah, Zephaniah, Habakkuk, and possibly Joel, as well of the earlier prophets Hosea, Amos, Micah and Isaiah, were concordant in their prophecies, for they presumed, if not always stated, that the people of Judah were subject to the obligations defined in the covenant with Yahweh. He would not abandon them, they said. But his favor was conditional. As the book of Deuteronomy stated, to have his goodwill they must obey his commandments: to worship him solely, keep his sabbaths, and practice his stipulated social requirements, honoring their parents, and refraining from murder, adultery, dishonesty, theft, and covetousness.

## Deuteronomist Thought Becomes Official

The fluorescence of Yahwism and the production of Yahwist writings in Josiah's time—which is manifest in his official inauguration of Yahwist rituals and in the numerous proclamations by the prophets, driven by the powerful influence of the Deuteronomists—indicates that Yahwism was becoming "the dominant ideology of the time," at least in the influential elements of the society.[33] It was during Josiah's regime that the Deuteronomists enjoyed the support of the crown and probably much of the society, for a coalition seemed to exist between the Jerusalem priests, the middle class of Judah, individual prophets, and the members of the royal family.[34]

31. Joel 2:19–27.
32. Joel 2:28–32a.
33. Lipschits, *Fall and Rise*, 288.
34. Albertz, *History*, 203.

Thus, the view that Yahweh should be worshipped and his standards of social behavior observed faithfully became the official, public position of the administration and the professional classes. "[T]hrough the involvement of influential circles within officialdom [the Deuteronomistic reform movement] gained a much wider influence and made more of an impact on society."[35] Yahwism was no longer a mere tradition of a few Israelite families, as it had been in previous times. It was now the official policy of the government and was embraced by the elite. Yahwism now provided the moral ground for justifying the actions or projects undertaken by the administration. It was now natural for officials to speak in the name of Yahweh, for individuals to invoke the name of Yahweh when swearing oaths, and for parents to give names to their children in deference to Yahweh. But whether the ordinary folks throughout the country intended to live in the fear of Yahweh was something else.[36] A point of view about how to interpret events in Judah was thus more or less in place once again in the discursive vocabulary of the Judahites by the end of Josiah's reign, to exist in the repertoire of presumptions and teachings taken for granted in the heritage of the community. It would be invoked in a later time. Whether these social practices would hold up in times when the society was tested by a disaster of inconceivable proportions remained to be seen. In reality idolatrous rituals remained in the community despite the policies of Josiah. Yahweh's rules for social interaction were apparently too onerous for many Judahites to apply to their everyday practices. The prophet Jeremiah, who began his ministry about this time, would later record his disappointment with how little Josiah's reforms had affected the consciousness and lifeways of the ordinary folks in Judah. People were still "committing adultery" with other gods, he lamented, and the ritual observances that were being performed under Josiah's leadership were not done "with all her heart, but only in pretense."[37] Jeremiah's comment was probably made after the world had

---

35. Albertz, *History*, 204.

36. Mark Smith (*Origins*, 164–65) argues that the process of making Yahweh Judah's only god was connected to broader social trends in the latter part of the seventh and the sixth centuries. As patrimonial authority weakened in Judah the individual became more accountable, a change that fostered notions of an individual deity. Also, because in this period Israel stood at "the bottom of its political power" its leaders exalted the national deity "inversely" in order to emphasize the new Israel's distinctiveness from the nations. Moreover, "the rise of supranational empires suggested the model of the super-natural god."

37. Jer 3:6–8.

## The Deuteronomist Movement

changed beyond recognition, and more dramatically than anyone could have imagined.

# 5

# Throes of Change

## Trouble Close to Home for the Assyrians

THE FLUORESCENCE OF YAHWIST activities in the time of Josiah, and the expanding of Judah's influence westward as far as Ashdod, whose port enabled access to the Mediterranean Sea, was possible because the Assyrians were being dangerously distracted by rebellious activities, again, among their Babylon subjects.[1] In 631 BCE Ashurbanipal died or at least ceded the throne to his son Ashur-etil-ilani, who soon also died in 627, leaving power to a brother, Sinsharishkun. About this time, the Chaldean chieftain Nabopolassar, who had rebelled unsuccessfully earlier, still thinking of rebellion, took advantage of the ambiguous power situation of the moment to organize a force in his city, Babylon, and in open defiance of his masters allowed himself to be proclaimed king (626 BCE). For the next several years Sinsharishkun's forces tried to bring the rebels under control but with little success. Nabopolassar's forces gained help from some disgruntled neighbors, Elamites whose base was to the southeast, and also Derites from across the Tigris. By 617 Nabopolassar had secured all the major cities of the region around Babylon, and in 616 his forces began pressing northward toward Assur, the Assyrians' home city and religious center.

The rising strength of the rebellion in Assyria alarmed Pharaoh Psamtik I, who was enjoying control of the city-states in the Levant in Syria-Palestine, fearing that his understanding with the Assyrians could be at

---

1. Ahmed, *Southern Mesopotamia*, 129.

risk. He preferred that the Assyrians remain strong enough in the east to buffer against the restive populations in southern Mesopotamia and Iran, so he proposed a mutual defense pact with the Assyrians in 616. To secure his position he advanced some forces northward into Syria-Palestine and established a base at Carchemish on the western banks of the Euphrates. It was a strategic move. In fact, he provided no help to the Assyrians when they needed it.

Nabopolassar's forces failed in the first attempt to take Assur, the ancient mother city of the Assyrians and still its religious center, but a Median army based on the east side of the Tigris came to help, and they independently possessed the city in 614 BCE. In the wake of this success the Babylonians and Medians formed a pact against the Assyrians; it seems that virtually all the peoples of southern Mesopotamia and their neighbors to the east were fed up with the Assyrians and ready to put them down.[2] Two years after the pact was sealed the combined forces crushed the Assyrian army in its own capital, Nineveh, forcing its remnants to flee westward to Haran, a town in Syria. There a rump group of Assyrian fighters prepared to defend against the assault that would surely come. The next year the Babylonians possessed Syria and plundered the lands around Haran. In late 610 BCE, with the help of the Medians, they besieged Haran. It took a year for the city to collapse, and when it did a ragtag group of Assyrian fighting men fled westward and crossed the Euphrates to find refuge with the Egyptian army which was encamped at Carchemish. The Babylon-Median army now held a position barely fifty miles away. A titanic struggle for control of Syria-Palestine was imminent.

## *Josiah's Untimely Death*

This was the context of a tragic loss to the country of Judah. The threat of a Babylonian presence in Syria-Palestine barely a couple-day's march away from Lebanon, which the Egyptians now claimed for themselves, induced a newly installed pharaoh, Necho II, to bring more forces from Egypt to support the garrison at Carchemish. He was in route to Carchemish, passing along the coast of the Sea, when he was intercepted on the plains of Megiddo by a hastily assembled Judahite army led by King Josiah, who objected to the Egyptian trespass across his territories. Necho declared he had no intention of invading Josiah's country. "What quarrel is there,

---

2. For more detail on these developments see Lipschits, *Fall*, 13–35.

king of Judah, between you and me? It is not you I am attacking at this time, but the house with which I am at war. God has told me to hurry; so stop opposing God, who is with me, or he will destroy you." It was a risky gamble and various readers have wondered why Josiah did this. The writer of Chronicles himself condemned Josiah for the move: "He would not listen to what Necho had said at God's command but went to fight him on the plain of Megiddo."[3] From our vantage point we wonder, could there have been a reason besides his stated objection to Necho's trespass? He may have regarded a possible victory by the Assyrian-Egyptian army as a threat to the anti-Assyrian reforms he had so zealously pursued in Judah.[4] In any case, whatever were his reasons for risking so much in this venture, his challenge to Necho cost him his life. His tragic death in battle at Megiddo marked a downturn in the affairs of Judah that in a few short years would culminate in its final end.

After the battle Necho proceeded on toward Carchemish and joined the forces there, perhaps soon enough to support an attempt in March 609 by a coalition of Assyrians and Egyptians to recapture Haran. The attempt failed. Thus ended the empire that had dominated the entire Near East for more than three hundred years.

It may have been after the failed attempt to retake Haran that Necho made his brief visit to Jerusalem to collect the cash to support his war and to put things in order in Judah. When he arrived he discovered that the notables of the country had already filled Josiah's office by appointing to it his second son, Jehoahaz.[5] This man Necho removed and instead appointed the older brother Eliakim to be king (a person whom the elders had passed over), giving him a new name, Jehoiakim, "raised up by Yahweh." Why did he make the change? Necho may have objected to the elders' decision to choose a king on their own. In any case, by appointing his own man he ensured that this man would be loyal and pay dues as required.[6] Also his decision effectively disempowered the notables who had passed over Jehoiakim to make his younger brother king.[7] In any case, Jehoiakim had

---

3. 2 Chr 35:22.

4. Albertz (*History*, 203) believes he opposed Pharaoh "to prevent a restitution of an independent Northern Kingdom with Egyptian support."

5. His other name was Shallom. He may have been the fourth son; see 1 Chr 3:15.

6. Miller and Hayes, *History*, 402.

7. Necho may have objected to the elders' decision to choose their own king, even though now Judah would be a vassal principality under his command (Miller and Hayes, *History*, 402). 2 Chr 36:1; 2 Kgs 23:31–36. Simon Sebag Montefiore (*Jerusalem*, 46) mistakenly says that Jehoiakim was Josiah's brother.

little choice but to tie his future to Necho. In fact, Jehoiakim's appointment as king was fateful for Judah because he would demonstrate in multiple ways why the notable leaders of his country had passed over him when choosing a successor to Josiah. Another cost to the country was the tax that Necho exacted as payment for the expensive interruption of his military plans. He carried away "a hundred talents" [7,500 pounds] of silver and "a talent" [seventy-five pounds] of gold. Also, Necho took with him the hapless former king, Jehoahaz, to his base camp at Riblah, a tragic figure who would never be heard from again.

## A New Prophetic Voice: Jeremiah

As many things of importance were taking place in Syria-Palestine, a young prophet of major importance to Judah had begun to speak out, and owing to his importance for everything that would take place in the next two decades, he needs an introduction. Jeremiah was a prophet with a unique calling. He was to be a meddlesome, irritating presence in Jerusalem during the reigns of five kings in Judah. He would live to see the final, total ruination of the country. Many times he would clash with the power elite over vital and immediate issues, and despite their recriminations he remained uncowed and unsilent. Jeremiah would be, for the successors of Josiah, a nettlesome pronouncer of worrisome, even frightening news to the people of the city. Against the power elite, Jeremiah was impertinent and subversive, willing to embarrass them in public, to make them subject to an increasingly alarmed public. He made declarations at inopportune moments, and exposed the stubborn refusal of Judah's leaders, the king and his advisors, to address challenges plainly facing the country.

It is because of his importance to my story, and the problems entailed in using the book ascribed to him that I must explain some details about the book of Jeremiah to which I will have to turn to explain the next events that take place in Judah.

## The Book of Jeremiah

The book of Jeremiah is an assemblage of several kinds of materials—essays, speeches, historical accounts, critical comments, notes—brought together by someone, or a group of individuals, and edited (possibly) at various times, in the attempt to salvage the story of Jeremiah's career and message. The structure of the book as we have it is not easily apparent. Events described in the book are out of order. Some incidents are described twice, from different points of view, and the corresponding accounts are displaced from each other. There are even two versions of the book, a Greek one (the Septuagint) and a Hebrew one (the Masoretic Text), and they are somewhat differently ordered.[8] And, moreover, the book seems at first glance to lack a single coherent scheme.[9]

But it has been pointed out that the text as we have it reflects the very turbulence of Jeremiah's times. As most of the leaders of the country distrusted, disliked, even despised Jeremiah, they insulted and abused him many times. The convoluted order of the book of Jeremiah, as Professor Kathleen O'Connor has suggested, exhibits in its very form the chaotic nature of the world he lived in. O'Connor likens the materials in the book to the flotsam of a terrible shipwreck. Debris from a once-extant society are scattered throughout the text, forcing the reader to construct—of course, tentatively and provisionally—a plausible narrative of the chaotic life and times of this magnificent prophet. The last we see of him in the story is his being dragged, against his will and advice, to Egypt by a renegade group of Judahites fleeing for their lives.

Jeremiah's life, in fact, presented in a majestic disorderly book, constitutes, according to Professor O'Connor, "a helpful text for survivors of disaster." People who are traumatized by events and are left to grope "for meaning, for words, images, metaphors, stories—interpretations of every kind" by which to rebuild their lives—will find in this book a helpful vocabulary of grief and heartache.[10] Here, in this book, one can find "words for wounds beyond speaking, and hope for the rebuilding" of broken lifeworlds,[11] so that one's "psychic numbing" after a traumatic experience can

---

8. On the general structure of Jeremiah, besides the authors cited here, see Hutton, *Jeremiah*, 1057-58.

9. The condescending references to its disorder are colorful. It is "literary chaos," "bumpy," "a hodgepodge thrown together without any discernible principle of arrangement," "a motley collection of materials ... all glued together by some not entirely clear connections to the prophet," "the longest and most tumultuous prophetic writing in the Bible," "unreadable" (see Stulman, *Jeremiah*, 1, 7-11; O'Connor, *Jeremiah*, 29; Brueggemann, *Like Fire*, 86). Middlemas (*Templeless*, 67-68) provides a general outline, but within her categories the material has no chronological order. Alberz (*Israel*) and Lipschits (*Fall*) provide a history of the various analyses of the book. Lipschits offers an explanation for how the book came to exist in two versions (*Fall*, 307-38).

10. O'Connor, *Jeremiah*, 31.

11. O'Connor, *Jeremiah*, 31.

be expressed in words.¹² "With poetic brutality and with quiet tenderness, the book names their wretched world and gives it meaning."¹³ For the people in exile, for whom the book was assembled, overtaken as they were with grief and bitterness for what had been lost, the language of this book must have been a source of succor.

Much effort has been expended to distinguish the prophet's original doings and sayings from the editorial attempts to produce a plausible narrative about his life.¹⁴ Some of it, as indicated, was salvaged from a time when Jeremiah was living in Jerusalem, but some of it must have been assembled and pieced together later. While the touch of editorial styluses on this work can be detected (at least, by some experts), still some passages read as if they were written down by someone observing events as they took place. In constructing my narrative from the materials available I acknowledge that—as is the case for all of this account anyway—it is *my* construction of how things went, and tracks closely with the text as we have it and the analyses of others.¹⁵

## *Jeremiah's Call and Early Prophecies*

Jeremiah came from a priestly family in a small town three miles outside of Jerusalem named Anathoth. He received a call to speak on behalf of Yahweh in the thirteenth year of Josiah's rule (about 627 BCE) when Yahweh told him that he was appointed to be a prophet to the nations. Jeremiah tried to refuse; he was young and afraid, he complained. But Yahweh insisted, saying that he would be with Jeremiah in the task. His assignment was indeed forbidding: he was to challenge the affairs of nations, even to tell nations that "they will be uprooted and torn down, destroyed and demolished, rebuilt and firmly planted."¹⁶ Here is the theme of his career: to announce the uprooting and demolishing of the political world around him, but also to foresee a time of rebuilding and renewal. Indeed, as he was receiving his

---

12. O'Connor, *Jeremiah*, 60.

13. O'Connor, *Jeremiah*, 31; see also Neimeyer et al., *Social Constructionist*.

14. Albertz (*Israel*) is a notable example. Some authors, rather than attempting to sort out when the various pieces in the book were produced, have tried to appreciate the "artful" coherence or dissonance in these texts (Diamond et al., *Troubling Jeremiah*; Stulman, *Jeremiah*).

15. The commentary of Louis Stulman (*Jeremiah*), for instance.

16. Jer 1:5–8, 10.

call, the uprooting and demolishing of a great empire was already in motion, far away in Babylon.

The first message that Yahweh gave him was two images whose significances would characterize the theme of his career. One of them consisted of two nearly homonymous words by which Yahweh was telling him something. He was asked what he could see; he saw "a branch of an almond tree," the word for almond being *shaqed*. Yahweh responded that he would be watching—*shoqed*—over his word so as to perform it. Apparently this wordplay was to help Jeremiah understand in the image of an almond tree that Yahweh would be active, present with Jeremiah through the troubling events of his life. The second image Jeremiah saw was a boiling pot "tilted away from the north." Yahweh explained that this was an image of his plans for Judah: he would bring a force from the north that would reach the gates of Jerusalem, for he was about to hold the people of Judah accountable for their apostasies.[17] Some commentators view "the north" here as a mythological place, perhaps the "mountains of the gods" referred to in legends.[18] But its most obvious reference seems to be northern Syria and Mesopotamia, the place from which imperial forces forming in Mesopotamia would many times be drawn into Syria-Palestine by a desire for tribute wealth. A new empire, in fact, was about to form even at that moment, and would soon burst into Jeremiah's world.

Jeremiah would be a vehicle of communication to the recalcitrant citizens of Judah. Yahweh said, "I, the LORD, hereby promise to make you as strong as a fortified city, an iron pillar, and a bronze wall. You will be able to stand up against all who live in the land, including the kings of Judah, its officials, its priests and all the people of the land. They will attack you but they will not be able to overcome you, for I will be with you to rescue you. . . ." And he was to warn them of a gathering danger ahead, and to urge the people of Judah to consent to Yahweh's will.[19]

I have noted that Jeremiah was not impressed by the impact of Josiah's reforms on the spiritual perceptions of the people of Judah. He likened Judah's sins to those of Israel.

> The LORD said to me, "Jeremiah, you have no doubt seen what wayward Israel has done. You have seen how she went up to every high hill and under every green tree to give herself like a prostitute

---

17. Jer 1:11–15.
18. Hutton, *Jeremiah*, 1059–60.
19. Jer 1:17–19 NET.

to other gods. Yet even after she had done all that, I thought that she might come back to me. But she did not. Her sister, unfaithful Judah, saw what she did. She also saw that, because of wayward Israel's adulterous worship of other gods, I sent her away and gave her divorce papers. But still her unfaithful sister Judah was not afraid, and she too went and gave herself like a prostitute to other gods. Because she took her prostitution so lightly, she defiled the land through her adulterous worship of gods made of wood and stone. In spite of all this, Israel's sister, unfaithful Judah, has not turned back to me with any sincerity; she has only pretended to do so," says the Lord.[20]

Jeremiah lamented that even though the people of Judah saw what happened to Israel because of its idolatries, they paid no attention. These reforms being instituted by Josiah had not touched the moral sensibility of the population of Judah. The people only "pretended to do so."

## *Jeremiah on Jehoahaz*

Soon after Jehoahaz was appointed king Jeremiah spoke to him. Calling him by his other name, Shallum, he urged him to rule with justice.

> The Lord says, "Do what is just and right. Deliver those who have been robbed from those who oppress them. Do not exploit or mistreat resident foreigners who live in your land, children who have no fathers, or widows. Do not kill innocent people in this land. If you are careful to obey these commands, then the kings who follow in David's succession and ride in chariots or on horses will continue to come through the gates of this palace, as will their officials and their subjects. But, if you do not obey these commands, I solemnly swear that this palace will become a pile of rubble."[21]

As we know, the official period of mourning for Josiah had not even ended when the hapless Jehoahaz was carted off by Necho. Jeremiah sympathized with the young deposed king, saying to his fellow Judahites, "Do not weep for the king who was killed [Josiah]. Do not grieve for him. But weep mournfully for the king who has gone into exile [Jehoahaz]. For he will never return to see his native land again."[22]

20. Jer 3:6–10 NET.
21. Jer 22:3 NET.
22. Jer 22:10 NET.

# Jerusalem Burning

## *Jeremiah and King Jehoiakim*

Jeremiah's relationship with the person whom Pharaoh Necho placed on the throne in Jehoahaz's place was altogether different. Jehoiakim had hardly assumed office when he revealed his true character. In order to pay the heavy tax that Necho levied on him he dragooned the money from his subjects rather than drawing the tax from his own treasury.[23] Furthermore, he commissioned a palace to be built for himself, and then shamelessly paid nothing to the builders. All this drew a rebuke by Jeremiah. Standing in the courtyard of the temple, where the notables normally gathered to talk about public affairs, he boldly spoke out to the king:

> Does it make you any more of a king that you outstrip everyone else in building with cedar? Just think about your father. He was content that he had food and drink. He did what was just and right. So things went well with him. . . . But you are always thinking and looking for ways to increase your wealth by dishonest means. Your eyes and your heart are set on killing some innocent person and committing fraud and oppression.

Jeremiah prophesied that Jehoiakim would die unmourned.[24]

Such was Jeremiah's impolitic introduction of himself to the new king. Jehoiakim was already, as I have implied, sensitive about his status, having been passed over by the notables in his own community only to be appointed king by an alien sovereign. Such a rebuke by a prophet standing in a public place would have stung. As it happened, the two men would never have any use for each other.

---

23. 2 Kgs 23:35; Jer 22:15–19 NET.
24. Jer 22:15. There is no record of how Jehoiakim died.

# 6

# Jehoiakim's Nemesis

*Jeremiah's Intolerable Themes*

IN FACT, JEREMIAH DID not endear himself to the notables of the city either, for throughout his career he denounced the ways they were breaking the standards of virtue that Yahweh had called them to. The early chapters of the book of Jeremiah appear to consist of such declarations, addressed at various times to the people of the city. His pronouncements would have been offensive to many, especially the notables. Here are some of his declarations in public (from those early chapters).

- Yahweh says, "I remember the devotion of your youth, how as a bride you loved me and followed me through the wilderness.... What fault did your ancestors find in me, that they strayed so far from me? They followed worthless idols and became worthless themselves."[1]
- "Long ago you broke off your yoke and tore off your bonds; you said, 'I will not serve you!' Indeed, on every high hill and under every spreading tree you lay down as a prostitute.... You are a swift she-camel running here and there, a wild donkey accustomed to the desert, sniffing the wind in her craving—in her heat who can restrain her? Any males that pursue her need not tire themselves; at mating time they will find her."[2]

1. Jer 2:1–5.
2. Jer 2:20–25.

- "Where . . . are the gods you made for yourselves? Let them come if they can save you when you are in trouble! For you, Judah, have as many gods as you have towns."[3]
- "In vain I punished your people; they did not respond to correction. Your sword has devoured your prophets like a ravenous lion."[4]
- "Does a young woman forget her jewelry, a bride her wedding ornaments? Yet my people have forgotten me, days without number."[5]
- "On your clothes is found the lifeblood of the innocent poor, though you did not catch them breaking in. Yet in spite of all this you say, 'I am innocent; he [Yahweh] is not angry with me.'"[6]
- You pretend to worship Yahweh, but in practice you "do all the evil you can."[7]
- "'Return, faithless Israel,' declares the LORD, 'I will frown on you no longer, for I am faithful. . . . I will not be angry forever. Only acknowledge your guilt. . . .'"[8]

By preaching such public condemnations of social practice Jeremiah of course would earn bitter resentment from the people of the city. Early in the reign of Jehoiakim, that is, in roughly 609–608 BCE, soon after the Babylonians had possessed Haran in Syria, but probably before the battle of Carchemish took place, Jeremiah was given a message that would not go down well in Judah. The struggle in Syria must have seemed far away and the Babylonians who were now challenging the Assyrians and Egyptians were newcomers to the region. The Assyrians, in contrast, were well known to Judah, as they had dominated the Near East for almost three centuries. From the viewpoint of folks in Judah it was hard to imagine a world in which Assyria did not exist as the hegemon of the region. It was in this context that Jeremiah began to predict that Judah would be overrun by the Babylonians. The text says that Yahweh directed the prophet to go to the gate of the temple courtyard where the notables of the city would have congregated and to declare in Yahweh's name:

3. Jer 2:28.
4. Jer 2:30.
5. Jer 2:32.
6. Jer 2:34.
7. Jer 3:5.
8. Jer 3:12.

## Jehoiakim's Nemesis

> Change the way you have been living and do what is right. If you do, I will allow you to continue to live in this land. Stop putting your confidence in the false belief that says, "We are safe! The temple of the Lord is here! The temple of the Lord is here! The temple of the Lord is here!" You must change the way you have been living.... Go to the place in Shiloh where I allowed myself to be worshiped in the early days. See what I did to it because of the wicked things my people Israel did. You also have done all these things, says the Lord, and I have spoken to you over and over again. But you have not listened! You have refused to respond when I called you to repent! So I will destroy this temple that I have claimed as my own, this temple that you are trusting to protect you. I will destroy this place that I gave to you and your ancestors, just like I destroyed Shiloh. And I will drive you out of my sight just like I drove out your relatives, the people of Israel.[9]

Here was a prediction that seemed unreal for the people of the city in that time, for they believed that Yahweh would never allow his temple to be destroyed, a belief from the time when the city was saved from Sennacherib's invasion in 701 BCE. The city, Jeremiah was saying, would fare no better than Shiloh, where the tabernacle that the temple replaced had once dwelt. Yahweh called them to "reform your ways and your actions," he said, lest their city become as barren and desolate as Shiloh. Specifically, "If you... deal with each other justly, if you do not oppress the foreigner, the fatherless or the widow and do not shed innocent blood in this place, and if you do not follow other gods to your own harm, then I will let you live in this place...." But in fact, said the prophet, they were stealing from and abusing each other, committing adultery and perjury; moreover, they were "burning incense to Baal and follow[ing] other gods." So, said Jeremiah, you have no grounds for claiming the safety of Yahweh's temple. Indeed, "you have become 'a den of robbers.'"[10] Indeed, says Yahweh, the people

> have set up their disgusting idols in the temple that I have claimed for my own and have defiled it. They have also built places of worship in a place called Topheth in the Valley of Ben Hinnom so that they can sacrifice their sons and daughters by fire. That is something I never commanded them to do! Indeed, it never even entered my mind to command such a thing! "So, watch out!" says the Lord. "The time will soon come when people will no longer

9. Jer 7:2-15 NET.
10. Jer 7:3-11 NET.

call those places Topheth or the Valley of Ben Hinnom. But they will call that valley the Valley of Slaughter, and they will bury so many people in Topheth they will run out of room. Then the dead bodies of these people will be left on the ground for the birds and wild animals to eat. There will not be any survivors to scare them away."

And Yahweh himself would bring it about: "I will put an end to the sounds of joy and gladness or the glad celebration of brides and grooms throughout the towns of Judah and the streets of Jerusalem. For the whole land will become a desolate wasteland."[11]

The wise and influential will not escape Yahweh's wrath, the prophet declared:

> Your wise men will be put to shame. They will be dumbfounded and be brought to judgment. Since they have rejected the LORD's message, what wisdom do they really have? So I will give their wives to other men and their fields to new owners. For from the least important to the most important of them, all of them are greedy for dishonest gain. Prophets and priests alike all practice deceit.... Are they ashamed because they have done such disgusting things? No, they are not at all ashamed! They do not even know how to blush. So they will die just like others have died. They will be brought to ruin when I punish them.... I will take away their harvests.... There will be no grapes on their vines. There will be no figs on their fig trees. Even the leaves on their trees will wither. The crops that I gave them will be taken away.[12]

Such a public denunciation of practices that were generally accepted in Judah was enough to turn most people in the city against Jeremiah the prophet. The notables would no longer tolerate such insults. Who in Judah could believe that the country would be overrun, that such things would happen in Jerusalem?[13] Jeremiah had barely finished his speech when religious authorities appeared ready to have him executed. "You must die!" they said. "Why do you prophesy in the LORD's name that this house will be like Shiloh and this city will be desolate and deserted?" And all the people crowded around Jeremiah in the house of the LORD. He was promptly brought to trial at the "new gate" of the temple. "When the officials of Judah

---

11. Jer 7:30–33 NET.
12. Jer 8:9–13 NET.
13. Jer 7:27.

## Jehoiakim's Nemesis

heard about these things, they went up from the royal palace to the house of the Lord and took their places at the entrance of the new gate of the Lord's house." There the officials offered their evidence against him: "This man should be sentenced to death because he has prophesied against this city. You have heard it with your own ears!" To this Jeremiah asserted that Yahweh had sent him "to prophesy against this house and this city." He was but performing what he had been told to do. Indeed, he took opportunity to urge them again: "Now reform your ways and your actions and obey the Lord your God. Then the Lord will relent and not bring the disaster he has pronounced against you." But if they should put him to death, he said, they would be spilling innocent blood, for everything he had said had come from Yahweh.

The officials did not relent. But some notable figures in the community arose to defend Jeremiah, pointing to the prophecy of Micah, proclaimed a century earlier on the grounds of the temple in Jerusalem. He had declared, "Zion will be plowed like a field, Jerusalem will become a heap of rubble, the temple hill a mound overgrown with thickets." Despite such an offensive prophecy, they noted, Micah was not put to death. Indeed, they said, "King Hezekiah and all the people of Judah did not put him to death, did they? Did not Hezekiah show reverence for the Lord and seek the Lord's favor? Did not the Lord forgo destroying them as he threatened he would? But we are on the verge of bringing great disaster on ourselves."[14]

To explain how precarious Jeremiah's plight was at this moment the editors of the book of Jeremiah inserted here a story about another prophet who had displeased king Jehoiakim.

> Now there was another man who prophesied as the Lord's representative against this city and this land just as Jeremiah did. His name was Uriah son of Shemaiah from Kiriath Jearim. When King Jehoiakim and all his bodyguards and officials heard what he was prophesying, the king sought to have him executed. But Uriah found out about it and fled to Egypt out of fear. However, King Jehoiakim sent some men to Egypt, including Elnathan son of Achbor, and they brought Uriah back from there. They took him to King Jehoiakim, who had him executed and had his body thrown into the burial place of the common people.[15]

---

14. Jer 26:8–19 NET.
15. Jer 26:20–23 NET.

Jeremiah would have suffered a similar fate to Uriah if a notable figure in the community had not spoken up in his defense. "Ahikam son of Shaphan used his influence to keep Jeremiah from being handed over and executed by the people."[16] This was probably the moment when Jeremiah was banished from the temple.

## A Plot

Even so, Jeremiah was not out of trouble, for this was a time of instability. The certainties of the social order in Judah had only a few months earlier been undermined by the death of their king in battle. And a large tax assessment had been taken by Necho, which left the city bankrupt. Furthermore, the person now occupying the throne enjoyed little respect among his own people, and his grip on affairs in the city may have been tenuous. The social order that might have constrained misbehavior, firmly intact under Josiah only a few months earlier, now had little salience. Ordinary rules of respect and decorum had frayed so that a cabal of priests and notables could contemplate murdering Jeremiah. They sent him a message: "Stop prophesying in the name of the LORD or we will kill you!"[17] It turns out that these criminals were his own relatives. Jeremiah had been born into a priestly linage in the town of Anathoth, which lay in the tribal territory of Benjamin, and his status may have provided him some prominence and protection—at least at first. But his support for Josiah's reforms, which included the destruction of "high places," like the one his relatives managed at Anathoth, and his blunt condemnation of the magical rites performed at such high places, made him odious to his own relatives. He says of their warnings, "I did not realize that they had plotted against me."[18] That was but the first of the threats that would assail him.

## Face-off at Carchemish

About this time, far away on the banks of the upper Euphrates a colossal clash between two great armies loomed, whose results would determine the future of Syria-Palestine. Only now, for the first time in three hundred

---

16. Jer 26:24 NET.
17. Jer 11:21 NET.
18. Jer 11:19–22.

years, the Assyrians were not represented, its army having vanished forever. The contestants in this case were the Egyptians, bivouacked on the west banks of the river, versus the upstart military coalition of Babylonians and Medes that had scarcely ever lost a battle. King Jehoiakim in Jerusalem was of course allied with the Egyptians, having been placed in office by Pharaoh himself. Also, while the elite of Jerusalem preferred the customs of the Egyptians, supposing their civilization to be superior to all others, they had little sense of what the Babylonians were like. To them they were unknown interlopers into Syria-Palestine from a place far away, so far away that Hezekiah had deemed their ambassadors unthreatening enough to permit them into his treasury to view it.

Necho had returned from his short visit to Jerusalem in order to be present for the great moment. Nebuchadnezzar, son of King Nabopolassar, was in command of the Babylonian army. It was in early summer 605 BCE that the battle was finally joined. The desperate clash of forces at Carchemish became a total rout of the Egyptians. The Babylonians chased stragglers from the field to the district of Hormath where, according to their Chronicles, "Not a single man escaped."[19]

---

19. Wiseman, *New Babylonian Chronicles*.

# 7

# The Prophet's Warnings

### *The Scene in 605 BCE*

MAY/JUNE OF 605 BCE was the fourth year of Jehoiakim's reign in Judah.[1] He was now facing a problem. The Assyrian Empire that had for three hundred years dominated the territory from Iran to Libya had vanished. The Pharaoh who had appointed him king of Judah and the army that had killed Josiah were limping home. In place of the usual external powers that Judah had to deal with—Assyria and Egypt—there was now a new one: the army that had defeated the military of the old empires. And this new army was led by a man whose personality was yet to be known. He and his soldiers stood supreme over the whole of Syria-Palestine, and would soon demand Jehoiakim's loyalty and dues.

But the Babylonians paused. Soon after the battle at Carchemish the king of Babylon, Nebuchadnezzar's father, unexpectedly died (July, 605 BCE). Nebuchadnezzar abruptly left his army and raced across the desert to claim the throne against his rivals in the capital city. The Babylonian distraction and the absence of an Assyrian hegemon in Syria-Palestine allowed the rulers of the small principalities of Syria-Palestine to enjoy relief from having to pay dues. There was time to plan how to act in the new

---

1. It is difficult to match the dates cited in the several sources, perhaps because of different calendars and different ways of referencing time. See Miller and Hayes, *History*, 419–20, for an attempt to reconcile dates cited in 2 Kings and Jeremiah.

## New Issues in Judah

Jehoiakim and his advisors in Judah were of course shaken by the results of the battle at Carchemish. And virtually every principality in Syria-Palestine knew that they would be asked to submit to Nebuchadnezzar, once he returned to lead his army as their new king. In fact, when within three weeks he returned he began to demand his tribute from each of the principalities in Syria-Palestine, and all of them, one by one, submitted to him and paid up—except for two rulers, Adon in Ashkelon and Jehoiakim in Judah. Adon pointedly refused to consent to Babylonian authority, supposing that, as there was a contingent of the Egyptian army in the city, the Babylonians would leave him alone. Jehoiakim for his part made no move; he was not ready to pay dues to this unknown force whose origins were several weeks' march away.[2]

Nebuchadnezzar displayed his personality in the way he dealt with Ashkelon. He brought the full force of his army against the city in 604 BCE and crushed all resistance. Then he sacked and razed city. Now he was poised to move against Jerusalem, only a two-days march away. Jehoiakim immediately offered fealty and sent dues to Nebuchadnezzar.[3] But he worried that his temporizing could have angered this unknown and terrifying conqueror. He anxiously proclaimed a national fast and invited the people to come and pray for the city.[4] Jehoiakim had now "gotten religion."

## Jeremiah Produces a Scroll

It was at this moment that, according to the book of Jeremiah, Yahweh commissioned the prophet to challenge the idolatrous practices in the country,

---

2. It took Ezra four months to bring a group of nine hundred from Babylon to Jerusalem. https://www.esv.org/resources/esv-global-study-bible/facts-ezra-7/.

3. Nebuchadnezzar's attack seems to have been notably vicious. One reason may be that virtually every other principality in Syria-Palestine had quickly submitted to Babylonian claims of suzerainty except Ashkelon and Judah, and another may have been the need to defeat the Egyptian military contingent stationed in Ashkelon (Lipschits, *Fall and Rise*, 40; Fantalkin, *Why Did Nebuchadnezzar II Destroy*).

4. Lipschits places the date of this fast as November/December 604 BCE.

and in even more blunt terms than ever. He had been banished from the temple, so he directed his assistant Baruch to write on a scroll everything that Yahweh had told him to say, from the time of Josiah up to that point. Yahweh's intention, he said, was that "perhaps when the people of Judah hear about all the disaster I intend to bring on them, they will all stop doing the evil things they have been doing. If they do, I will forgive their sins and the wicked things they have done."[5] Baruch went to the temple courtyard and began to read the scroll aloud for all to hear; there must have been a sizable audience for him at this time, because the city was stirring over the public ceremonies of the official fast that was soon to take place. The text says that Baruch placed himself where all the people could hear him and began to read aloud the following:[6]

> For the last twenty-three years, from the thirteenth year that Josiah son of Amon was ruling in Judah until now, the LORD's messages have come to me and I have told them to you over and over again. But you would not listen. Over and over again the LORD has sent his servants the prophets to you. But you have not listened or paid attention. He said through them, "Each of you must turn from your wicked ways and stop doing the evil things you are doing. If you do, I will allow you to continue to live here in the land that I gave to you and your ancestors as a lasting possession. Do not pay allegiance to other gods and worship and serve them. Do not make me angry by the things that you do. Then I will not cause you any harm." So, now the LORD says, "You have not listened to me. But you have made me angry by the things that you have done. Thus you have brought harm on yourselves."
>
> Therefore, the LORD of Heaven's Armies says, "You have not listened to what I said. So I, the LORD, affirm that I will send for all the peoples of the north and my servant, King Nebuchadnezzar of Babylon. I will bring them against this land and its inhabitants and all the nations that surround it. I will utterly destroy the land, its inhabitants, and all the surrounding nations and make them everlasting ruins. I will make them objects of horror and hissing scorn. I will put an end to the sounds of joy and gladness and the glad celebration of brides and grooms in these lands. . . . [Also] to the sound of people grinding meal . . . [and] to lamps shining in their houses. This whole area will become a desolate wasteland.

---

5. Jer 36:2, 3 NET. The contents of the scroll seem to be the message that appears in chapter 25. I therefore tack between chapters 25 and 36.

6. The time must have been toward the end of Jehoiakim's fourth year, for the book of Jeremiah says it was read in "the fifth year."

## The Prophet's Warnings

> These nations will be subject to the king of Babylon for seventy years. . . . But when the seventy years are over, I will punish the king of Babylon and his nation for their sins. I will make the land of Babylon an everlasting ruin. I, the Lord, affirm it! I will bring on that land everything that I said I would. I will bring on it everything that is written in this book. I will bring on it everything that Jeremiah has prophesied against all the nations. For many nations and great kings will make slaves of the king of Babylon and his nation too. I will repay them for all they have done."[7]

The prediction that the army of Nebuchadnezzar, stationed only a few miles away, would possess and destroy the city was enough to alarm anyone who heard it, and the scroll was quickly taken to the notables in Jehoiakim's court.[8] The danger to the author of this scroll was apparent to his friends, so they sent word to Jeremiah and Baruch to hide. The scroll was taken to the king and read to him as he was sitting in his winter apartment warming himself at a burning brazier. As the scroll was read to him he sliced off portions of it, piece by piece, and pitched them into the fire. At this point the editor(s) of the book of Jeremiah pause to point out how offensive this behavior was. Even Jehoiakim's own advisors implored him to desist, they note, but he had no respect for Jeremiah. And moreover, he sent his aids to go find him.[9]

The specificity of the way this story is told reveals how significant it was to the editors of the book of Jeremiah. They identified the individuals by name (Gemariah, Micaiah, Elishama, Delaiah, Elnathan, Zedekiah, Jehudi, Nethaniah), and note the location where each event took place (king's house, winter apartment, secretary's chamber, Gemariah's chamber, the new gate). They provide certain specific details about each situation: Baruch is told to "sit down and read"; the scroll is left in Elishama's chamber; it is the ninth month; a fire burns in the brazier; three or four spans of the scroll as they are read aloud are sliced off and burned.

To be precise, the scroll was addressed to the people of Judah, not the king. But no one failed to recognize the threat it was for the king and his advisors; it was a direct challenge to the king's policies, and his authority. Jeremiah's prediction that Jerusalem would be "a desolate wasteland and

---

7. Jer 25:1–14 NET.
8. Jer 36:16.
9. Jer 36:1–26.

these nations will serve the king of Babylon seventy years"[10] was good reason to arrest Baruch and Jeremiah. Fortunately for them, they could not be found.

In response to the destruction of the scroll Jeremiah produced another and added even more to it. And in this scroll he pointedly addressed the king himself. He told him that because he had resisted Yahweh's counsel he would have no heirs on the throne and would meet a humiliating end.[11]

This second edition of Jeremiah's critique of the behavior of the citizens and the king was a declaration that Yahweh had made up his mind: Judah would be crushed for its apostasy. Even so Jeremiah appealed to King Jehoiakim, yet again, to submit to the Babylonians in hopes that through Yahweh's mercy he and his people would survive. The response of the king and his advisors to his warnings and appeals was only contempt.

Fortunately for Jehoiakim the Babylonians took no action against the city despite Jehoiakim's delay in offering fealty and dues. But Jeremiah's open critique of the king's policies and authority sealed Jehoiakim's enmity for him.

## Jehoiakim's Folly

Jehoiakim's submission to Nebuchadnezzar, reluctant as it was, spared Judah from attack. And yet he had not given up hope of escaping the grip of the Babylonians on Judah. He seemed unable to internalize how definitely the geopolitical world around him had changed. He seemed to regard the Babylonian invasion of Syria-Palestine as a temporary incursion. Egypt was still, in his mind, the political and military enduring hegemonic force in the southern portion of Syria-Palestine. And anyway, its civilization was manifestly superior to that the invaders. He waited and watched for a chance to bolt from Babylonian control, supposing the pharaoh would protect him. And as it happened, it was not long before an opportunity seemed to appear. The Babylonians recognized that their hold on Syria-Palestine, especially in the southern territories, was not secure as long as Egypt could be active in the region. In March-April 601 BCE Nebuchadnezzar brought his army back to Syria-Palestine to collect tribute. By November/December he had subjected Tyre and Sidon, and supposing the Egyptians would not be fully reorganized, he suddenly attacked Egypt. But the Babylonians were

---

10. Jer 25:11.
11. Jer 26:30.

stunned by the ferocious Egyptian response. It was a terrible battle, and both sides suffered heavy losses. The Babylonians were forced to withdraw.

The battle tarnished the Babylonian reputation for invincibility, and Egypt was thereafter broadly recognized as the de facto hegemon of southern Philistia.[12] Several principalities in Syria-Palestine started paying dues to Egypt, betting that it would continue to be dominant in Philistia, of course spurning the Babylonians. This was the opportunity Jehoiakim had been waiting for. He joined the general rebellion and after three years stopped his paying dues to Nebuchadnezzar. Like the others, he supposed that the Egyptians' strength would protect him.[13] In truth, the Egyptians were unready to engage in any further fighting. When Judah on its western flank was harassed by Moabite and Ammonite marauders, it got no help from the pharaoh.[14]

## Nebuchadnezzar Besieges the City

In the meantime Nebuchadnezzar had not given up on his plan to subdue Egypt. But as many of the kingdoms in Syria-Palestine were now paying tribute to pharaoh, he had to confront each one separately again. Eventually, in spring, 597 BCE, he arrived at the gates of Jerusalem. Jehoiakim refused entry and awaited help from pharaoh. The Babylonians set up siege works around the city to starve it into submission. The siege lasted about three months and in that period several things took place. For one thing, King Jehoiakim disappeared from the scene.[15] The writer of Chronicles, written several generations later, says that he was *bound in chains* and taken to Babylon.[16] The authors/editors of the book of Kings say that he "passed away and his son Jehoiachin [also known as Jeconiah] replaced him as

---

12. Lipschits, *Fall*, 48–51.

13. Here I follow Miller and Hayes, *History*, 406–8. It may have been in this context that Jeremiah prophesied against the Egyptians (Jer 46:7–26).

14. 2 Kgs 24:2; this may have been the reason the Rechabites whom Jeremiah dealt with ended up in Jerusalem (Jer 35:11).

15. *New Bible Dictionary*, 547. Miller and Hays (*History*, 408) and Bright (*Jeremiah*, xlix) believe that Jehoiakim died during the siege and was replaced by Jehoiachin (Jeconiah), who was captured by Nebuchadnezzar after a reign of only three months, which they justify by reference to Jer 22:18–28 and 36:30–32. Cf. 2 Chr 36:6; 2 Kg 24:6. See also Green, *Fate of Jehoiakim*. Hirsh et al. (*Nebuchadnezzar*) say that Nebuchadnezzar "probably slew him, casting out his dead body unburied."

16. 2 Chr 36:6.

king."[17] Based on these statements, Professor Bright believes that Jehoiakim was assassinated in December 598 (that is, just as the siege began).[18] Other scholars suppose that he died before the Babylonians got into the city. In any case, it was his son Jeconiah, along with his mother, his servants, his officials, and his eunuchs, who surrendered to the invaders.[19]

Even as Jeconiah was assuming the role of king, Jeremiah announced that he would hardly enjoy any time in power. Yahweh will soon "deliver you into the hands of those who want to kill you, [he said].... I will hurl you and the mother who gave you birth into another country, where neither of you was born, and there you both will die. You will never come back to the land you long to return to."[20]

Jeconiah was eighteen years old, and the authors/editors of the book of Kings condemned his policies.[21] Actually, he had little opportunity to do much because once Nebuchadnezzar entered the city he removed Jeconiah and carried him off to Babylon, along with his mother and other notables. Nebuchadnezzar then placed Josiah's third son, Mattaniah, on the throne, giving him a new name, Zedekiah ("Yahweh is just"), and forcing him to swear fealty to Nebuchadnezzar in the name of his own god Yahweh. Here, placed in authority over Judah, at a time when the challenge for the country would be existential, was yet another personality who was eminently unsuited for the office.

## The First Deportation

Nebuchadnezzar carried away, according to the Babylonian Chronicles, "heavy booty . . . and sent it to Babylon."[22] The book of Kings says that he took "the treasures from the temple of the Lord and from the royal palace, and cut up the gold articles that Solomon king of Israel had made for the temple of the Lord." And he also exacted a heavy toll in human capital from the country. Besides the king and his mother, he took "all the officers and fighting men, and all the skilled workers and artisans—a total

17. 2 Kgs 24:6.
18. Bright, *Jeremiah*, xlix.
19. 2 Kgs 24:12; Miller and Hays (*History*, 408) list other possible ways that Jehoiakim may have died.
20. Jer 2:26–27.
21. 2 Kgs 24:9.
22. Miller and Hays, *History*, 408.

of ten thousand. Only the poorest people of the land were left."[23] Judah was deprived of its finest talent, including notably two young men, Daniel and Ezekiel.

In the end, this deportation of Judah's best talent may have turned out for the Judahites' benefit, for it preserved the learned class whose descendants would take prominent roles several decades later when they would be joined by survivors of a later disaster to be trying to reconstitute a new society. Jeremiah even suggested this when he described the citizens of Judah who had been deported in 597 as the "good figs," dubbing those who were left in Judah as "bad figs, . . . so bad they cannot be eaten." Of the good figs he says, Yahweh's "eyes will watch over them for their good . . . [and] he will bring them back to this land. . . ." More importantly, "I will give them a heart to know me, [Yahweh says] . . . [and] they will return to me with all their heart." By "bad figs" he meant the new king Zedekiah and his advisors as well as "the survivors from Jerusalem, . . . [who] will become a reproach and a byword, a curse and an object of ridicule."[24] The promise to bring back the captives taken to Babylon is reproduced in another chapter of the book of Jeremiah, where Yahweh promises he will "gather the remnant of my flock out of all the countries where I have driven them and will bring them back to their pasture, . . . [and] they will no longer be afraid or terrified. . . . [Also] I will raise up for David a righteous Branch, a King who will reign wisely and do what is just and right in the land. In his days Judah will be saved and Israel will live in safety."[25]

## Jeremiah's Letter to the Exiles

The captives, who would be known as the "golah" (Hebrew, "exile") had scarcely been carried off to Babylon when Jeremiah composed a letter for "the elders of the golah." He urged them to commit to their host country.[26] They should "Build houses and settle down; plant gardens and eat what they produce. Marry and have sons and daughters. . . . They are to [i]ncrease in number there. . . . And they are to seek the peace and prosperity of the city

---

23. 2 Kgs 24:13–14. The book of Daniel, written centuries later, says that it was about this time that Nebuchadnezzar took a group of promising young men, including Daniel and several friends, to Babylon to be trained for his bureaucracy (Dan 1:1–4).
24. Jer 24:4–10.
25. Jer 23:3–8.
26. Albertz, *Israel*, 100.

to which I have carried you into exile, ... because if it prospers, you too will prosper." They should not expect to return soon to Judah, because they will be there for seventy years. After that, Yahweh says, "I will bring you back from captivity. I will gather you from all the nations and places where I have banished you." Indeed, for these folks in captivity Yahweh promises that he has "plans to prosper you and not to harm you, plans to give you hope and a future.... You will seek me and find me when you seek me with all your heart."[27] Such were the promises to those who languished far from home in Babylon in 597 BCE.

For those who remained in Judah, says the prophet, they will suffer "the sword, famine and plague, they will be a curse and an object of horror, of scorn and reproach ... [because, says Yahweh] they have not listened to my words, ... words that I sent to them again and again by my servants the prophets."[28] But eventually, Yahweh promises, the people of Judah will be joined by the tribes of the north (Israel) to enjoy his favor. "So do not be afraid, Jacob my servant; do not be dismayed, Israel, ... I will surely save you out of a distant place.... Jacob will again have peace and security, and no one will make him afraid."[29]

Yahweh had glorious plans for his people, he says, even the descendants of the Northern Kingdom:

> In a far-off land the LORD will manifest himself to them. He will say to them, "I have loved you with an everlasting love. That is why I have continued to be faithful to you. I will rebuild you, my dear children Israel, so that you will once again be built up. Once again you will take up the tambourine and join in the happy throng of dancers. Once again you will plant vineyards on the hills of Samaria. Those who plant them will once again enjoy their fruit. Yes, a time is coming when watchmen will call out on the mountains of Ephraim, 'Come! Let us go to Zion to worship the LORD our God!'" Moreover, the LORD says, "Sing for joy for the descendants of Jacob. Utter glad shouts for that foremost of the nations.... I will bring them back from the land of the north. I will gather them in from the distant parts of the earth. Blind and lame people will come with them, so will pregnant women and women about to give birth. A vast throng of people will come back here. They will come back shedding tears of contrition. I will bring them back

---

27. Jer 29:10–14.
28. Jer 29:5–19.
29. Jer 30:10.

praying prayers of repentance. I will lead them besides streams of water, along smooth paths where they will never stumble. I will do this because I am Israel's father...."[30]

Jeremiah's letter to the exiles in Babylon was not, however, appreciated by the notables among the captives in Babylon, for they looked forward to a quick return to Jerusalem. The idea that they were favored by Yahweh by being situated far away in captivity made little sense to them, neither did the claim that Jerusalem would suffer plague, sword, and famine. Other prophets among the captives arose to assure everyone that they would soon return to their homeland, and they claimed, like Jeremiah, to be spokesmen for Yahweh.[31]

Resentment among the exiles in Babylon against the letter to the captives would cause Jeremiah trouble at home. A notable person among the golah named Shemaiah wrote to the high priest in Jerusalem demanding that Jeremiah be silenced; he even urged that he be put in the stocks. And there were plenty of folks in Jerusalem who thought that was a good idea; many people wanted Jeremiah to be curbed. But did anyone take notice of what he was saying? This may have been one of the times when the prophet shouted out in exasperation, "O land, land, land, hear the word of the Lord!"[32]

---

30. Jer 31:3–17 NET.
31. Jer 29:5–19.
32. Jer 22:29.

# 8

## Prophet in Babylon
*Ezekiel*

EVEN AS JEREMIAH WAS crying out to be taken seriously, a distinctive, formidable new prophetic voice was appearing among the captives in Babylon. And he would be as disparaging as Jeremiah. This was Ezekiel, one of the talented young men imported by Nebuchadnezzar for his own service in Babylon. Ezekiel came from the Zadokite lineage of priests who controlled the ritual services in the temple. They traditionally represented the belief that Jerusalem was a sacred locality, that the temple was the proper locus of Yahweh worship, that the household of David should forever occupy the throne, and that the people of Israel had a privileged relationship with Yahweh, established through a covenant with their ancestors in the ancient past. They were among the Yahwists who had committed themselves to worship Yahweh alone and to obey his commandments, hoping that they would be blessed for their obedience. It was Ezekiel's lot to live at a time when these fundamental religious dogmas were contradicted by events.

What we know of Ezekiel comes essentially from the book ascribed to him.[1] Compared to most of the other prophetic writings in the Bible this book has been only lightly edited; in some ways it could be read as a diary of notable events in his life. The book seems to have survived because it was considered useful for contemporary and succeeding generations

---

1. Albertz (*Israel*, 346) describes the book as a much more "unified composition" and the work of a "strong and consistent creative will."

of the golah. Unlike the books of Isaiah and Jeremiah it tracks events in chronological order. It even provides dates for certain notable events, such as Ezekiel's birth (623 BCE), and his call to prophesy (593 BCE).[2] Here I follow Ezekiel's prophetic activities in Babylon down to the point when he hears that Jerusalem had fallen to the Babylonians (587 BCE); in a later chapter I note the new themes taken up by Ezekiel after that event.

## Ezekiel's Call

Ezekiel received his call from Yahweh through a terrifying vision, so awesome that he records where and when it took place: "on the fifth day of the month[,] . . . the fifth year of King Jehoiachin's exile" (July 31, 593 BCE),[3] while he was living in Tel-abib by the river Chebar.[4] The vision presented Yahweh as a majestic, powerful, beautiful, mysterious composite of images: a storm, lightening, billowing clouds, brilliant light, flames of fire, five peculiar creatures, each with four faces and four wings that gleamed "like polished bronze"; a fluttering sound like "rushing waters," like "the voice of the Almighty," or like "the tumult of an army"; and wheels within wheels, each with rims "full of eyes all around" that glowed "like gleaming jasper" and moved without turning; and above all this there was a mysterious figure, "a man," enveloped in a fiery glow and a brilliant rainbow, sitting on a throne that gleamed like sapphire. Ezekiel was so shaken by the apparition that he collapsed face down on the ground.

That this apparition—an image of Yahweh?—would have appeared to him in Babylon, a pagan country far from the temple of Solomon, impressed upon the young man the sense that Yahweh was indeed a god beyond the lands of Judah. Here was a previously unimagined concept: Yahweh existed even here, in a gentile country; he had not been left behind by the Babylonian exiles; he was here with them. The importance of such a notion, says theologian Keith Carley, could "hardly be exaggerated for those who were accustomed to link the presence of God with a particular country (Judah) or building (the Temple). Until that time Ezekiel and the other exiles would

---

2. Ezek 1:1.

3. Block, *Book of Ezekiel*, 87. If Block's date is correct, Ezekiel was called seven years to the month before the fall of Jerusalem.

4. Despite the specific references to Babylon in the text some scholars argue that he was actually situated in or near Jerusalem, or (according to some) even in the city before it fell (*New Bible Dictionary*, 353–55). I here follow Weir (*Aspects of the Book of Jeremiah*).

have felt at a loss owing to their distance from their sacred temple, but the vision suggested that Yahweh could reveal himself elsewhere, even among the golah living in a pagan land." Yahweh was present, even in Babylon. "No longer, the vision suggested, should the exiles suppose that true worship of Yahweh had to be limited to Jerusalem. Their God was present and accessible even in a foreign land."[5]

The terrifying image was enough to compel awe, worship, and submission, but to enforce Yahweh's claim on his life he subjected Ezekiel to further ordeals.[6] He was lifted up in a vision and placed on his feet; he was warned against refusing to comply (as some of his compatriots had done); he was commanded three times to eat a "scroll" set before him, and then force-fed the scroll. He was lifted up with a "strong hand" and warned (again!) against refusing to comply; and he was warned against defending his people. How could he have refused such a call?[7]

The fundamental message in Ezekiel's early years would be directed to the concerns of the golah who wanted to return to Jerusalem. That, he said, would not happen, for Yahweh had determined to destroy Jerusalem and his temple. Another focus of Ezekiel's prophecies to the golah was the reasons for Yahweh's decision to enact such a radical plan. It was because God's people had betrayed the covenant that Yahweh had made with their ancestors. According to the terms of that covenant, if they disobeyed his commandments they would endure many disasters. And yet—and this would be the theme of Ezekiel's latter years—Yahweh's intentions were benevolent; they had always been benevolent. He was working to win back their devotion to him, that they would commit themselves to him as his people, and for him to be their god, their only god. By extreme measures he would transform their inner dispositions toward him: he would change their hearts. And once their hearts toward him had changed he would bless them and bring them back to their country. This was the substance of Ezekiel's prophetic message.

But it would fall upon obdurate ears. The people of Israel were committed to disobeying Yahweh's commands. Yahweh told him, "You are not being sent to a people of obscure speech and strange language, but to the people of Israel . . . [who] are not willing to listen to you because they are not willing to listen to me, for all the Israelites are hardened and obstinate.

5. Carley, *Book of the Prophet Ezekiel*, 19.
6. Block, *Book*, 122.
7. Ezek 2–3.

But I will make you as unyielding and hardened as they are.... So you need not be daunted by them."[8]

## *Ezekiel's Style: Pantomime*

Ezekiel presented his messages through exaggerated displays or fantastic visions that were vivid, gross, sometimes even lewd.[9] Indeed, Ezekiel himself would become a sign for his people; his life would display a kind of portent of things to come in order to "transform his audience's perception of their relationship with Yahweh."[10] He challenged the captives' delusions of their own innocence by acting out Yahweh's disgust and abhorrence of their ways of life.

One of Ezekiel's earliest symbolic pantomimes was a sandcastle, built on a brick slab as a representation of the city of Jerusalem. He constructed siege works around the city and posted images of soldiers with battering rams next to it. Then he set up an iron frying pan to stand for the defensive walls around the city. Eventually, he would destroy the whole construction in the sand, to illustrate what would happen to the city.

Another pantomime depicted the length of time that the Judahites would remain in captivity: he lay on his left side for 390 days, representing the time of Yahweh's patience before destroying the Northern Kingdom of Israel. Then Ezekiel lay on his right side for forty days, to represent a length of time, in years, that Judah would be in captivity.[11]

In yet another symbolic action he was told to bake a loaf of bread that exemplified how austere the situation would be for the residents of the city under siege. The small ration of water showed how little water they would have to drink.

## *What the Pantomimes Meant*

To make sure that the meanings of these actions were understood by his audience, Yahweh told Ezekiel, "I am about to cut off the food supply in Jerusalem. The people will eat rationed food in anxiety and drink rationed

---

8. Ezek 3:5–9.

9. *New Bible Dictionary*, 354.

10. Block, *Book*, 11, 14.

11. Ezek 4:1–8. The interpretive problems with this passage are discussed in Block, *Book*, 170–72.

water in despair, for food and water will be scarce. They will . . . waste away because of their sin." The reason for Yahweh's anger at Judah was its betrayal of the covenant with Yahweh:

> Because of all your detestable idols, I will do to you what I have never done before and will never do again[:] . . . parents will eat their children, and children will eat their parents. I will . . . scatter all your survivors to the winds. . . . [Indeed,] because you have defiled my sanctuary with all your vile images and detestable practices, . . . I will not look on you with pity or spare you. . . . I will make you a ruin and a reproach among the nations around you, in the sight of all who pass by I will send famine and wild beasts against you, and they will leave you childless. Plague and bloodshed will sweep through you, and I will bring the sword against you.[12]

Furthermore, he says,

> I am about to bring a sword against you, and I will destroy your high places. Your altars will be demolished and your incense altars will be smashed; and I will slay your people in front of your idols. I will lay the dead bodies of the Israelites in front of their idols, and I will scatter your bones around your altars. . . . [T]he towns will be laid waste and the high places demolished. . . . Your people will fall slain among you, and you will know that I am the LORD.[13]

This formula, "they will know that I am the LORD," is repeated nine times in chapters 5 to 9 of the book of Ezekiel. It seems to be a way to emphasize Yahweh's unshakable commitment to bring to pass what he had promised.

### Yahweh's Bill of Particulars

In the second year of his call Ezekiel was given a vision of Yahweh's complaints against the people of Judah, the "abominable" practices that would bring his wrath upon them, presented in a series of images.

- He was taken to the altar gate where he saw "an idol of jealousy." Whatever it was, its appearance obviously was a blatant offence to Yahweh, for he asked, "Do you see what they are doing—the utterly detestable

---

12. Ezek 5:7–17.
13. Ezek 6:3b–7.

things the Israelites are doing here, things that will drive me far from my sanctuary?"[14]

- In a hidden place inside the temple Ezekiel saw, "portrayed all over the walls, all kinds of crawling things and unclean animals and all the idols of Israel. In front of them stood seventy elders of Israel. . . . Each had a censer in his hand, and a fragrant cloud of incense was rising [from it]." Then Yahweh asked, "Son of man, have you seen what the elders of Israel are doing in the darkness, each at the shrine of his own idol? They say, 'The Lord does not see us; the Lord has forsaken the land.'"[15]

- In the north gate he "saw women sitting there, mourning the god Tammuz. He said to me, 'Do you see this, son of man? You will see things that are even more detestable than this.'"[16]

- In the inner court of the temple and "at the entrance to the temple, between the portico and the altar, were about twenty-five men. With their backs toward the temple of the Lord and their faces toward the east, they were bowing down to the sun in the east. He said to me, 'Have you seen this, son of man? Is it a trivial matter for the people of Judah to do the detestable things they are doing here? Must they also fill the land with violence and continually arouse my anger? . . . Therefore I will deal with them in anger; I will not look on them with pity or spare them. Although they shout in my ears, I will not listen to them.'"[17]

---

14. Block, *Book*, 286, translates Yahweh's words as an exclamation: "Look at what they are doing . . . !"

15. Ezek 8:9–10.

16. Ezek 8:14–15. Easton (*Illustrated Bible Dictionary*) describes Tammuz as "a corruption of Dumuzi, the Acadian sun-god (the Adonis of the Greeks), the husband of the goddess Ishtar. In the Chaldean calendar there was a month set apart in honor of this god, the month of June to July, the beginning of the summer solstice. At this festival, which lasted six days, the worshippers, with loud lamentations, bewailed the funeral of the god, they sat 'weeping for Tammuz.'" http://www.biblestudytools.com/dictionary/tammuz/.

17. Ezek 8:16, 17.

# Jerusalem Burning

## The Executioners

Here was the point: Yahweh had determined to bring judgment on the city of Jerusalem because of the common practice there of worshipping other gods. To reinforce this message, that disaster lay ahead, Ezekiel was shown a vision of six executioners. One of them was sent out into the city to "put a mark on the foreheads of those who grieve and lament over all the detestable things that are done in it." The other five were sent to "[f]ollow him through the city and kill, without showing pity or compassion. Slaughter the old men, the young men and women, the mothers and children, but do not touch anyone who has the mark. Begin at my sanctuary."

Ezekiel was shocked at the carnage, and he fell on his face and cried out, "Alas, Sovereign LORD! Are you going to destroy the entire remnant of Israel in this outpouring of your wrath on Jerusalem?" Yahweh answered that "The sin of the people of Israel and Judah is exceedingly great; the land is full of bloodshed and the city is full of injustice."[18]

## Yahweh Abandons the Temple

Ezekiel had another vision of the terrifying image of God. Only this time the mysterious, terrifying apparition that appeared to him at first was leaving the temple. "[T]he glory of the LORD departed from over the threshold of the temple and stopped above the cherubim. While I watched, the cherubim spread their wings and rose from the ground, and as they went, the wheels went with them. They stopped at the entrance of the east gate of the LORD's house, and the glory of the God of Israel was above them."[19] Then the image vanished.

The significance of this vision was ominous: Yahweh would no longer dwell in the temple built in his honor. The city and the temple would be left without his protection. That was in direct contrariety to the story that had circulated among the people of Jerusalem since the time of Hezekiah, that Jerusalem would be spared, as it was when Sennacherib threatened it.[20] What could the departure of the apparition from the temple mean?

---

18. Ezek 9:3–11.
19. Ezek 10:1–20.
20. Klein, "Ezekiel," 3.

# Prophet in Babylon

## *The Elders Plot Evil*

Again Yahweh gave Ezekiel a vision of the reason for his determination to destroy Jerusalem. He was brought to the east gate of the temple where he saw twenty-five notables gathered to "plot evil and to offer wicked advice within the city." To these notables Yahweh declared, "I know what is going through your mind. You have killed many people in this city and filled its streets with the dead." Yahweh then declared that he would drive these men out of the city. He would bring "the sword" against them and deliver them into the hands of foreigners. "I will execute judgment on you at the borders of Israel . . . for you have not followed my decrees or kept my laws but have conformed to the standards of the nations around you."

Even as this message was being pronounced, one of the elders died, prompting Ezekiel in desperation to cry out for mercy: "Then I fell face down and cried out in a loud voice, 'Alas, Sovereign LORD! Will you completely destroy the remnant of Israel?'"[21] Yahweh responded that he was for now "a sanctuary for [the Israelites] in the countries where they have gone," but eventually he would "bring [them] back from the countries where you have been scattered, and I will give you back the land of Israel again."

This plan—punishment and renewal—was to correct their obstinacy: Yahweh was going to change their hearts. At that time "I will give them an undivided heart and put a new spirit in them; I will remove from them their heart of stone and give them a heart of flesh. Then they will follow my decrees and be careful to keep my laws. They will be my people, and I will be their God. Even so, as for those whose hearts are devoted to their vile images and detestable idols, I will bring down on their own heads what they have done."[22]

## *Another Pantomime: Packing for Travel*

Ezekiel, prophesying to his fellow Judahites in Babylon, warned them against supposing that they would ever return to their homeland. It was a warning that would presumably be shared with their relatives in Judah. In fact, the next pantomime directly applied to the relatives in Jerusalem. Ezekiel was told to

---

21. Ezek 11:5b–13.
22. Ezek 11:16–21.

pack your belongings for exile, ... go from where you are to another place. Perhaps they will understand, though they are a rebellious people. During the daytime, while they watch, bring out your belongings packed for exile. Then in the evening, while they are watching, go out like those who go into exile. While they watch, dig through the wall and take your belongings out through it. Put them on your shoulder as they are watching and carry them out at dusk. Cover your face so that you cannot see the land, for I have made you a sign to the Israelites.

Then Yahweh revealed what this pantomime meant. The "prince" of Judah—King Zedekiah—"will put his things on his shoulder at dusk and leave, and a hole will be dug in the wall for him to go through. He will cover his face so that he cannot see the land. Even though he will try to escape I will spread my net for him, and he will be caught in my snare; I will bring him to Babylonia, the land of the Chaldeans ..."—and here Yahweh predicts what will happen to Zedekiah and his associates: "I will scatter to the winds all those around him—his staff and all his troops—and I will pursue them with drawn sword...." A few will survive this disaster "so that in the nations where they go they may acknowledge all their detestable practices. Then they will know that I am the LORD." Again he distills the point in a few words: "The inhabited towns will be laid waste and the land will be desolate. Then you will know that I am the LORD."[23]

Some folks among the golah seemed to believe that these tragic developments would take place only in the distant future, but Yahweh insisted that none of "my words will be delayed any longer; whatever I say will be fulfilled, declares the Sovereign LORD."[24]

There was among the golah a general appearance of piety, but Ezekiel confronted a group of men who presented themselves to him appearing to be eager for a word from Yahweh, but it was mere pretense. In truth "these men have set up idols in their hearts [Yahweh told him] and put wicked stumbling blocks before their faces." Yahweh appealed to them: "Repent! Turn from your idols and renounce all your detestable practices! ... I will set my face against them and make them an example and a byword. I will remove them from my people."[25]

---

23. Ezek 12:12–20.
24. Ezek 12:28.
25. Ezek 14:1–6.

# Prophet in Babylon

## *Allegory: The Adulterous Lover*

In a long discourse about Yahweh's love for the Israelites, Ezekiel presents Yahweh's case against them in the form of an allegory. A passerby rescues a helpless child and raises her up, falls in love with her, and marries her, only to be jilted by her. Yahweh said, on "the day you were born your cord was not cut, nor were you washed with water to make you clean, nor were you rubbed with salt or wrapped in cloths. No one looked on you with pity or had compassion enough to do any of these things for you. Rather, you were thrown out into the open field, for on the day you were born you were despised."

But Yahweh saved this child from her pathetic condition. "Then I passed by and saw you kicking about in your blood, and as you lay there in your blood, I said to you, 'Live!' I made you grow like a plant of the field. You grew and developed and entered puberty. Your breasts had formed and your hair had grown, yet you were stark naked."

Yahweh fell in love with this young woman and betrothed her in marriage. "[W]hen I looked at you and saw that you were old enough for love, I spread the corner of my garment over you and covered your naked body. I gave you my solemn oath and entered into a covenant with you, . . . and you became mine."

Then Yahweh bathed her and decked her with beautiful clothing and jewels. "So you were adorned with gold and silver; your clothes were of fine linen and costly fabric and embroidered cloth. . . . You became very beautiful and rose to be a queen. And your fame spread among the nations on account of your beauty."

Famous for her beauty, she betrayed him.

> But you trusted in your beauty and used your fame to become a prostitute. You lavished your favors on anyone who passed by and your beauty became his. You took some of your garments to make gaudy high places, where you carried on your prostitution. . . . You also took the fine jewelry I gave you, the jewelry made of my gold and silver, and you made for yourself male idols and engaged in prostitution with them. And you took your embroidered clothes to put on them, and you offered my oil and incense before them. Also the food I provided for you—the flour, olive oil, and honey I gave you to eat—you offered as fragrant incense before them.

Yahweh's lover even sacrificed her children to her idols.

You slaughtered my children and sacrificed them to the idols. In all your detestable practices and your prostitution you did not remember the days of your youth, when you were naked and bare, kicking about in your blood. Woe! Woe to you, declares the Sovereign Lord. In addition to all your other wickedness, you built a mound for yourself and made a lofty shrine in every public square. At every street corner you built your lofty shrines and degraded your beauty, spreading your legs with increasing promiscuity to anyone who passed by. You engaged in prostitution with the Egyptians, your neighbors with large genitals, and aroused my anger with your increasing promiscuity. So I stretched out my hand against you and reduced your territory; I gave you over to the greed of your enemies, the daughters of the Philistines, who were shocked by your lewd conduct. You engaged in prostitution with the Assyrians too, because you were insatiable; and even after that, you still were not satisfied. Then you increased your promiscuity to include Babylonia, a land of merchants, but even with this you were not satisfied. You adulterous wife! You prefer strangers to your own husband! . . . [Y]ou give gifts to all your lovers, bribing them to come to you from everywhere for your illicit favors.

But there would be consequences:

Because you poured out your lust and exposed your naked body in your promiscuity with your lovers, and because of all your detestable idols, and because you gave them your children's blood, therefore I am going to gather all your lovers . . . against you from all around [and] I will sentence you to the punishment of women who commit adultery and who shed blood. . . . Then I will deliver you into the hands of your lovers, and they will tear down your mounds and destroy your lofty shrines. They will strip you of your clothes and take your fine jewelry and leave you stark naked. They will bring a mob against you, who will stone you and hack you to pieces with their swords. They will burn down your houses and inflict punishment on you in the sight of many women.

Even then, however, Yahweh was committed to his unfaithful wife. He wanted to establish a new and enduring covenant with her. "Yet I will remember the covenant I made with you in the days of your youth, and I will establish an everlasting covenant with you." The effect of his generosity, Yahweh says, will overwhelm his bride with shame. "So I will establish my covenant with you, and you will know that I am the Lord. Then, when I make atonement for you for all you have done, you will remember and be ashamed and never again open your mouth because of your humiliation, declares the Sovereign LORD."[26] Daniel Block concludes his discussion of this passage with the observation that "The disputational form and hortatory style press readers in every age to decision. To those who presume on the grace of God, it sends a stern warning; to those who despair of life, it offers hope."

This god, Ezekiel says, is committed to his people; they are his beloved. It is only in frustration that he punishes them, only to correct and restore a relationship with them. He pleads, he argues, he complains, he appeals—all to the end that his people would return to him. He punishes with deep reluctance, and only as a last resort. "Repent! Turn away from all your offenses; then sin will not be your downfall. Rid yourselves of all the offenses you have committed and get a new heart and a new spirit. Why will you die, people of Israel? For I take no pleasure in the death of anyone, declares the Sovereign LORD. Repent and live!"[27]

But Yahweh's courting of his beloved is driven by another motive: his reputation. Judah, his bride, will be a vehicle through which to demonstrate his generosity to the world. That has been his intention in all his works with the people of Israel, says the prophet. Even in the ancient past, when he saved them from Egypt, "I did it to keep my name from being profaned in the eyes of the nations. . . . Therefore I led them out of Egypt and brought them into the wilderness. I gave them my decrees and . . . my laws, by which the person who obeys them will live. Also I gave them my Sabbaths as a sign between us, so they would know that I the LORD made them holy."[28]

## The Obstinacy of His People

But Yahweh's relationship with the Israelites was plagued by their stubborn unfaithfulness. The terms of the covenant between them entailed obligations on both sides, and the Israelites had repeatedly refused to fulfill their side of the covenant. Yahweh's favor was conditional from the beginning, but they had from very early ignored (forgotten?) their stipulated obligations to him. The prophet reminds the Israelites in their captivity in Babylonia that their ancestors had often rebelled against him. "They did not follow my decrees but rejected my laws . . . and they utterly desecrated my

26. Ezek 16. Cf. Block, *Book*, 589.
27. Ezek 18:30-32.
28. Ezek 20:4-12.

Sabbaths." This is why Yahweh had been angry at them. But he could not bring himself to destroy them.

> I said I would pour out my wrath on them and destroy them in the wilderness. But for the sake of my name I did what would keep it from being profaned in the eyes of the nations. [So] I swore to them in the wilderness that I would not bring them into the land I had given them—a land flowing with milk and honey, the most beautiful of all lands—because they rejected my laws and did not follow my decrees and desecrated my Sabbaths. For their hearts were devoted to their idols. Yet I looked on them with pity and did not destroy them or put an end to them in the wilderness.

He then spoke to the children of the current generation. "I said to their children in the wilderness, 'Do not follow the statutes of your parents or keep their laws or defile yourselves with their idols. I am the Lord your God; follow my decrees and be careful to keep my laws. Keep my Sabbaths holy, that they may be a sign between us. Then you will know that I am the Lord your God.'"[29]

The covenant between Yahweh and his people was not working out. He had wanted to favor them with his mercy, but they had shown little interest in him and his entreaties. "They did not follow my decrees, they were not careful to keep my laws, . . . and they desecrated my Sabbaths." Yet, despite their long history of disobedience, Yahweh's commitment to them was undying. Eventually, he will turn them into an obedient people, he insists. "[A]fterwards you will surely listen to me and no longer profane my holy name with your gifts and idols. For on my holy mountain, the high mountain of Israel, . . . all the people of Israel will serve me, and there I will accept them. . . . I will accept you as fragrant incense when I bring you out from the nations and gather you from the countries where you have been scattered, and I will be proved holy through you in the sight of the nations."[30]

### *Another Pantomime: Disaster Ahead*

As affairs proceeded toward the event that would mark the end of Judah, Ezekiel was directed to display the privations that the people of Judah would bear when their city would be under siege. Yahweh tells the prophet

---

29. Ezek 20:13–20.
30. Ezek 20:21–44.

that he was about to "draw my sword from its sheath and cut off from you both the righteous and the wicked. . . . Therefore groan, son of man! Groan before them with broken heart and bitter grief. And when they ask you, 'Why are you groaning?' you shall say, 'Because of the news that is coming. Every heart will melt with fear and every hand go limp; every spirit will become faint and every leg will be wet with urine.' It is coming! It will surely take place, declares the Sovereign LORD."[31]

Yahweh even appeals directly to the people in Jerusalem. To King Zedekiah: "You profane and wicked prince of Israel, whose day has come. . . . Take off the turban, remove the crown. . . ."[32] And to the people in Jerusalem: "You have become guilty because of the blood you have shed and have become defiled by the idols you have made. You have brought your days to a close, and the end of your years has come. Therefore I will make you an object of scorn to the nations and a laughingstock to all the countries."[33]

To ensure that the people in Jerusalem understood the reasons for Yahweh's wrath Ezekiel drew a scandalous image of the offenses for which Yahweh would bring Judah down. They have "shed blood," referring to the sacrifice of children to Canaanite gods; they have "treated father and mother with contempt; oppressed the foreigners, orphans, widows; desecrated my Sabbaths; slandered their neighbors"; venerated shrines where they have committed lewd acts (possibly sex acts at their shrines); they have slept with women forbidden to them (neighbors' wives; sisters; menstruating women); they accept bribes; they take interest from the poor.[34]

So many offenses! For these Yahweh ordained captivity for the people of Judah. "I will disperse you among the nations and scatter you through the countries; and I will put an end to your uncleanness."[35]

And yet, Yahweh still had plans for his people. "When I gather the people of Israel from the nations where they have been scattered, I will be proved holy through them in the sight of the nations. Then they will live in their own land, . . . in safety and will build houses and plant vineyards. . . . And when I inflict punishment on all their neighbors who maligned them. . . . Then they will know that I am the LORD their God."[36]

31. Ezek 21:2b–7.
32. Ezek 21:25, 26.
33. Ezek 22:3b–4.
34. Ezek 22:6–12.
35. Ezek 22:15.
36. Ezek 28:24–25.

Such were the prophecies of Ezekiel among the golah in Babylon. He had things to say to Judah's neighbors, specifically to Ammon, Moab, Seir, Edom, Philistia, Tyre, Sidon, and Egypt. As a distinctive personality, with distinctive skills, his warnings and predictions of Yahweh's frustration against the people of Israel and the disaster that would soon overwhelm Judah were in the critical tradition of the Yahwistic prophets who preceded him. Now, as the warnings were soon to be dramatically and tragically objectified, he had spoken with a raw bluntness, crudeness, even a lewdness that scandalized the sensibilities of his countrymen, but his gross vocabulary should have prepared the citizens of the city for what would soon take place. His proclamations, when put into writing, were for some folks in the community too offensive to be read aloud in their sacred assemblies. But his critiques were hardly different in substance from those of Zephaniah, Habakkuk, Huldah, the unfortunate Uriah, and Jeremiah.[37] Their declarations would together be preserved in the collective memory of the survivors of the disaster so that when a disaster took place of the sort they had warned about there was a reservoir of cultural resources—concepts, critiques, warnings, prophecies—from which to craft a way to understand what had happened to them. But also the repeated assertion by the prophets that Yahweh had an enduring commitment to his people would enable the survivors of the disaster to believe that there was reason for hope. Yahweh had grand plans for his people, the prophets had claimed, and despite the tragic losses the Judahites would suffer they could know, because of the ministries of Ezekiel and Jeremiah, that their story was not over.

---

37. Some scholars believe that the similarities in the prophetic texts have been created by editors who in later times were promoting the Deuteronomic critique.

# 9

# Zedekiah

IN JUDAH THE COMMUNITY that had suffered the siege of the city because of Jehoiakim's rebellion was trying to reconstitute itself after the disruptive Babylonians' siege of Jerusalem. The famished citizens were still short on food; the treasury was empty; the most promising young elite of the country had been taken away; Jehoiakim had vanished from the scene, and his son had been carried away with the others. Zedekiah had been appointed king by an alien invader, and in fact he seemed uncomfortable in his position. He had been forced to swear loyalty to Nebuchadnezzar in the name of his own god—a ritual performance aimed at ensuring that he, unlike his predecessor, would not betray his patron conqueror. In fact, his new name—which meant "Yahweh is [my] righteousness"—was a cognomen for which he would prove unworthy.[1] The citizenry seemed, even from the beginning, to see him as a barely legitimate king; many of them, especially those in Babylon, reckoned calendrical time from the date of Jeconiah's accession to the kingship, not Zedekiah's.[2]

Hardly had Zedekiah come into office that he was given news that the town of Ramah-Negev on his southern frontier was being threatened

---

1. 2 Kgs 24:17. Lipschits, *Fall*, 55–68. The name could also mean "Yahweh is my justice," a phrase that suggests that betrayal of an oath to him could require punishment.

2. 2 Kgs 25:27. Babylonian inscriptions have been found referring to Jehoiachin as "the king of the land of Judah." That Ezekiel dates events from the time of Jehoiachin's ascension seems to indicate that he regarded Jehoiachin as still the rightful king of Judah (Block, *Book*, 6).

by Edomite marauders. The record of this episode is recorded on ostraca found at Arad. To respond to the threat Zedekiah ordered the commander at nearby Kinah to send troops to help defend Ramah-Negev. This commander pointedly refused, arguing that he was barely able to hold his own position, as he was also being harassed by Edomites. The king sent back a new order: send troops or die. There is no record how this dispute turned out, other than that somewhat later both of the locations along the southern frontier had been overrun by Edomites, possibly in 587 BCE, that is, during the time that Jerusalem was being besieged for a second time by the Babylonians. What this affair demonstrates is how vulnerable the country of Judah was at the time, and how clumsy the new king was in his role. He did not perform with wisdom when confronted by a critical problem.[3]

## Debate with Hananiah

Moreover, Zedekiah was not a man of his word. Indeed, hardly had Nebuchadnezzar's troops quit the city (March, 597 BCE) that Zedekiah revealed his true character. He invited representatives from the neighboring countries of Edom, Moab, Ammon, Tyre, and Sidon to confer with him on how to break away from their new master.[4] Jeremiah was opposed to the whole idea.[5] He was told by Yahweh to picket the conference. "Make a yoke out of straps and crossbars and put it on your neck." Then he was to announce to the envoys of these nations that Yahweh would hand their countries over to Nebuchadnezzar. In fact, he said, any country that refuses to submit to Nebuchadnezzar would suffer "sword, famine and plague." Further, Jeremiah says to Zedekiah and his advisors, "do not listen to your prophets, your diviners, your interpreters of dreams, your mediums or your sorcerers. . . . They prophesy lies to you that will only serve to remove you far from your lands; . . . But if any nation will bow its neck under the yoke of the king of Babylon and serve him, I will let that nation remain in its own land to till it and to live there, declares the LORD." This was what the prophet declared in public for the benefit of the envoys from the countries who were conferring on the grounds of the temple. But to King Zedekiah Jeremiah sent

---

3. https://www.bible.ca/ostraca/bible-ostraca-ostracon-Arad40-letters-edomite-threat-send-troops-Gemariah-Nehemiah-Malchijah-Eshijah-Ramah-Negev-Tel-Ira-Kinah-Horvat-Uza-YHWH-597BCE.htm.

4. I rely on Lipschits, *Fall*, in recounting this sequence of events.

5. Jer 27.

an appeal: "Bow your neck under the yoke of the king of Babylon; serve him and his people, and you will live." Otherwise, he said, the price for refusing to submit would be the total demise of Judah. This he also said to the priests and the public. "Serve the king of Babylon, and you will live." He even specified some of the precious items in the temple that would be lost to Judah if the country rebelled: the pillars, the bronze Sea, the movable stands, and other sacred articles would all be lost to the Babylonians, he said. And the "nobles of Judah" would be taken to Babylon where they would remain until the time that "I will bring them back and restore them to this place."[6]

Jeremiah's speeches on the temple grounds caught the attention of the whole city. And in response a "prophet" named Hananiah, who also claimed to speak in the name of Yahweh, challenged him. Hananiah asserted that the secret pact being sealed among the emissaries would prevail.[7] Within two years, he said, they would be free of the Babylonian claim on their treasuries. Nebuchadnezzar would even bring back all the sacred objects of the temple that he had taken in the previous raid. And King Jeconiah would return, he said, as well as all the other notables that had been taken away.[8] Jeremiah responded that the proof of a prophecy was whether it comes to pass, so events in the next two years would demonstrate whether Hananiah's prophecy came from Yahweh or not. Hananiah then took Jeremiah's props to dramatize how wrong his prophecies were. He "took the yoke off the neck of the prophet Jeremiah and broke it, and he said before all the people . . . : 'In the same way I will break the yoke of Nebuchadnezzar king of Babylon off the neck of all the nations within two years.'"[9] Jeremiah at first walked away from the argument, but as he was leaving the temple grounds he got a directive on how to answer Hananiah. Yahweh would give the Babylonians control of everything in the region, he said. And to emphasize the point he said they would even have control over the wild animals. As for Hananiah himself, said Jeremiah, he would be "removed from the face of the earth."[10]

---

6. Jer 27:2–22.

7. According to the *New Oxford Annotated Bible*, 1103, this confrontation took place in August 594 BCE.

8. Jer 28:1–4.

9. Jer 28:10–11.

10. Jer 28:13–17.

This confrontation on the grounds of the temple, phrased as prophecy in the name of Yahweh, was essentially about how to interpret Judah's predicament, whether or not to consent to the hegemonic demands for submission and tribute payments to the Babylonians. Jeremiah was insisting that Judah must accept their dominance and pay the tribute; Hananiah was saying that the current ascendance of the Babylonians was an aberration that would soon be corrected. Judah and its neighbors would soon be relieved of the Babylonian demands.

It would not take long for a change in the situation to shift the debate.

## Jeremiah Foretells Babylon's Demise

In his fourth year king Zedekiah was called away to Babylon (for unknown reasons), and his journey provided Jeremiah with an opportunity, through courier channels, to send a message to the golah in Babylon.[11] He gave the courier a scroll and told him to read it aloud to the golah, and then to tie it to a stone and throw it into the Euphrates, declaring to those who watched that in this way Babylon would sink, to rise no more.[12] The contents of this scroll were probably the prophecy against Babylon that appears in chapters 50 and 51 of the book of Jeremiah. This message may have been intended to give hope to the golah at a time when many of them were discouraged, for in those chapters the prophet declared that Babylon itself would be overcome by another power, and the Israelites would have a fresh relationship with Yahweh. He predicted that they would return "and bind themselves to the LORD in an everlasting covenant that will not be forgotten."[13]

## Zedekiah Takes a Risk

For a while after his invasion of Judah Nebuchadnezzar was distracted by trouble in his own homeland. In 596 BCE Elamites were harassing his eastern frontier, forcing him to engage with these rebels.[14] And soon after subduing those marauders some of his own troops mutinied (December 595

---

11. Jer 29:1–23.
12. Jer 51:61–64.
13. Jer 50:2–5. Miller and Hays, *History*, 410–11.
14. Lipschits, *Fall*, 62.

to April 594 BCE).¹⁵ These distractions meant that the local rulers of cities in Syria-Palestine were free to manage affairs as they liked; there would be no harassment by the Babylon emissaries demanding to be paid dues. Also, in Egypt a new pharaoh arose, Psammetichus II (r. 595–589 BCE) who, after putting down a Kushite rebellion in Nubia, turned his attention to expanding his influence northward into Syria-Palestine. In 592 BCE he led a naval expedition up the coast of Palestine to Phoenicia, perhaps to test the situation.¹⁶ From Zedekiah's perspective the emerging situation looked promising for the escape from Nebuchadnezzar's demands for tribute that he had been plotting. When Psammetichus II died (589 BCE) Zedekiah sent a congratulatory delegation to his successor, Pharaoh Hophra, as he was celebrating his accession to power. It was a subterfuge; the real reason was to propose an alliance with Egypt.¹⁷

Zedekiah's gambit did not stay a secret for long. Even among the golah in faraway Babylon Ezekiel heard about it, and he pronounced it folly: "[T]he king rebelled . . . by sending his envoys to Egypt to get horses and a large army. Will he succeed? . . . Will he break the treaty and yet escape? In fact, he shall die in Babylon, in the land of the king who put him on the throne, whose oath he despised and whose treaty he broke." This, the prophet said, was one more example of the king's indifference to the oath of loyalty he had sworn in the name of his god Yahweh. "He despised the oath by breaking the covenant, . . . he shall not escape."¹⁸ This was the second time Nebuchadnezzar had been betrayed by a king of Judah and his reaction was decisive: According to the book of Kings, "in the ninth year of Zedekiah's reign, on the tenth day of the tenth month, Nebuchadnezzar king of Babylon marched against Jerusalem with his whole army. He encamped outside the city and built siege works all around it."¹⁹

At this critical moment Zedekiah exhibited a fundamental flaw in his personality. Having precipitated a crisis, he dithered. He asked Jeremiah to approach Yahweh for guidance on what to do. And he got back a ferocious

---

15. Lipschits, *Fall*, 63.

16. Lipschits, *Fall*, 63n. Cf. Lloyd, "Late Period," 381; Miller and Hays, *History*, 412.

17. The writer of Lachish letter 3 (*Lachish Letters*) says, "The commander of the army, Konyahu son of Elnatan, has gone down to go to Egypt and he sent to commandeer Hodawyahu son of Ahiyahu and his men from here." This appears to refer to Zedekiah's solicitations of Pharaoh Hophra.

18. Ezek 17:15.

19. 2 Kgs 25:1,2. The date, according to Lipschits (*Fall*, 74), was early January 587 BCE.

answer. Yahweh, the prophet said, will himself "fight against you.... [Yahweh said] I will strike down those who live in this city—both man and beast—and they will die of a terrible plague. After that I will give Zedekiah king of Judah, his officials and the people in this city ... into the hands of Nebuchadnezzar [and] he will put them to the sword; he will show them no mercy or pity or compassion."[20]

Jeremiah now spoke out to the public and urged people to flee the city. "Whoever stays in this city will die by the sword, famine, or plague. But whoever goes out and surrenders to the Babylonians ... will live; they will escape with their lives. [Yahweh said,] 'I have determined to do this city harm and not good.... It will be given into the hands of the king of Babylon, and he will destroy it with fire.'"[21] In this situation, with the city under siege by an angry master who has been betrayed for a second time, Jeremiah's appeal to the people to flee the city and to the king and his elders to capitulate to the besiegers was regarded as treason.

At this moment, when Jeremiah could have feared being lynched, Yahweh told him to do something that would guarantee it. To obey what Yahweh commanded at this moment required extraordinary courage. Jeremiah led the notables of the city out to the Valley of Ben Hinnom, where sacrifices—even of children—were being made to the Canaanite gods, and he declared to them, in the name of Yahweh, that because they have "forsaken me and made this a place of foreign gods, [and] have burned incense in it to gods ... [and even] have built the high places of Baal to burn their children" Yahweh will allow them to be killed in that very place. Yahweh "will devastate this city and make it an object of horror and scorn; ... I will make them eat the flesh of their sons and daughters, and they will eat one another's flesh." At this point Jeremiah broke a jar and declared in Yahweh's name, "I will smash this nation and this city just as this potter's jar is smashed and cannot be repaired. They will bury the dead in Topheth [the place of Canaanite sacrifices] until there is no more room.... The houses in Jerusalem and those of the kings of Judah will be defiled like this place." Even then Jeremiah was not finished. From the valley of Ben Hinnom he marched back into the city and into the courtyard of the temple and proclaimed the same seditious message to the citizens of the city. Yahweh, he announced, would "bring on this city and all the villages around it every

---

20. Jer 21:6–8.
21. Jer 21:1–10.

disaster I pronounced against them, because they were stiff-necked and would not listen to my words."[22]

No surprise, then, that Jeremiah was reined in by the authorities. When the priest of temple security heard Jeremiah's prophecy he seized him and had him flogged. He then locked him up in the stocks for all in the city to see. The affair attracted attention throughout the city, and when Jeremiah was released he declared that in fact the country of Judah would be captured by Nebuchadnezzar, and many would be killed, the wealth of the country would be taken away, and the official who tormented him would die in Babylon.[23]

## Jeremiah's Collapse

The prophet had reached his limit. He was exhausted. The clash with Hananiah, the public challenge to the elders at Topheth, the public declarations at the temple, and the abusive treatment he had suffered from the officials drained the prophet of all his energy. He had courageously obeyed Yahweh's commands. He had proclaimed the coming disaster as directed, and for doing as he was told he was abused and publicly humiliated. He collapsed into self-pity, and complained to Yahweh, "You deceived me. . . . I am ridiculed all day long; everyone mocks me. Whenever I speak, I cry out proclaiming violence and destruction. So the word of the LORD has brought me insult and reproach all day long." At the same time Yahweh's word had gripped him: "if I say, 'I will not mention his word or speak anymore in his name,' his word is in my heart like a fire shut up in my bones. I am weary of holding it in; indeed, I cannot." Furthermore, the citizens of the city consented in the abuses he had suffered. "All my friends are waiting for me to slip, saying, 'Perhaps he will be deceived; then we will prevail over him and take our revenge on him.'"[24] Such friends!

Jeremiah's emotions whipped him back and forth between exultation in Yahweh and utter desolation. On one hand, "the LORD is with me like a mighty warrior; so my persecutors will stumble and not prevail. . . . Sing to the LORD! . . . He rescues the life of the needy from the hands of the wicked." On the other hand he lamented even his birth: "Cursed be the day I was born! May the day my mother bore me not be blessed! Cursed be the man

22. Jer 19.
23. Jer 20:1–6.
24. Jer 20:7–10.

who brought my father the news. . . . May he hear wailing in the morning, a battle cry at noon. For he did not kill me in the womb, with my mother as my grave. . . . Why did I ever come out of the womb to see trouble and sorrow and to end my days in shame?"[25]

## The Lachish Letters

As Jeremiah had proclaimed terror and destruction to come and struggled with his personal moments of despair and humiliation, he was being decried by people far and wide. At least it would seem so, for a set of letters that were found in 1935 among the ruins of an ancient guard room outside the old city of Lachish (Teel ed-Duweir) reveal that Jeremiah's declarations were infamous even outside the city. Although fortified, Lachish would be destroyed by the Babylonians in 588–587 BCE when they invaded Judah. In the debris of the city potsherds were found on which notes had been written in ink during the last months of the city's defense by a Judean commander named Hosha'yahu. He was writing to his superior officer while hunkered down in this stronghold.[26] Hosha'yahu was supposed to be relaying fire signals from the nearby towns at Azekah and Lachish during the time of the siege, the only cities at the time besides Jerusalem that had not yet fallen.[27] And Hosha'yahu complains about some individuals, apparently in Jerusalem, whose opinions "are of a kind to slacken your courage and to weaken that of the men. . . ." And he wished his superior would silence such people. He was worried by the claims of those urging capitulation: "As YHWH your God lives, ever since your servant read the letters he has not had [a moment of peace]."[28]

25. Jer 20:11–18.

26. The letters reflect the disturbed and excited condition of the country just before the fall of Lachish at the end of Zedekiah's reign. Professor Albright plausibly suggests the late summer of 589 BCE as the date of the letters, the period just before the arrival of the main body of Nebuchadnezzar's army which laid siege to Jerusalem in the middle of January, 588 BCE. The presence of a great number of burnt olive stones in the nearby ruins suggests that it was in autumn that the city was destroyed, "after the conclusion of the olive harvest" (Haupert, *Lachish Letters*). John W. Adey (*Social and Historical Aspects*) says of the letters, "Regarding the contribution of the LL [Lachish Letters] to historical aspects of Jeremiah's time, . . . 'could be interpolated into the Book of Jeremiah with no noticeable difference.'"

27. http://www.bible-history.com/archaeology/israel/lachish-letters.html. Jer 34:7.

28. Miller and Hayes, *History*, 418. The way the author uses the name of God in this letter suggests that in his day it was common to use Yahweh's name in ordinary speech. In this sense, the recognition of Yahweh as their god seems to have been perfunctory.

## Zedekiah

The book of Jeremiah says that there was a time when Jerusalem and the fortified cities of Lachish and Azekah "were the only fortified cities of Judah that remained" besides Jerusalem, so that Hosha'yahu's letter complaining to his superior about some people in the city discouraging everyone may have been written even at the very time Jeremiah was calling upon the citizens of the city to capitulate.[29] It was also about the time that Jeremiah is being told to deliver a personal message from Yahweh to King Zedekiah: "I am about to give this city into the hands of the king of Babylon, and he will burn it down. You will not escape from his grasp but will surely be captured and given into his hands. You will see the king of Babylon with your own eyes, and he will speak with you face to face. And you will go to Babylon." However, "You will not die by the sword; you will die peacefully." This message was meant to reassure the king that it would be well for him if he would give himself into the hands of the Babylonians.[30] But Zedekiah could not bring himself to capitulate. His inability to act would cost him dearly.

### Zedekiah Again Consults the Prophet

One reason that Zedekiah was still hoping to withstand the siege was that it looked like Egypt would finally come to his aid. Pharaoh indeed at about that time did bring an army into Palestine, approaching Jerusalem as if to challenge the Babylonians. His move forced the Babylonians to lift the siege of the city and reposition themselves against the advancing forces. Zedekiah took this as great news and appealed to Jeremiah to confirm his hopes. But again, the prophet provided no comfort. "Pharaoh's army, which has marched out to support you, will go back to its own land, to Egypt. Then the Babylonians will return and attack this city; they will capture it and burn it down." Again the prophet urged the king and his advisors to accept his advice. "Do not deceive yourselves, thinking, 'The Babylonians will surely leave us.'" No matter what the Judahites do, the prophet was saying over and over, if they did not capitulate, the Babylonians would burn down their city.[31] As it happened, the Egyptians had no heart for another fight with Nebuchadnezzar, and as soon as the Babylonians positioned themselves to resist the Egyptians they turned back.

29. Jer 34:7.
30. Jer 32:3–4.
31. Jer 37:7b–10.

# Jerusalem Burning

## *The Elite Betray Their Slaves*

In this brief interlude, when the Babylonians had quit the siege in order to confront the Egyptians, a couple of notable events took place inside the city. One was an issue that arose between the slaves and their masters.[32] During the height of the siege, as everyone was struggling to survive, the notable families freed their slaves. They made the act of emancipation official by performing a ritual of emancipation in the temple. In truth, it was an act of desperation, for these well-to-do families no longer had the means to provide for their slaves. By freeing them they were releasing themselves from obligation, for they themselves were in desperate condition. Anyway, it was an act that appeared to be in obedience to Yahweh's rules, which limited the amount of time a master could hold a slave, a rule the elite had conveniently been ignoring.

But when the siege dissolved, when the Babylonians left the city to reposition themselves against the Egyptian army, the citizens in the city believed that the siege had ended. They could now get provisions for themselves and resume living as they had been before. It was in this situation that the former slave-owners demanded that the slaves return to their service. It was a betrayal of their oath of emancipation. To this Jeremiah denounced the slave-owners. In Yahweh's name he declared that they had "profaned my name" by such behavior. Therefore, they will gain a freedom for themselves: a "'freedom' to fall by the sword, plague and famine. [Furthermore,] I will make you abhorrent to all the kingdoms of the earth. . . . And your dead bodies will be food for the birds and wild animals."[33] And, said the prophet, the king himself would suffer at the hands of the Babylonians. The Babylonians had left the siege, he said, but Yahweh himself would bring them back! "I will deliver Zedekiah king of Judah and his officials into the hands of their enemies who want to kill them, to the army of the king of Babylon, . . . I will bring [the Babylonians] back to this city. They will fight against it, take it and burn it down. And I will lay waste the towns of Judah so no one can live there."[34]

---

32. Lipschits (*Fall*, 75–76) regards this event as an insertion in the text from a later time.

33. Jer 34:8–11.

34. Jer 34:13b–22.

# Zedekiah

## Jeremiah Tries to Leave

Not a good way for a prophet to behave when he has already earned the enmity of most of the notables of the city. Indeed, he would soon need powerful friends, because the other thing that took place in the city while the Babylonians had lifted the siege was Jeremiah's altercation with the officials over his attempt to leave the city. Ostensibly, at least, he was acting to claim "his share of the property among the people," for he had been given an option to buy some land. But he was stopped at the gate and apprehended by the captain of the guard, who accused him of deserting to the enemy.[35] Professor Lipschits takes this move by Jeremiah to be an attempt, along with many other folks, to escape the city while the siege was lifted. Jeremiah himself denied that he was deserting, but Lipschits believes that he might have been trying to move to the town of Mizpah a few miles north of the city where refugees from the city were gathering under Babylonian protection. It would become a protected enclave for folks who were defecting to the Babylonians. Eventually, Lipschits believes, the only people left in the city would be those who still believed that it would never fall to invaders.

Jeremiah was brought to the officials for trial. We already know what they thought of him. They had repeatedly been publicly condemned and embarrassed by Jeremiah's condemnation of their idolatries and their indifference to Yahweh's commandments. And moreover, he had in open defiance of state policy persistently appealed to the citizens of the city to surrender to the enemy. His attempt to leave the city constituted further proof in their eyes that he was disloyal. And also there was a problem of appearances: if a notable member of the city like Jeremiah were to flee during this hour of trial, other citizens might lose their resolve and flee as well. What Jeremiah was doing was manifestly subversive. The officials needed no encouragement to condemn him, for he was clearly betraying his country. They had him flogged—that would be the second time—and locked up in a nobleman's house.[36]

---

35. Jer 37:11–12.

36. Jer 37:12–16. Lipschits (*Fall*, 316–30) examines Jer 37–38 closely and believes that the story of the prophet in the cistern is a folkloristic addition, but he takes the similarities and duplications in the two incidents (prison, cistern) to indicate that something actually happened. In both stories Jeremiah was opposed by officials who wanted him punished/killed, he met the king to warn him, he affirmed twice (37:8; 39, 17,18) that if Zedekiah would not surrender Jerusalem would be burned. These subtleties do not touch my concerns, as my interest in these texts is the interpretive perspective of how Yahweh came to be the cause for the city's destruction.

# JERUSALEM BURNING

## *Zedekiah Again Asks for Advice*

Jeremiah was kept in this prison, according to the text, "for a long time," and in the meantime the Babylonians, having chased off the Egyptians, returned to Jerusalem and again set up siege works around the city. Zedekiah was pressed to do something, so—again!—he turned to Jeremiah for advice. He ordered that Jeremiah be brought in secret in order to avoid the criticism of his advisors. And he asked him if he had any word from Yahweh. Jeremiah told him what he had said before: Zedekiah would be "delivered into the hands of the king of Babylon." Not what he wanted to hear.

But Jeremiah used the opportunity to ask for the king's mercy: "What crime have I committed against you or your attendants or this people, that you have put me in prison? Where are your prophets who prophesied to you, 'The king of Babylon will not attack you or this land?'" And he begged not to be sent back to the house of the nobleman where he had been locked up "or I will die there." Apparently, his host had been so inhospitable that the prophet feared for his own life if he was to go back. The king assigned him to the courtyard of the guard and ordered that he be given a loaf of bread daily until the flour ran out.[37]

## *The Cistern*

Now Jeremiah was better off—or so it seemed. But a clique of notables that despised him had not given up on doing him in. They had heard him declare that whoever stayed in the city would be killed but whoever leaves it would save their lives. They proposed to the king that he be put to death because, as they said, he was "discouraging the soldiers who are left in this city, as well as all the people. . . . This man is not seeking the good of these people but their ruin." Zedekiah lacked the courage to speak up for Jeremiah, and he responded, "He is in your hands, I can do nothing against you." So Jeremiah was put into "the cistern of Malkijah, the king's son, which was in the courtyard of the guard."[38] Now, at least this scandalous voice would be silenced; whether he would die in the cistern was of little concern to his tormentors.

Was everyone in Judah cowed by this gang? Surely the king knew what was happening, as well as many others, and yet no native Judahite came

---

37. Jer 37:17–21.
38. Jer 38:4–6.

forward to help the prophet in this moment of helplessness. It was an alien, an Ethiopian eunuch, who mustered the courage to act. "Ebed-Melek, ... an official in the royal palace, heard that they had put Jeremiah into the cistern...." And he implored the king on Jeremiah's behalf. In response, the king allowed for the prophet to be saved from the cistern. He sent an aid to find some men to help Ebed-Melek pull the prophet out.

The project is described in some detail in the book of Jeremiah: "Ebed-Melek took the men with him and ... took some old rags and worn-out clothes from there and let them down with ropes to Jeremiah in the cistern. Ebed-Melek ... said to Jeremiah, 'Put these old rags and worn-out clothes under your arms to pad the ropes.' Jeremiah did so, and they pulled him up with the ropes and lifted him out of the cistern. And Jeremiah remained in the courtyard of the guard."[39] He was saved, pulled out of the pit, but he was still confined to the courtyard of the guard.

## Yet Again Zedekiah Consults Jeremiah

The city had been under siege for months (it would last eighteen months), the people were starving, and the king could not bring himself to act. Again he had Jeremiah brought to him and he asked him to promise to tell him the truth. Jeremiah's response was, "If I give you an answer, will you not kill me? Even if I did give you counsel, you would not listen to me." But the king swore an oath that he would not kill or hand him over to his enemies if he would but give him a word from Yahweh. Jeremiah then said what he had said before: "If you surrender ... your life will be spared and this city will not be burned down; you and your family will live. But if you will not surrender ... this city will be given into the hands of the Babylonians and they will burn it down; you yourself will not escape from them."[40]

Zedekiah's earlier comment to the elders, "the king can do nothing against you," reveals how intimidated he was by the notables in the city, but he was also fearful of the Judahites who had already gone over to the Babylonians. He confessed to Jeremiah, "I am afraid of the Jews who have gone over to the Babylonians, for the Babylonians may hand me over to them and they will mistreat me." Jeremiah reassured him that he need not fear his own people. He only needed to do what Yahweh had been telling him to do. But "if you refuse to surrender ... [a]ll the women left in the palace ... will

39. Jer 38:2–13.
40. Jer 38:14–20.

be brought out to the officials of the king of Babylon." Moreover, "All your wives and children will be brought out to the Babylonians. You yourself will not escape from their hands but will be captured by the king of Babylon; and this city will be burned down." How many times had Jeremiah said that if Zedekiah continued to refuse to surrender, his capital city would be burned the ground? This was the third time that Jeremiah had brought the same message to Zedekiah, but the king could not bring himself to take his advice. Was he paralyzed by fear? He seemed to be afraid of his own advisors. He told the prophet to tell no one about their conversation. He knew that some of his officials would ask what he and Jeremiah had talked about, and he told him to say that he had only pled with the king not be sent back to the house of the inhospitable nobleman. The editors of the text add that Jeremiah remained "in the courtyard of the guard until the day Jerusalem was captured."[41]

At some point, when Jeremiah was still "shut up in the court of the guard," Yahweh gave him a word for the Ethiopian eunuch who had saved his life. He said to Ebed-Melek: "I am about to fulfill my words against this city—But I will rescue you on that day, . . . ; you will not be given into the hands of those you fear. I will save you; you will not fall by the sword but will escape with your life."[42]

---

41. Jer 38.
42. Jer 39:16b–18.

# 10

# On the Verge

### *Jeremiah Purchases Land*

THE SIEGE WAS TAKING its toll.[1] The besiegers' control of all traffic in and out of the city left it helpless and desperate. As inside the city the citizens were starving, outside the city I surmise that the local population was being used as forced labor. Also, their lands were trampled on and overgrazed by the invaders' livestock and their fodder, produce, and meat were being demanded by the invaders. Inside the city the man who was supposed to be managing on behalf of these desperate populations needed someone to blame. He complained to the hapless prophet whose warnings he had persistently refused to accept. "Why do you prophesy as you do? . . . [that] the LORD says: 'I am about to give this city into the hands of the king of Babylon, and he will capture it. Zedekiah king of Judah will not escape the Babylonians. . . . If you fight against the Babylonians, you will not succeed.'" The king could not have been the only one wanting to throttle this pesky, annoying prophet.

In this moment Jeremiah took pains to offer hope to the desperate people of the city. He had gotten a note from a cousin who wanted to sell some property to which Jeremiah had the first right of refusal. Jeremiah took this offer as a sign from God. "I bought the field at Anathoth from my cousin. . . . I signed and sealed the deed, had it witnessed, and weighed out the silver on the scales." He then took his deed, and in the presence of many

---

1. 2 Kgs 25:3.

in the community, probably on the courtyard of the temple, he directed his assistant: "Take these documents, both the sealed and unsealed copies of the deed of purchase, and put them in a clay jar so they will last a long time." And he announced to those observing him on the courtyard that a day would come when land in Judah would be bought and sold as before. However tragic might be the course of events now, the city would someday be alive and vital again. Property would again be bought and sold, he said. And he prayed to Yahweh aloud before the people, recalling the many ways that Yahweh had protected his people in the past. And even though the city would face a terrible time—when many would suffer the sword, famine, plague, and fire—a day would come when Yahweh would show his people mercy. The prophet announced a message from Yahweh to his audience: "I will surely gather them from all the lands where I banish them in my furious anger . . . ; I will bring them back to this place and let them live in safety. They will be my people, and I will be their God."

Yahweh's real agenda, the prophet said, was to change the hearts of his people so that he could show them favor. "I will give them singleness of heart and action, so that they will always fear me and that all will then go well for them and for their children after them. I will make an everlasting covenant with them: I will never stop doing good to them, and I will inspire them to fear me, so that they will never turn away from me."[2] The prophet who had predicted so much calamity ahead was reminding the elders who had gathered on the temple grounds that Yahweh still had plans for his people. Their descendants would someday come back. Jeremiah's purchase of land, secured in a deed that would be protected for a distant future, was a declaration and demonstration of the surety of Yahweh's promise.

## Yahweh's Promises

During this time, even as the situation was desperate, with the buildings of the city, even the palace, being torn down by Judah's military for materials to construct defensive structures against the siegeworks, Jeremiah received another word from Yahweh. Yes, truly, as already predicted, it said, "the houses in this city and the royal palaces of Judah that have been torn down to be used against the siege ramps and the sword . . . will be filled with the dead bodies of the people I will slay in my anger and wrath. I will hide my face from this city because of all its wickedness." But after that time "I will

---

2. Jer 32:16–44.

bring health and healing to [this city]; I will heal my people and will let them enjoy abundant peace and security." Yahweh even promised to bring the two kingdoms of Israel back together in their revived homeland: "[I will] bring Judah and Israel back from captivity and [will] rebuild them as they were before. Moreover, I will cleanse them from all the sin they have committed against me and will forgive all their sins of rebellion against me. Then this city will bring me renown, joy, praise, and honor before all nations on earth that hear of all the good things I do for it; and they will be in awe and will tremble at the abundant prosperity and peace I provide for it."

The day would come, the message was saying, when sounds of "joy and gladness, the voices of bride and bridegroom will be heard in the city; also, the voices of those who bring thank offerings to the house of the LORD, . . . 'For I will restore the fortunes of the land as they were before,' says the LORD." Moreover, "in all its towns there will again be pastures for shepherds to rest their flocks. In the towns of the hill country, of the western foothills and of the Negev, in the territory of Benjamin, in the villages around Jerusalem and in the towns of Judah, flocks will again pass under the hand of the one who counts them." At that time a descendant of David will sit on the throne of Israel: "I will make a righteous Branch sprout from David's line; he will do what is just and right in the land. . . . [Indeed,] David will never fail to have a man to sit on the throne of Israel, nor will the Levitical priests ever fail to have a man to stand before me continually to offer burnt offerings, to burn grain offerings and to present sacrifices."

These promises, fantastic as they would have sounded in this locked-in, starving community, were sealed by an oath: "If you can break my covenant with the day and my covenant with the night, . . . then my covenant with David my servant—and my covenant with the Levites who are priests ministering before me—can be broken and David will no longer have a descendant to reign on his throne." Yahweh made even more fantastic claims: "I will make the descendants of David my servant and the Levites who minister before me as countless as the stars in the sky and as measureless as the sand on the seashore."[3]

Who could believe this?

---

3. Jer 33:5–26.

# Jerusalem Burning

## *Caldrons Near and Far*

For at least eighteen months Jerusalem was shut off from the world.[4] The siege began "in the ninth year, in the tenth month, on the tenth day of the month" (of Jeconiah's reign), that is January 5, 587 BCE.[5] And as the tourniquet tightened, the prophetic messages in both communities became more urgent and shrill, in Judah from Jeremiah, and in Babylon from Ezekiel.

Ezekiel was given another pantomime to perform: to act out, for the benefit of his fellow exiles, what the city of Jerusalem was going through. He placed a pot on a burning fire, filled it with the best pieces of meat and "choice bones," and brought the broth to a boil. Then he poured out the water and allowed the bones and the pot to be burned up. Here was a picture of what was going on in Judah. The folks in Jerusalem were the meat in the pot, being roasted. They will be in this caldron, Yahweh said, "till [the pot] becomes hot and its copper glows, so that its impurities may be melted, and its deposit burned away"—so severe would be the purge of the idolatrous practices of the people of Judah. Their worship of other gods "has frustrated all efforts [said Ezekiel]; its heavy deposit has not been removed, not even by fire." Indeed, said Yahweh, "[b]ecause I tried to cleanse you but you would not be cleansed from your impurity, you will not be clean again until my wrath against you has subsided." And here Yahweh declared his resolve to bring judgment on Judah owing to its apostasy: "'I will not have pity, nor will I relent. You will be judged according to your conduct and your actions,' declares the Sovereign LORD."[6]

As it would happen, Ezekiel himself would suffer deeply under Yahweh's command, for he would suffer like the citizens in Jerusalem. Yahweh told him that "with one blow" he would take away "the delight of your eyes." What could that mean? The phrase "The delight of your eyes" can be read as "the dearest thing you have."[7] Of this terrible loss, whatever it would be, the prophet was disallowed from showing grief. "Yet do not lament or weep or shed any tears." The assignment he was being given, of all the many onerous

---

4. The length of the siege is unclear. Scholars differ over whether it was eighteen months or thirty months. See Malamat, *Last Kings of Judah*.

5. NET note at Ezek 24:1. Lipschits (*Fall*, 74n) reckons it to have been in December 588/January 587 BCE.

6. Ezek 24:13; Block, *Book*, 781.

7. Carley (*Book*, 166) says, "This moving passage has sometimes been taken to indicate the prophet's heartlessness in turning personal grief in an act of prophecy. In fact, the depth of his personal feeling is quite evident."

tasks he had been given, would be the most painful and grievous of all. Yes, he must carry on as if nothing had happened, Yahweh said. "Groan quietly; do not mourn for the dead. Keep your turban fastened and your sandals on your feet; do not cover your mustache and beard or eat the customary food of mourners." Ezekiel would have wondered what was about to happen. He didn't have to wait long.

In the evening of that very day Ezekiel's wife died. The directives he had received had been for this situation. He was to act as he always had before. He could express no grief, not even a trace of the customary rituals of lament for his precious wife, "the delight of your eyes." Ezekiel had obeyed Yahweh faithfully through the years, and had barely whimpered, only once complaining that his neighbors were "saying of [him], 'Is he not a maker of allegories?'"[8] But now he was to bear a crushing personal loss without revealing his heartbreak. His behavior would be a stunning surprise to his friends, those who knew his wife and his love for her. In astonishment they asked why he was behaving so strangely. "Why are you acting like this?" He replied in Yahweh's name that this was to announce what was about to happen to the folks in Jerusalem. Yahweh was about to desecrate the temple,

> the stronghold in which you take pride, the delight of your eyes, the object of your affection. The sons and daughters you left behind will fall by the sword. And you will do as I have done. You will not cover your mustache and beard or eat the customary food of mourners. You will keep your turbans on your heads and your sandals on your feet. You will not mourn or weep but will waste away because of your sins and groan among yourselves.

Yahweh says to them, "Ezekiel will be a sign to you; you will do just as he has done. When this happens, you will know that I am the Sovereign LORD."[9]

Ezekiel's attempt to quench his grief was a climactic display to the exiles as well as the citizens who heard about it in Judah, whoever would hear of his behavior. That was what, in truth, the people of Jerusalem would be forced to endure. When the terrible moment finally would come, they would suffer the sudden loss of everything they held dear, "the delight of their eyes," their capital city and its majestic temple, their loved ones, their homes, their lands, their livestock—all of it, just as Ezekiel had lost his wife. And, like him, they would not be free to go through the formalities of

---

8. Ezek 20:46.
9. Ezek 24:15–27.

grieving, for there would be no time to grieve. Even as they were suffering the shock of all they had just seen and all that was lost, they were being forced to gather up their families and whatever valuables were left as they were forced out of the city and directed to set out on the journey to Babylon. The suffering prophet, holding back his tears, was a living exposition of how deeply the Israelites—those at home and those in exile—would have to manage their feelings over the loss of the city, its temple, and their way of life as they trudged away from the ruin that the Babylonians had made of the "delight of their eyes." For them there would no longer be a city to return to, or a temple to worship in.

## *Distress in Judah*

Meanwhile, as Ezekiel was acting out his pantomime of what Yahweh had told him would soon happen, the citizens of Jerusalem, still under siege, were barely surviving. Conditions among the peasants in the suburbs of the city must have been scarcely better. Their lands would have been overgrazed and heavily trampled on by the livestock of the invaders, and they would have been forced to supply food for the besieging army. As the siege ground on, the resources around the city were gradually depleted, obliging the invaders to reach further out to provide for themselves and their animals. This applied also to the built environment around the city, as the houses near the city were, I suppose, dragooned for the construction of the siege-ramps which were built at the gates and at other vulnerable sites along the defensive walls.[10] As time passed more of the houses were probably claimed by the invaders.

All the while, the king sat on his hands, his advisors having rejected any move to conciliate. Jeremiah remained locked up in the courtyard of the guards. And the flight of people from the city had ceased, those left in the city still believed against all hope that it would be somehow delivered. Pharaoh might still come to the rescue. And, of course, every soul in the city was calling upon higher powers for deliverance. Some were supplicating their gods, as least this I suppose from the debris that they would leave behind for archaeologists to find centuries later. Of course, contrary to the warnings of Jeremiah, the hope that kept many of them in the city was the belief that the sacred power of their temple would save them.

10. Lipschits (*Fall*) finds no evidence of lasting damage to the environment around the city left by the invaders. Cf. 108n10.

It was during this time that Ezekiel in Babylon was given a vision of the idolatrous behavior that some Judahites were practicing in secret. He was shown men worshipping the sun god; others worshipping images of gods engraved on the walls of a secret hideout; women attaching knitted garments to a sacred pole dedicated to the goddess Asherah ("Queen of Heaven," regarded by the Canaanites as the feminine consort of Yahweh). The women were also, in order to become fertile, lying with male prostitutes in the temple. Some families were apparently burning their children as an offering to Molech in the "valley of the son of Hinnom."[11]

---

11. Ezek 8.

# 11

# Collapse

AFTER AT LEAST EIGHTEEN months of siege the resistance crumbled, and events took place in rapid succession.[1] The editor of the book of Jeremiah says that when the Babylonians broke through the wall, they ensconced themselves in the middle gate. Zedekiah with his troops fled by night through an opening in the wall and headed for the desert.[2] They were chased down on the plane of Jericho and brought to Nebuchadnezzar's headquarters in Riblah, which would have been at least a day's journey by horseback. According to Josephus, when Zedekiah was presented to Nebuchadnezzar, the Babylonian ruler reviled him, calling him "a wicked wretch and a covenant-breaker, someone who had forgotten his former promise to keep the country for him."[3] Then they slaughtered Zedekiah's sons in front of him, blinded him, and took him away in bronze chains to Babylon.[4]

About a month after the original entry of the troops into the city a "commander of the guard" named Nebuzaradan arrived in Jerusalem and set about to destroy it. Totally. As the Romans so thoroughly wrecked Carthage that it would never rise again, the Babylonians set out to destroy Jerusalem, the city that had twice rebelled against Nebuchadnezzar. The task

---

1. The siege is believed by some to have been thirty months. Block (*Book*, 254n80) calculates the date of the collapse to be July 14, 587 BCE. NET calculates it to be July 18, 587 BCE.
2. The NIV says they fled to the Arabah, a word that means a desolate area.
3. Josephus, *Works*, 275b.
4. 2 Kgs 25:7.

## Collapse

was undertaken systematically, thoroughly. First, his troops pillaged what was left of its wealth. Most troubling to the writer(s) of the book of Kings was what they took from the temple: two bronze pillars, the movable stands and the big bronze basin called "the Sea," and many other accoutrements of the temple. The writer(s), troubled by the loss and destruction of so many sacred objects, describe how some of the valuables were desecrated. The pillars that were taken and broken up had been, the authors noted, twenty-seven feet tall and decorated with bronze latticework and pomegranate-shaped ornaments. The total amount of bronze carried away was beyond measure, they say. Once the city had been stripped of its valuables it was torched—the temple, the palace, all the "large houses." Then they broke down the defensive walls around the city. They left the city a desert.

Lipschits takes the delay of a month before the troops began destroying the city to be evidence that the task had been carefully planned. The city was not destroyed spontaneously but after a "considered political decision." The point was to "obliterate the center of rebellion."[5] It seems worth noting, also, how disciplined the Babylonian troops had been for that month of delay. They took no action against the city and its inhabitants as they waited for orders. No wonder this army was so effective in battle.

Next, Nebuzaradan dealt with the notables who had refused to capitulate. He had seized the chief priest and his deputy, the commander of the palace guard, several personal advisors to the king, the clerk in charge of military records, and as many as sixty others. Now he took them to Nebuchadnezzar at his headquarters in Riblah. The text does not say so, but it can be surmised that as these notables were presented to the king he could have insulted and berated them as he had Zedekiah. In the end, every one of them was slaughtered.[6] In the meantime many of the citizens of the city were forced to set out on the long trek to Babylon.[7] Left behind were the poorest of the people, who were directed to care for the farmlands and

---

5. Lipschits, *Fall*, 80.

6. Jer 39:2–7.

7. There were altogether three deportations: the deportation after Jehoiakim's rebellion when those with Jeconiah (Jehoiachin) were taken (598 BCE); the deportation after the fall of Jerusalem (587 BCE); and another a few years later (Jer 52:30). Problems of reconciling the dates of these deportations in Kings and Jeremiah are discussed in Miller and Hayes, *History*, 419–20, and Albertz, *Israel*.

vineyards around the city. The desolation was total.[8] Lipschits says that the city would remain "desolate and abandoned" for many years.[9]

The ruins that remained reeked of charred wood, smoldering embers, billowing smoke, its stone walls strewn around helter-skelter. Further out, what had been the city's suburban lands were, I suppose, trampled clean of foliage.[10] This desolate ruin would be here, visible from the Ridge Road, for several generations.[11] Travelers on this road would be left to surmise what had happened at that place. For the first few years many of the passers-by well knew of the great city that had been there, and what had happened to it. But as time passed memory would have faded and more and more travelers would have had little or no knowledge of what had gone on at that place. They would surmise that this place had once been a great city where commercial activity was brisk, social affairs were alive, where births and marriages were celebrated, and a sovereign and his nobles had presided over ceremonies, made public pronouncements, formally signed treaties, deliberated over public issues. It was obviously a place where religious figures were given generous gifts by individuals seeking blessing, cleansing,

---

8. Lipschits, *Fall*, 270: "the destruction of Jerusalem and the end of the kingdom of Judah brought about the gravest demographic crisis in the history of the kingdom...."

9. Lipschits, *Fall*, 112.

10. Many scholars believe that a considerable social and political life continued in Judah after the Babylonian raid, contrary to the image presented by virtually all the writings of the Judeans themselves about the country during this period. These works present Judah as "an occupational vacuum awaiting repopulation from those taken into exile and [they assume] that all the major impulses of the time came from the returnees" (Miller and Hays, *History*, 444–50). Barstad (*After the Myth*, 3–5) believes, as do Miller and Hays, that the image of a land left barren by the invaders was a creation of the exilic writers. I wonder: What was the condition of the country after the occupation of the region for eighteen (or thirty?) months by several thousand troops and their livestock? Middlemas (*Templeless*, 17), who stresses the continuance of social and economic activity in Judah during the exile period, nevertheless acknowledges that the city itself had only "minimal habitation." On the basis of archaeological evidence, Ephraim Stern ("Babylonian Gap") believes there was much more significant devastation than Barstad and others allow for. He argues that "Judah was almost entirely destroyed and its Jewish population disappeared from most of the kingdom's territory (except, perhaps, for the area of Benjamin)."

11. There is reason to believe that the folks left in Judah after the deportation of 587 BCE formed a community and perpetuated many of the pre-Babylonian customs. "[T]he situation in Judah [was] sufficiently stable to support general well-being and theological activity." Middlemass (*Templeless*, 18; cf. Jer 41:5) says that there was "spontaneous and sporadic worship at the ruins of the Sanctuary." Also, as will be indicated below, a community took form in Egypt, or at least expanded during this period. My focus, in any case, will be the community that formed among the survivors in Babylon.

or healing, and offered sacrifices to the gods. Beyond all that, what was most evident was that this once-great city had been attacked and burned, perhaps never to rise again.[12]

## *Witnessing*

The survivors who had been forced to make the weeks-long trek into southern Mesopotamia well knew what had happened at that site. It had been their honored city, capital of their country, admired by neighboring countries. For them the whole affair had been traumatic beyond words. They had starved under siege, they had been physically, even sexually abused, and their homes had been looted by invading troops. They had witnessed the slaughter of family members, neighbors, local leaders; they had watched the great mansions of the city and their majestic temple burning to the ground. The only world they knew had been reduced to ashes. If, as Lipschits believes, the folks who had remained in the city to the very last had clung the most tenaciously to the belief that the city would never be breached by alien troops, then it was those folks who experienced the full measure of the devastation. These people witnessed what for them had been unthinkable.[13] These were the folks who came away from their burning city in a state of shock, traumatized, much of what they had believed in having been radically contradicted by one great terrible event. Trauma of this sort, we are told, can leave people helpless, violated, bitter, consumed with fury.[14]

## *The Lamentations*

We get a sense of how traumatic the event had been from the writings that were composed in the disaster's aftermath. People gave voice to their anguish through dirge-like poems, such as those collected in the book of

---

12. The writer of Chronicles described Yahweh's response to Solomon's prayer by stating that the ruins of the city would stand before those who passed by them as a witness to the unfaithfulness of his people. "This temple will become a heap of rubble. All who pass by will be appalled and say, 'Why has the Lord done such a thing to this land and to this temple?' People will answer, 'Because they have forsaken the Lord, the God of their ancestors, who brought them out of Egypt, and have embraced other gods, worshiping and serving them—that is why he brought all this disaster on them'" (2 Chr 7:21–22).

13. Middlemas, *Templeless*, 8, 47; *New Bible Dictionary*, 355a; Berlin, introduction to *Four Essays*, xxxii.

14. Norman and Maguen, *Moral Injury*.

Lamentations.[15] No one knows how the dirges came to be, but their themes apply well to the time and the situation of Jerusalem's destruction. Kathleen O'Connor merely says, "Anonymous poets and survivors of the destruction produced it."[16] They reveal the sense of shock, grief, pain, guilt, and humiliation that had overwhelmed the citizens inside the city when it collapsed.[17] The laments describe the sense of dismay, despair, terror, trauma that the authors experienced. Racked with fury, they helplessly called out for vengeance. Brilliant poets had crafted these laments. They describe their sacred city as an abused woman—her skirts besotted with blood, her children starving, her streets barren, her jewels strewn on the ground, her gates unhinged, her palace walls broken down. Whoever the authors were, they had been there. They had beheld and been appalled by Jerusalem in its most pathetic, ravaged, debased, despoiled moment.[18] Their grief and anger are palpable. But beyond their feelings of a world blown away there was the sense of *abandonment*. The experience of seeing their city trampled by foreign troops, their precious things vandalized, their temple burned—all this objectified the sense that God was not there. Yahweh was silent. And without him, there was no ground for understanding. Only a bitter, infuriating, blankness prevailed.

"Lamentations is about the collapse of a physical, emotional, and spiritual universe of an entire people," says O'Connor.[19] She notes that when people are traumatized, like those who had experienced the attack on the city, they are left without the vocabulary to put their feelings into words. What they experience is "literally unspeakable because profound pain destroys victims' capacity for speech. It renders victims numb, wordless, and further isolates them in their pain." But when words can be found, she said, they become "a poetry of truth-telling." The poetry of Lamentations was, for those who voiced it, an act "of survival that [testified] to the human requirement to speak the unspeakable, to find speech in traumatized numbness."[20] Through verse these poets expressed their sense of shock, grief, anger, and

15. The Septuagint in a prefatory note attributes the Lamentations to Jeremiah: "after Israel had been taken captive and Jerusalem had been laid waste, Jeremiah sat weeping and lamented this lament over Jerusalem . . ." (NET Lam 1:1, n3). Few scholars believe this.

16. O'Connor, *Lamentations*, 15.

17. No one knows who produced these dirges or when. They seem eminently to apply to the time of the second Babylonian attack on Jerusalem (587 BCE), but some scholars have insisted that they could have been produced at other times (O'Connor, *Lamentations*, 6–7).

18. Cf. O'Connor, *Lamentations*, 15.

19. O'Connor, *Lamentations*, xiv.

20. O'Connor, *Lamentations*, 5–6.

confusion. The dirges "above all else highlight[ed] the human tragedy" of what the survivors had experienced.[21] They emote what it was like to starve under siege, to watch one's loved ones violated, one's cherished belongings pillaged, one's world torn down and torched.[22] Each dirge was constructed to evoke deep feelings—as if, says O'Connor, they were "prayers that erupt from wounds, burst out of unbearable pain, and bring it to language."[23] They consisted of rhythmic "short, sobbing lines," so as to express and enhance weeping and the grieving process.[24] They mimic the shock, pain, and grief of one who is helplessly violated.[25] Each lament was constructed in a "carefully wrought, highly artificial" style. The first four of the Lamentations were acrostic poems, each line beginning with a letter of the Hebrew alphabet, except for chapter 3, which consisted of three lines for each letter.[26] Today the Lamentations are recited as confessional dirges in the Jewish month of Ab, as if "to bring about a complete cleansing of the conscience through a total confession of sin."[27]

Here is what they depict.

- "All her people groan as they search for bread; they barter their treasures for food to keep themselves alive."[28]

- "They say to their mothers, 'Where is bread and wine?' as they faint like the wounded in the streets of the city, as their lives ebb away in their mothers' arms."[29]

- "Look, LORD, and consider: Whom have you ever treated like this? Should women eat their offspring, the children they have cared for? Should priest and prophet be killed in the sanctuary of the LORD?"[30]

21. Middlemas, *Templeless*, 45.

22. By reproducing these poems in this form of course I violate the acrostic nature of the originals. The point here is merely to note the sentimental representations of the Judean experience.

23. O'Connor, *Lamentations*, 9.

24. *New Bible Dictionary*, 662. The rhythmic beat is called *qinah* or "limping" meter in Hebrew (O'Connor, *Lamentations*, 11).

25. They thus constitute a theodicy of suffering (Boase, *Constructing Meaning*).

26. Chapter 5 is not an acrostic, but it does have 22 verses in the form of one, though its contents more closely resemble a psalm. Cf. Pss 44 and 80.

27. Norman Gottwald, quoted in *New Bible Dictionary*, 662.

28. Lam 1:11.

29. Lam 2:12.

30. Lam 2:20.

- "Young and old lie together in the dust of the streets."[31]
- "Because of thirst the infant's tongue sticks to the roof of its mouth; the children beg for bread."[32]
- "Those who once ate delicacies are destitute in the streets. Those brought up in royal purple now lie on ash heaps."[33]
- "But now they are blacker than soot; they are not recognized in the streets. Their skin has shriveled on their bones; it has become as dry as a stick."[34]
- "Those killed by the sword are better off than those who die of famine; racked with hunger, they waste away for lack of food from the field."[35]
- "With their own hands compassionate women have cooked their own children."[36]

They provide images of the city at various instants during the attack.

- "How deserted lies the city, once so full of people! How like a widow is she, who once was great among the nations! She who was queen among the provinces has now become a slave. All the splendor has departed from Daughter Zion. Her princes are like deer that find no pasture; in weakness they have fled before the pursuer. In the days of her affliction and wandering Jerusalem remembers all the treasures that were hers in days of old."[37]
- "Arise, cry out in the night, . . . ; pour out your heart like water in the presence of the Lord. Lift up your hands to him for the lives of your children, who faint from hunger at every street corner."[38]
- "Women have been violated in Zion, and virgins in the towns of Judah. Princes have been hung up by their hands; elders are shown no respect. Young men toil at the millstones; boys stagger under loads of wood."[39]

31. Lam 2:21.
32. Lam 4:4.
33. Lam 4:5.
34. Lam 4:8.
35. Lam 4:9.
36. Lam 4:10.
37. Lam 1:6, 7.
38. Lam 2:19.
39. Lam 5:11–13.

- "The kings of the earth did not believe, nor did any of the peoples of the world, that enemies and foes could enter the gates of Jerusalem."[40]
- "The enemy laid hands on all her treasures; she saw pagan nations enter her sanctuary—those you had forbidden to enter your assembly."[41]
- "All who pass your way clap their hands at you; they scoff and shake their heads at Daughter Jerusalem: 'Is this the city that was called the perfection of beauty, the joy of the whole earth?'"[42]
- "Is it nothing to you, all you who pass by? Look around and see. Is any suffering like my suffering that was inflicted on me, that the LORD brought on me in the day of his fierce anger?"[43]

Survivor sentiments can also be found in some of the psalms. The writer of Psalm 74 presents himself as a witness of the destruction of the temple. "Your foes roared in the place where you met with us; they set up their standards as signs. . . . They smashed all the carved paneling with their axes and hatchets. They burned your sanctuary to the ground; they defiled the dwelling place of your Name. . . . They burned every place where God was worshiped in the land."[44]

The author of Psalm 79 was similarly horrified by the desecration of the sacred temple and city. "God, the nations have invaded your inheritance; they have defiled your holy temple, they have reduced Jerusalem to rubble. They have left the dead bodies of your servants as food for the birds of the sky, the flesh of your own people for the animals of the wild. They have poured out blood like water all around Jerusalem, and there is no one to bury the dead."[45]

The writer of Psalm 137—a voice from the golah, in contrast to those representing the situation in the ruined city (Lamentations)—was grief-stricken by the loss of the city and its temple. "By the rivers of Babylon we sat and wept when we remembered Zion. There on the poplars we hung our harps, for there our captors asked us for songs, our tormentors demanded

---

40. Lam 4:12.

41. Lam 1:10.

42. Lam 2:15. The short critique of Judah's neighbors by Obadiah may have been produced in this context.

43. Lam 1:11–13.

44. Ps 74:4–8.

45. Ps 79:1–8.

songs of joy; they said, 'Sing us one of the songs of Zion!' How can we sing the songs of the LORD while in a foreign land?'"

This psalmist imagines the city and the temple as the locus of worship. "If I forget you, Jerusalem, may my right hand forget its skill. May my tongue cling to the roof of my mouth if I do not remember you, if I do not consider Jerusalem my highest joy."

For this poet the gloating of Judah's neighbors still rankled.[46] "Remember, LORD, what the Edomites did on the day Jerusalem fell. 'Tear it down,' they cried, 'tear it down to its foundations!'"

And he cursed the Babylonians for what they had done: "Daughter Babylon, doomed to destruction, happy is the one who repays you according to what you have done to us."[47]

## Yahweh's Role in the Disaster

The writers of the Lamentations knew that the catastrophe was evidence of Yahweh's wrath owing to their sins.

- "My sins have been bound into a yoke; by his hands they were woven together. They have been hung on my neck, and the LORD has sapped my strength. He has given me into the hands of those I cannot withstand."

- "[H]e has summoned an army against me to crush my young men. In his winepress the LORD has trampled Virgin Daughter Judah. . . . The LORD has decreed for Jacob that his neighbors become his foes; Jerusalem has become an unclean thing among them."[48]

- "The LORD has given full vent to his wrath; he has poured out his fierce anger. He kindled a fire in Zion that consumed her foundations."[49]

---

46. Torry, *Edomites*, 18. "Edom rejoiced in his brother's calamity; laid hands on his property when he was in distress; entered into possession of . . . a part of the territory of Israel, when the land was weakened. It has been generally agreed that we have in these passages the evidence of an Edomite invasion of Judah, following the Babylonian conquest." "Archaeological evidence has confirmed that Edom invaded and conquered extensive territory of Judah while the Chaldaeans were besieging Jerusalem" (De Moor, *Rise of Jahwism*, 199n2).

47. Ps 137 (selections).

48. Lam 1:14–17. See also 1:5b, 12b, 15; 2:1–2, etc.

49. Lam 4:11.

## Collapse

- "Jerusalem sinned grievously, so she has become a filthy thing; all who honored her despise her."[50]
- "The Lord is in the right, for I have rebelled against his word."[51]

Even so, among the dirges there appears an affirmation of hope. The writer of the third dirge "has seen affliction by the rod of the Lord's wrath." But he still believes that Yahweh is merciful. "Because of the Lord's great love we are not consumed, for his compassions never fail. They are new every morning.... I say to myself, 'The Lord is my portion; therefore I will wait for him.' The Lord is good to those whose hope is in him, to the one who seeks him; it is good to wait quietly for the salvation of the Lord."[52] This writer is confident that Yahweh will eventually show mercy. "For no one is cast off by the Lord forever. Though he brings grief, he will show compassion, so great is his unfailing love. For he does not willingly bring affliction or grief to anyone."[53]

The composer of Psalm 74, cited above, fully aware that Yahweh was displeased with his people, nevertheless appealed to his kindness:

> Remember the nation you purchased long ago, the people of your inheritance, whom you redeemed.... Turn your steps toward these everlasting ruins, all this destruction the enemy has brought on the sanctuary.... [D]o not forget the lives of your afflicted people forever. Have regard for your covenant, because haunts of violence fill the dark places of the land. Do not let the oppressed retreat in disgrace; may the poor and needy praise your name. Rise up, O God, and defend your cause.[54]

This hope that repentance and renunciation of sins would open up a new relationship with their god was shared by the writer of the third Lament. "Let us examine our ways and test them and let us return to the Lord. Let us lift up our hearts and our hands to God in heaven, and say: 'We have sinned and rebelled.'"[55]

---

50. Lam 1:8.
51. Lam 1:18.
52. Lam 3:22–26.
53. Lam 3:31–33 (selections).
54. Ps 74 (selections).
55. Lam 3:40–42.

# 12

# Chaotic Aftermath

### *The News Reaches Babylon*

IN BABYLON THE JUDAHITE captives who had been brought there in 597 BCE after Nebuchadnezzar's first attack on the city were anxiously waiting for news. Could Jerusalem hold out against the siege? It took five months for the news to reach the Israelite community in exile. When it came, it was heartbreaking. Ezekiel records the date when it reached him. "In the twelfth year of our exile, in the tenth month on the fifth day, a man who had escaped from Jerusalem came to me and said, The city has fallen!"[1] All of Ezekiel's foreboding had finally been realized. A stream of exhausted human beings from the disaster began to arrive with whatever they had brought with them, including their flocks, cattle, camels, and donkeys. It must have been a motley scene.

Although Ezekiel had been predicting the catastrophe, he was shaken by the news, like everyone else in his community. As he heard in detail how much had been lost, what his countrymen had suffered, he began to receive from Yahweh messages of a different sort. Heretofore he had been trying to disabuse his countrymen of their hopes of returning home. The city, he had told them many times, would be destroyed. Now it had happened. He had done his best to describe Yahweh's complaints against his people, but now he needed to promote the news that Yahweh had more positive plans for

---

1. Ezek 33:21. NET gives the date as January 19, 585 BCE, that is, twenty-two weeks and four days after the city fell.

them. Ezekiel's visions and revelations hereafter would promise hope for the people of Israel. A new, glorious city and a majestic temple would rise upon the ruins of Jerusalem, he said. And Yahweh would show them mercy.

But Ezekiel would not spare the leaders who had brought upon Judah such a disastrous and shameful end. Even as they were arriving in their desperate condition he declared, "Woe to you shepherds of Israel who only take care of yourselves! . . . You have not strengthened the weak or healed the sick or bound up the injured. You have not brought back the strays or searched for the lost. You have ruled them harshly and brutally."[2] Yahweh says, "I will hold them accountable for my flock. I will remove them. . . ."

But Yahweh would not be angry at his people forever. Through Ezekiel Yahweh would give the captives in Babylon visions of hope. Even as they would languish far from their homeland, living under gentile dominion, Yahweh would say, "I myself will search for my sheep and look after them. . . . I will rescue them from all the places where they were scattered. . . . I will bring them out from the nations and gather them from the countries, and I will bring them into their own land."[3] Here was reason for hope.

## Terror in Mizpah

But events would not go well back in Judah where some of the survivors were reorganizing. The city of Jerusalem being unlivable, the place where people had gathered was at the town of Mizpah, about ten miles northwest of Jerusalem.[4] A man named Gedaliah was appointed to manage the town. It was here that the folks who fled the siege congregated.[5] Gedaliah was the son of a man whose family had been involved in court affairs since the time of Josiah, in fact the grandson of the man who oversaw the refurbishment of the temple for Josiah.[6] Renegade Judahite troops who had survived the attack joined the Judahites at Mizpah as Gedaliah reassured everyone that they would be safe there. The book of Jeremiah says that the refugees

---

2. Ezek 34:2–5.

3. Ezek 34:11–13.

4. Lipschits, *Fall*, 84–102. The exact location of this ancient town is uncertain, but the most likely site is Tell an-Nesbeh about ten miles from Jerusalem (*New Bible Dictionary*, 775a).

5. Jer 40:7–8.

6. Lipschits, *Fall*, 88–102.

arrived there in time to help in the harvest and that the community had copious amounts of wine, dates, and figs.[7]

In the meantime Jeremiah was found by Nebuzaradan, the captain of Nebuchadnezzar's royal guard, and given protection. He had been in chains among a group of Judahites slated to be herded to Babylon, but Nebuzaradan invited him to go with him as his guest to Babylon. He could go anywhere he liked, he said.[8] Jeremiah chose to stay in Mizpah with the others.

The community was barely getting organized, however, when it was disturbed by the attempt of a collateral member of the royal family to claim the vacated throne for himself. The king of Ammon, often a nemesis to Judah, had encouraged this man, Ishmael the son of Nethaniah, who was from a collateral line of the royal family and had served as an officer in Zedekiah's army, to assume control of the community. Ishmael conspired to assassinate Gedaliah, but the plot reached the ears of an officer in the Judean army named Johanan who warned Gedaliah of the plot and proposed to find Ishmael and kill him, arguing that if Ishmael would succeed in killing Gedaliah "what remains of Judah" would dissolve.[9] Gedaliah could not believe the story and forbade Johanan from taking any action against Ishmael. A fateful decision.

Johanan's intelligence was correct. Ishmael paid a visit to Gedaliah and his community with ten of his men, and Gedaliah invited them for a meal. But during the meal he and his men rose up and killed the governor and all the fighting men with him, even some Babylonian soldiers who happened to be there. The rebels left no survivors among the troops and took the civilians of the city captive. The next day, when eighty men from various places in the north arrived, they also were treacherously slaughtered, except for several men who proposed to lead Ishmael to a cache of wheat, barley, olive oil, and honey. The offer was too tempting for Ishmael to pass up, for regular payoffs were necessary to keep his ad hoc band with him. But it meant a delay in his plans to take his captives back to Amon, and that delay gave the Judahite general Johanan time to organize an avenging force. They intercepted Ishmael and his men and rescued the hostages, although Ishmael and eight of his men got away.[10]

7. Jer 40:12.
8. Jer 39:12—40:6.
9. Jer 40:13-16.
10. Jer 41; 2 Kgs 25:22-26.

# Chaotic Aftermath

## *Flight to Egypt*

But now Johanan had a problem. He and his men feared they would be blamed for the murder of the Babylonian soldiers. Might the Babylonians hold them responsible for the betrayal of the governor and those with him? Fear seems to have overtaken him and many in the community at Mizpah, and they decided to flee to Egypt.

They were so sure this was the best thing to do that they approached Jeremiah to authorize the idea. They asked him to pray to Yahweh for guidance on what they should do, promising to do whatever he would report. Jeremiah agreed to pray about it. When Jeremiah came back with a report that Yahweh told them to remain in the area, they responded that no matter what Jeremiah said they were leaving. The prophet warned them against rejecting Yahweh's will. If they insisted on fleeing anyway, he said, the troubles they had feared would catch up with them in Egypt; they would starve and die there, for Yahweh, he said, would pour out his wrath on them. They would become an object of ridicule and horror.[11] Jeremiah then became more specific: if they persisted, he said, they would die by war, starvation, and disease. The leaders of this group had no use for such admonitions, and they blamed Jeremiah's assistant, Baruch, for persuading him to take this position. Despite Jeremiah's advice and severe warnings, the captain who had bravely avenged Gedaliah and the others was so frightened of the Babylonians that he eagerly led his officers, men, the other Judahites in a flight to Egypt. And they dragged Jeremiah and Baruch with them.[12] The prophet brought some large stones from Judah with him and, once there, buried them at the entrance to Pharaoh's residence, announcing that Nebuchadnezzar would come down to Egypt and set his throne over those very stones. The Judahites that had fled to Egypt, he said, would die of disease and war as the temples of Egypt were burned down.[13] And here Jeremiah reminded them of the reason for the many tragic events they and their people had already suffered. It had been because of the "wickedness of the people": they had offered sacrifices to other gods, despite the warnings of the prophets, and had flouted Yahweh's commandments. Why would they bring harm to themselves—every man, woman, child, and baby among them—by refusing to obey Yahweh's direction? They would be regarded

---

11. Jer 42.
12. Cf. 2 Kgs 25:26.
13. Jer 43.

with disdain and ridicule by the nations, he claimed. They were as stubborn as ever, he said, in resisting the laws and statutes of Yahweh. For that reason, Yahweh has a message for them: they would suffer disaster—not one of them would see Judah again.

In response, the women in this troop defiantly told Jeremiah they were still soliciting the favor of the "Queen of Heaven," not Yahweh, for she seemed be a better source of wellbeing to them. Jeremiah replied that Yahweh had endured their idolatries for a time but eventually would make their lands a curse and a desolate waste. He challenged them, "Go ahead then, do what you promised! Keep your vows!" But, he said, Yahweh had sworn that they would all perish. The sign of that would be that Pharaoh Hophra, like Zedekiah, would be overtaken by his enemies. The disasters only recently visited upon Jerusalem would be visited upon these immigrants to Egypt as well.[14]

This is the last we see of Jeremiah. He disappears from history still remonstrating with the refugees for their idolatrous habits, still being rebuffed and scorned by his own people. He had carried out all that Yahweh had called upon him to do: he had been, as Yahweh had told him, a vehicle for the "uprooting and tearing down of nations and the building and planting" of something new.[15] This had been God's message for the times through Jeremiah from start to finish, even extending beyond the span of his own life.[16] The promises and predictions he uttered would be fulfilled in due time.[17] But his urgent warnings had been repeatedly rejected by his people, for they, at least many of them, could not grasp that Yahweh would bring down the city and temple that were associated with his name. This was the burden of Jeremiah's lifetime. We see him down to the very end, still warning his countrymen, still calling them to turn back from practices that offended Yahweh. For his pains, to the very last, he was treated with scorn and indifference.

---

14. Jer 44.
15. Jer 1:10.
16. Stulman, *Jeremiah*, 15.
17. I have felt free to use the texts of the book of Jeremiah here as at least one authority. Lipschits (*Fall*, 304–47) believes that much of it was written down in Egypt soon after these interactions took place.

# Chaotic Aftermath

## Another Deportation

This was the tragic end of Judah. Josephus concluded his description of the second Babylonian attack on Judah with the comment, "Such was the end of the nation of the Hebrews." He added that the Babylonians—unlike the Assyrians before them, who imported gentiles into the lands of Israel—had left the land of Judah untouched, and that "Judea and Jerusalem, and the Temple, continued to be a desert for seventy years."[18]

A coda has been added to the book of Jeremiah about another invasion of Judah by the Babylonians five years later (581 BCE). It says that at that time the invaders took another 745 people back to Babylon.[19] Josephus explains that "On the fifth year after the destruction of Jerusalem, . . . [Nebuchadnezzar] made an expedition against Coelesyria; and when he had possessed himself of it, he made war against the Ammonites and Moabites; and when he had brought all those nations under subjection, he fell upon Egypt, in order to overthrow it; and he slew the king that then reigned, and set up another; and he took those Jews that were there captives, and led them away to Babylon. . . ."[20] Apparently Nebuchadnezzar had felt, again, that his grip on his western flank was at risk and so had invaded in order to secure his control of Egypt as well as the small principalities in Syria-Palestine. But the captives taken from Judah would not have been the only ones taken to Babylon; their neighbors such as the Ammonites, Moabites, and other peoples in the west would have been forced to give up captives to them as well.[21]

---

18. Josephus is following Jer 29:10.
19. Jer 52:30.
20. Coelesyria was an ancient region centering on Baqa in Lebanon.
21. Josephus, *Works*, 287a, b. Cf. Albertz, *Israel*, 95–96.

# 13

# Struggle to Comprehend
## *The Problem of Understanding*

THE DESTRUCTION OF JERUSALEM was a "massive rupture in the history of Israel,"[1] a threshold event, a "dismantling" of the Judahite system of power and meaning that would allow a different frame of meaning to be constructed in its place, about their identity as a people, the nature of their god, and the world that confronted them.[2] The symbols of Israelite identity had vanished. No sacred city remained, no holy temple, no God-given homeland. The last king in the line of David was blind and shackled in Babylon.[3] Despite the many prophetic warnings, the totality of the affair overwhelmed. The trauma of the moment damaged the inner moral compass of those who survived. How were they to grasp what happened without any familiar frames of reference?[4] The comprehensive wrecking of their world, especially for those who had supposed that the city and its

---

1. Albertz, *Israel*, 90.

2. Brueggemann (*Hopeful Imagination*, 4) presents the destruction of Judahite society on 587 BCE as a metaphor for "the dismantling of any system of meaning and power" so that a new system could take its place.

3. Cf. Middlemas, *Templeless*, 49.

4. Cf. Norman and Maguen, *Moral Injury*. Goodman (*History of Judaism*, 241–60) indicates that after the destruction of Jerusalem by the Romans in 70 CE many of the survivors sought for a "religious explanation" for it.

sacred temple were inviolate, constituted for them, as Daniel Block puts it, a "theological shock."[5]

Terrence Fretheim has unpacked the many issues that the survivors were confronted with.[6] They included the following:

- *Identity*: Are we still a people of God, or has God abandoned us, perhaps forever?
- *Guilt*: What went wrong? Are we to blame? Can such heinous sins be forgiven?
- *Theodicy*: Has God been fair to us? Does his punishment fit the crime? Were his actions justified? Are we being punished for the sins of others?
- *Hope*: Is there any basis for hope, or are we condemned to despair?
- *Divine faithfulness*: Will God remain true to the ancient promises? Do promises of land, prosperity, etc., still hold, or have they been annulled by our sins?
- *Divine presence*: Without a temple, is God present with his people anymore? Is God available where we now are?[7]
- *Divine power*: Given our defeat at the hand of enemies, who serve other gods, what does that reveal about the power of our god, Yahweh? Does Yahweh have the ability to deliver us?
- *Idolatry and syncretism*: Has it paid us to worship Yahweh? Would it not have been better to worship other gods?
- *Purity*: What should be our relationship to other peoples, given the troubles such mixing has occasioned for us in the past? Should we be separatistic?
- *Continuity and change*: To what extent can we count on old truths? Will long-standing symbols of the faith (such as the temple) remain a part of what it means to be the people of God?

---

5. Block, *Book*.
6. Fretheim, *Deuteronomic History*, 46–47. I have edited and truncated his list.
7. Stein (*Collapsing Structures*) discusses the implications of an absent temple for the development of the moral sensibility of the Judeans after the catastrophe. Middlemass, *Templeless* is a compact discussion of the many issues entailed in the event.

- *How to begin again:* What ought to be the shape of the community on the other side of the exile? What can we do to make sure that this does not happen again?
- *Leadership:* Given past patterns of leadership, what is appropriate for today and for the future?

Such were the conceptual issues the surviving community faced as they settled down in Babylon. They would for some time be groping for a way to encompass their experience in terms that would make sense for them. But the trauma they had experienced made the search for understanding all the harder. The horrors they had witnessed addled their attempts to rationally explain what happened. Kathleen O'Connor says that "To survive [a] disaster and its lingering consequences requires the remaking of language, a turning of suffering into words. . . . It is the speech itself for which survivors struggle. . . . To find language that begins to embrace historical reality is to find a kind of 'redemption.'"[8] That was their struggle as they tried to put order into their lives in the strange world of Babylon. Finding a way to talk about their deepest feelings would take time. It would entail letting go of the world that God had taken from them and receiving from him "a new world, which [they] did not believe possible, and which was not the one [they] would have preferred or chosen."[9] But once they found their voice the way they would frame their experience became "the decisive shaping reference point for the self-understanding of Judaism."[10]

## Life in Babylon

When they arrived, they found kinsmen already in the region who had been brought there by other imperial armies.[11] Families from Galilee and Transjordan had been brought into Mesopotamia by Assyrians who invaded the Northern Kingdom in 733–732 BCE. Descendants of the 27,000 captives brought from Samaria in 722 BCE by Sargon II were there.[12] The

---

8. O'Connor, *Jeremiah*, 136.
9. Brueggemann, *Hopeful*, 4.
10. Brueggemann, *Like Fire*, 116.
11. Miller and Hays, *History*, 430.
12. "Deportation was a punitive response enacted by ruling states for treaty violations . . . [and] was perfected by the Assyrians. Whole families were deported and resettled elsewhere in the empire" (Middlemas, *Templeless*, 23).

descendants were there from the 200,000 persons that Sennacherib had in 701 BCE, claimed as booty from "Hezekiah's towns."[13] And of course they found their own relatives and friends who had been brought to Babylon only a decade earlier, after Jehoiakim's rebellion, including such notable figures as Daniel, Ezekiel, King Jeconiah, and the queen mother.

For the most part conditions in Babylon were not harsh, and the new immigrants suffered little or no abuse. They settled together in communities, mostly near the heartland of Babylon, and remained culturally distinct. They called themselves the "golah," the Hebrew word for "a minority among aliens."[14] And they did what Jeremiah had urged the captives of the previous invasion to do: they settled down, built houses, planted gardens, took wives, and multiplied—activities that suited their Babylonian hosts, who gave them land. As "tenants to the king [they] ... provided labor, paid taxes, and served in the military."[15] They learned Accadian and Aramaic,[16] and they began in their public interactions to use the Babylonian calendar, although among themselves they dated events from the accession of King Jeconiah.[17] Most of the captives tilled the soil, although some established themselves in mercantile and banking.[18]

## Religious Meetings and the Growing Consensus

Religious practices were adapted to fit the new setting. They met on the Sabbath[19] for worship, encouraged by the prophet Ezekiel, in which the sacred writings were read aloud. Even before the new refugees had arrived, Ezekiel had been reassuring his community in the words of Yahweh: "Although I sent them far away among the nations and scattered them among the countries, yet for a little while I have been a sanctuary for them in the

---

13. Shea, *Sennacherib's Description of Lachish*.
14. Middlemas, *Templeless*, 24.
15. Miller and Hays, *History*, 433.
16. The Babylonians spoke Akkadian but adopted Aramaic in their communications with the subject peoples; it would become the lingua franca of the whole Near East for many generations.
17. Miller and Hayes, *History*, 433–34; Ezekiel, we have noted, dated events from Jeconiah's ascension.
18. Block, *Book*, 5, 6.
19. The Jewish Sabbath (Saturday) begins at sundown the previous day, so the meetings would have been on what we think of as Friday evenings.

countries where they have gone."[20] The refugees far from home began to understand that their god was accessible even in such a faraway land as Babylon and could be worshipped in their convocations, which eventually would become known as Synagogues.[21] In these sessions Yahweh was venerated as their god—their only god.

The Friday-evening assemblies enabled people to talk about vital issues, common problems, and to take stock of their situation.[22] Their status in this society, demeaned and disenfranchised as they were—and also being inarticulate in the languages and unaccustomed to the customs—worked to tie them together. Their sense of commonality was further strengthened as they debated the questions they shared about their situation and their future. What were their options from here? What could they do for their families? How would they educate their children, to socialize them into the customs of their ancestors? Much had been taken for granted previously; now they had to think about how to make sure their children were socialized into their customs and beliefs, and the history of their people. Of course, there was always an implicit issue in their discussions: Why were they in Babylon and why had they had suffered such losses? The abrupt debasement before their neighbors rancored. Some may also have been asking a question natural to the assumptions of their time: What about the spirits and unseen forces they had always solicited for protection and prosperity in uncertain circumstances?[23]

As they discussed and debated what had happened and why they were trapped in Babylon, many in the community came to agree that the ultimate cause of the demise of their society had been the wrath of their god Yahweh. Common understandings, says Fredrick Bailey, "emerge in human interaction and especially in argument," when "claim and counterclaim continually modify a shifting mass of propositions and directives about the way our world is and the way it should be."[24] Indeed, this is what we

---

20. Ezek 11:16.

21. This term first appeared in Greek inscriptions in Egypt in the third century BCE. (*New Bible Dictionary*, "Synagogue," 1142a). Goodman (*History*, 39) describes the synagogue as one of the "most striking religious innovations in antiquity."

22. Middlemas, *Templeless*, 140.

23. Lester (*Back from the Edge of Existence*) and Abramowitz (*The Poor Have Become Rich*) describe similar cases in which the sense of trauma affected the development of shared beliefs about their circumstances.

24. Bailey, *Prevalence of Deceit*, 17. See Halbwachs, *On Collective Memory* on the melding of individual and collective memories.

presume throughout the history of the Israelites. It is plausible to suppose that Israelite history was alive with local and immediate controversies.[25] As the exiles recalled the predictions of those who spoke out in Yahweh's name, they would note that the wreckage of their society corresponded to the predictions they had heard from the Yahwist prophets but had mostly ignored. Was the disaster not what Jeremiah and Ezekiel had foretold? Who could have forgotten Jeremiah's declaration, "This city . . . is filled with oppression. . . . Violence and destruction resound in her; her sickness and wounds are ever before me. Take warning, O Jerusalem, or I will turn away from you and make your land desolate so no one can live in it."[26] Also he had stated in Yahweh's name, "I will pronounce my judgments on my people because of their wickedness in forsaking me, in burning incense to other gods and in worshiping what their hands have made."[27] He was clear about what was to happen. "The Babylonians who are attacking this city will come in and set it on fire; they will burn it down, along with the houses where the people aroused my anger . . ."[28] Yahweh had already declared what lay ahead: "I will thrust you from my presence, just as I did all your fellow Israelites."[29] All this the prophet had declared publicly many times; but who paid attention? Most of the city elders were in fact infuriated at Jeremiah for such pronouncements.

Likewise for Ezekiel, whose grotesque metaphors for the idolatrous practices of Israel had offended his fellow countrymen in exile. Like Jeremiah he had explained that it was their ways of life, their indifference to the claims of Yahweh, that would incur Yahweh's wrath and bring about the final demise of their country. He was even more blunt than Jeremiah: Judah had prostituted herself.

> Because you poured out your lust and exposed your naked body in your promiscuity with your lovers, and because of all your detestable idols, . . . I am going to gather all your lovers, with whom you found pleasure, . . . and will strip you in front of them, and they will see you stark naked . . . and they will tear down your mounds and destroy your lofty shrines. They will strip you of your clothes

---

25. Albertz, *History*, 18.

26. Jer 6:6b–7.

27. Jer 1:16. See also Jer 7:6, 9, 18; 11:10; 13:10; 16:11, 13; 19:13; 22:9; 25:6; 32:29; 35:15; 44:3, 5, 8, 15.

28. Jer 32:29.

29. Jer 7:15.

and take your fine jewelry and leave you stark naked.... They will burn down your houses and inflict punishment on you in the sight of many women.[30]

And besides the prophecies of Jeremiah to the folks in Jerusalem and of Ezekiel to his fellow exiles in Babylon there were the prophetic warnings of the Yahwist prophets who had preceded them. *Isaiah* had specifically challenged the abuses of those who held strong positions in Judah. "Because you have ... relied on oppression and depended on deceit, this sin will become for you like a high wall, cracked and bulging, that collapses suddenly, in an instant."[31] *Micah* had similarly warned those who used their power to steal from the weak: "Those who plan iniquity, ... those who plot evil on their beds! They covet fields and seize them, and houses, and take them. They defraud people of their homes, they rob them of their inheritance.... [And so] I am planning disaster against this people, from which you cannot save yourselves. You will no longer walk proudly, for it will be a time of calamity. In that day people will ridicule you; they will taunt you...."[32] To the leaders of Judah "who despise justice," Micah said, "because of you, Zion will be plowed like a field, Jerusalem will become a heap of rubble, the temple hill a mound overgrown with thickets."[33] *Zephaniah* had prophesied, "I will stretch out my hand against Judah and against all who live in Jerusalem. I will destroy every remnant of Baal worship in this place, the very names of the idolatrous priests.... [Therefore, o]n the day of the Lord's sacrifice I will punish the officials and the king's sons, ... [all those] who fill the temple of their gods with violence and deceit."[34]

Moreover, the warnings of the prophets Hosea and Amos, uttered against the nation of Israel, had been so radically fulfilled that Israel's demise should have frightened the citizens of Judah, for they had been as guilty in their ways of life as the people of Israel. Hosea had objected to those who "make idols for themselves to their own destruction. Samaria, throw out your calf-idol! My anger burns against them."[35] Amos had challenged the rich and powerful of "trampl[ing] on the heads of the poor as on the dust of the ground and deny[ing] justice to the oppressed. Father

30. Ezek 16:35–42.
31. Isa 30:8–14.
32. Mic 2:1–5.
33. Mic 3:8–12.
34. Zeph 1:4–9.
35. Hos 8:4b–5, 11–12, 14b.

and son use the same girl and so profane my holy name. . . . Now then, I will crush you as a cart crushes when loaded with grain. The swift will not escape, the strong will not muster their strength, and the warrior will not save his life."[36] When those predictions came true in the tragic and total destruction of Israel, rather than bringing about a national act of repentance in Judah, the event made no difference in their religious observances or in the abuses they meted out on the weak. The Judahites persisted in worshipping other gods and flouting Yahweh's commandments. Jeremiah grieved that the people of Judah learned nothing from the demise of their kinsmen. He said, in the voice of Yahweh, "I gave faithless Israel her certificate of divorce and sent her away because of all her adulteries. Yet . . . Judah had no fear; she also went out and committed adultery."[37] Yahweh had revealed his wrath by bringing both of them down. The compelling explanation for why the peoples of both countries had suffered such total destruction and were now servants of gentile masters seemed undeniable: Yahweh had in fury crushed them. The writers of some of the laments, written soon after the event, knew that instantly. The writer of the first lament speaks in the voice of the abandoned city, "Is any suffering like my suffering that was inflicted on me, that the LORD brought on me in the day of his fierce anger? . . . My sins have been bound into a yoke; by his hands they were woven together. They have been hung on my neck, and the LORD has sapped my strength. He has given me into the hands of those I cannot withstand."[38] It was all Yahweh's doing, as Jeremiah saw it.

But what about the other gods? Why had they been silent? Clearly, only Yahweh could have produced this disaster, for only the prophets of Yahweh had predicted it. The attack itself effectively authorized their predictions. No other unseen spirit had warned them of such an event. The predictions uttered in Yahweh's name coupled with the event had, for these survivors, made Yahweh a living force, a spiritual reality unlike any other. This god, as Nahum said, could bring down a nation as well as activate a storm. No other god was worth considering. In fact, now they knew that there was no other.

---

36. Amos 2:7–8, 13–16.
37. Jer 3:8.
38. Lam 1:12–15.

## More Reason for Hope?

But had Yahweh rejected them *forever*? Was this the end of the relationship of the Judahites with Yahweh, as it had seemed to be for the people of the Northern Kingdom? To this question the prophets had also given an answer: Yahweh was committed to the Children of Israel. He would not leave them bereft forever. Jeremiah had purchased property in his village to demonstrate that in future, "houses, fields and vineyards will again be bought in this land."[39] Yahweh promised that he would "bring Judah and Israel back from captivity and will rebuild them as they were before."[40] His commitment to the Children of Israel was unshakable: "I have loved you with an everlasting love; I have drawn you with unfailing kindness."[41] The prophets had iterated this from ancient times. Isaiah had declared, "the LORD longs to be gracious to you; therefore he will rise up to show you compassion."[42] Micah had said, "I will gather the lame; I will assemble the exiles and those I have brought to grief. I will make the lame my remnant. . . . The LORD will rule over them . . . from that day and for ever."[43] Zephaniah had assured his generation that "the LORD your God is with you, the Mighty Warrior who saves. He will take great delight in you; in his love he will no longer rebuke you, but will rejoice over you with singing."[44] Joel had foreseen a time when Yahweh will "restore the fortunes of Judah and Jerusalem."[45] Hosea, in his prophecies to the Northern Kingdom had stated, speaking in the voice of Yahweh: "How can I give you up, Ephraim [Israel]? How can I hand you over, Israel? . . . [My] children will come trembling from the west. They will come from Egypt, trembling like sparrows, from Assyria, fluttering like doves. I will settle them in their homes,' declares the LORD."[46]

Ezekiel had explained that, in fact, Yahweh had a grand and subtle agenda in his work with the Children of Israel: to produce a people with a different moral sensibility, to instill in them "a new heart," one that would desire to please him. "I will give them an undivided heart and put a new

---

39. Jer 32:15.
40. Jer 33:7.
41. Jer 31:3.
42. Isa 30:18.
43. Mic 4:1–7.
44. Zeph 3:11–17.
45. Joel 3:1–3.
46. Hos 11:8–11.

spirit in them; I will remove from them their heart of stone and give them a heart of flesh. Then they will follow my decrees and be careful to keep my laws. They will be my people, and I will be their God."[47] Jeremiah (in Yahweh's voice) had similarly predicted a time when "I will make a new covenant with the people of Israel and with the people of Judah.... I will put my law in their minds and write it on their hearts. I will be their God, and they will be my people ... [and] I will forgive their wickedness and will remember their sins no more."[48]

Jeremiah had even given the Judahites who had been captured in 597 BCE a timeframe for how long their bondage would last:

> When seventy years are completed for Babylon, I will come to you and fulfill my good promise to bring you back to this place.[49] "For I know the plans I have for you," declares the Lord, "plans to prosper you and not to harm you, plans to give you hope and a future.... You will seek me and find me when you seek me with all your heart ... and [I] will bring you back from captivity. I will gather you from all the nations and places where I have banished you...."[50]

## *The Dry Bones*

Ezekiel, in fact, was now telling a new story. "The mountains of Judah would someday be plowed and planted" again, he said. The people of Judah would multiply, their towns would be populated, and their city rebuilt.[51] Yahweh emphasized this view of a future time for the exiles now languishing in captivity by presenting Ezekiel with two visions. In the first Ezekiel saw a valley filled with dry bones. He "brought me out by the Spirit of the Lord and set me in the middle of a valley; it was full of bones, ... bones that were very dry." Yahweh asked him if those bones could ever live again. Ezekiel did not know. "Then he said to me, 'Prophesy to these bones and say to them, "Dry bones, hear the word of the Lord! ... I will make breath enter you, and you will come to life. I will attach tendons to you and make

---

47. Ezek 11:17–18. Cf. Ezek 36:25–28.
48. Jer 31:31–34.
49. The meaning of seventy years has been debated. An extended discussion is in Winkle, "Jeremiah's Seventy Years" and "Jeremiah's Seventy Years II."
50. Jer 29:14.
51. Ezek 36:8.

flesh come upon you and cover you with skin; I will put breath in you, and you will come to life. Then you will know that I am the LORD.'"" In response to Ezekiel's voice, "there was a noise, a rattling sound, and the bones came together, bone to bone . . . and tendons and flesh appeared on them and skin covered them, but there was no breath in them. Then he said to me, 'Prophesy to the breath.' . . . 'Come, breath, from the four winds and breathe into these slain, that they may live.' [And] they came to life and stood up on their feet—a vast army."

To ensure that the meaning of this vision was clear, Yahweh explained it: "Son of man, these bones are the people of Israel. . . . My people, I am going to open your graves and bring you up from them; I will bring you back to the land of Israel. . . . I will put my Spirit in you and you will live, and I will settle you in your own land. Then you will know that I the LORD have spoken, and I have done it."[52] Here was a promise that the Israelites would become a nation again that would "walk around."

Moreover, the two Israelite peoples, Israel and Judah, would be united in the reconstituted Israel of the future, said Yahweh. "I am going to take the stick of Joseph—which is in Ephraim's hand—and of the Israelite tribes associated with him, and join it to Judah's stick. I will make them into a single stick of wood, and they will become one in my hand. . . . I will gather them from all around and bring them back into their own land. I will make them one nation in the land. . . . There will be one king over all of them and they will never again be two nations or be divided into two kingdoms. . . . They will be my people, and I will be their God."[53] They would be ruled by "David my servant" and bound to Yahweh by an "everlasting covenant. 'My servant David will be king over them, . . . [and] I will make a covenant of peace with them; it will be an everlasting covenant.'"[54]

## Temple of the Future

The other vision of hope given to Ezekiel was of a new majestic temple in the future Jerusalem. In his vision he was standing inside the temple and saw the same awesome apparition of Yahweh that had appeared to him before, the image of wheels within wheels presided over by storms and a human figure; only now the mysterious image that Ezekiel had seen leave

---

52. Ezek 37.
53. Ezek 37:19–26. See also Isa 11:12; Jer 3:18; 23:6; 30:3; 31:31; 33:14.
54. Ezek 37:24.

the temple was coming back, and it would fill a new temple, one that would be immense and glorious. As before, the prophet collapsed at the sight of it. But, as on the previous occasion, he was lifted up, and he heard a voice that announced that this temple would be Yahweh's dwelling place for ever. "I will put my sanctuary among them forever. My dwelling place will be with them; I will be their God, and they will be my people, . . . when my sanctuary is among them forever."[55]

Such were the visions of hope that Ezekiel presented to the golah in exile. The Children of Israel would not be bereft indefinitely, for Yahweh had planned a glorious future ahead for them.[56] Before the second Babylonian attack on Jerusalem Ezekiel had been busy trying to dispel his countrymen's hopes of ever seeing Jerusalem again. Now, with the city in ruins, he was reassuring them that there would be a time when another temple would exist, which would be more magnificent than before, and the peoples of Judah and Israel would be brought together to form a new nation. The temple would be in a new Jerusalem and Yahweh's awesome presence would dwell there.

In fact, according to Ezekiel, Yahweh was exposing to the exiles in Babylon what really animated him in all these activities: he was restoring his reputation, for the citizens of Israel and of Judah had demeaned his reputation by their idolatries and the behaviors that broke his commandments. "It is not for your sake [Yahweh was saying] . . . that I am going to do these things, but for the sake of my holy name, which you have profaned among the nations. . . . I will show the holiness of my great name, which has been profaned among the nations. . . . Then the nations will know that I am the LORD, . . . when I am proved holy through you before their eyes."[57] To restore his reputation Yahweh would purge his people of their idolatrous inclinations, and he would transform their moral sensibility so that they would live out the virtues enjoined upon them by his commandments: he will put a new spirit in them, he says, and he will make them *want* to keep his laws.[58] As the Children of Israel would learn to observe his statutes he would honor them and save them from disgrace. As their commitment to him became more authentic, more from the heart, they would be ashamed

---

55. Ezek 37:26b–28.
56. Duguid, *Ezekiel and the Leaders of Israel*, 141.
57. Ezek 36:22–23.
58. Ezek 36:26–27.

of what they had done, the many times and many ways they betrayed him and his commandments, which brought upon them his wrath.[59]

When would that be? Seventy years, said Jeremiah to the Judahites carried away after Nebuchadnezzar's first attack on Jerusalem.[60] The elderly in exile could know, that is, that they would never see Judah again.[61] It seems that even early in the period of captivity there was a voice proposing how to appeal to the god who had brought them to ruin. The writer of the third lament in the book of Lamentations reminded his kinsmen that in response to their repentance and repudiation of their past habitual offenses Yahweh would show them mercy: "Let us carefully examine our ways, and let us return to the LORD. Let us lift up our hearts and our hands to God in heaven: 'We have blatantly rebelled.'"[62] They would have to wait for better times. Having been shaken by events in which Yahweh had seemed to shout out his disapproval, the next several decades he would be silent.

---

59. Exek 43:10–11. Cf. Daniel's prayer of repentance for Israel (Dan 9).

60. The term "seventy years" may have merely meant, as some have said, "a long time." The actual period between Nebuchadnezzar's second attack on the city and the time when the Jews were invited to come home (539 BCE) was forty-eight years; from the time of the first attack (597 BCE) it was fifty-eight years. Lipschits (*Fall*, 185–86) notes that the Babylonian Empire lasted only seventy years, from 609–539 BCE.

61. Glass, *Judean Mindset*.

62. Lam 3:40–42.

# 14

## Cyrus and a New Prophet
### Two New Actors

As the decades passed, the composition of the exile community in Babylon changed as those who had experienced the catastrophe were gradually replaced by their children and grandchildren, who were becoming ever more deeply ensconced into the Babylonian world. They learned the language and customs of the gentiles around them. For the folks among them who still pined to return to their home country the release of King Jehoiachin from prison in 562 BCE might have given them hope that better things might soon come.[1] But the prospect dimmed as the community became ever more accustomed to life in Mesopotamia.

As for the Babylonians, there was nothing on the horizon to suggest that their grip on their far-flung empire could be at risk. King Nabonidus (r. 556–539 BCE), an Assyrian who had seized the Babylonian throne in 556, felt confident enough after a few years to leave the capital city into the hands of his son Belshazzar and move to Tayma, a town on the edge of the Arabian desert, so that he could refurbish its temples to the god Sin.[2]

But the situation was not a secure as it seemed. On the Iranian plateau to the east a rebellion was brewing that would gather strength and

---

1. 2 Kgs 25:27–30.
2. Albertz, *Israel*, 111, connects several passages in Second Isaiah (Isa 44:27; 49:14; 50:1) with the situation in Babylon during this time, to suggest that after 553 BCE the exiles were losing hope.

eventually burst into the Babylonian world to reshape the configuration of power throughout the greater Near East. Among the several tribes of the Medes, who together dominated most of the land to as far east as the Indus River, there was a chieftain of Fars (or Pars), a principality in southwestern Iran, named Cyrus (a descendent of a notable ancestor, Achaemenes), who in about 553 BCE began to organize a force of his own in order to rebel against Astyages, the Median king. In 550 his forces seized the Median capital Ecbatana where he named himself king of the Medes and the Persians. Cyrus may soon afterwards have forayed into Central Asia to subdue some quarrelsome nomadic tribes, but in 547 BCE a Lydian army led by the famed King Croesus invaded lands in the west, prompting Cyrus to cross the Tigris and attack the Lydians. After defeating them he turned against their allies, the Babylonians. The decisive battle was fought at Opis a few miles south of Babylon, and on October 12, 539 BCE, his troops invested the capitol city without a fight. Cyrus himself marched triumphantly into the city fifteen days later, exulting that he had been chosen by the supreme god "Asuramazda" to be "king of the world."[3] In truth, he sat astride the largest span of territory of any empire before him, from the Mediterranean Sea to the borders of India.

## The Invitation

Cyrus soon invited the Jews who had been displaced into Mesopotamia, along with some other displaced groups in his newly acquired empire, to return to their homeland.[4] The invitation was significant enough for the authors of the books of Chronicles and Ezra, written decades later, to quote

---

3. The book of Daniel presents a scene before the collapse of Babylon in which Belshazzar, son of and co-regent with Nabonidus, was sponsoring a boisterous party for "a thousand nobles" that included wives and concubines. Belshazzar and his guests were drinking from the gold and silver goblets looted from the temple in Jerusalem and offering praises to "gods of gold and silver, bronze, iron, wood, and stone" when a bodiless hand appeared and began to write on the wall opposite the king. Belshazzar in terror demanded someone be found to interpret the writing, generating a frantic search among the wizards and magicians of the realm to interpret the writing. No one was found, but the Queen mother pointed out that a Jewish captive in his own bureaucracy, Daniel, was noted for his ability to interpret dreams. Daniel's interpretation was unsettling: the words meant that the kingdom was being taken from Belshazzar. And in fact that very night, according to the passage, the kingdom fell to Cyrus and Belshazzar was killed (Dan 5).

4. The offer was also made to other communities that had been subject to Babylon. See the Cyrus Cylinder (a translation is in Paul, *Isaiah 40–66*, 15).

## Cyrus and a New Prophet

from it: "This is what King Cyrus of Persia says: 'The LORD God of heaven has given me all the kingdoms of the earth. He has appointed me to build a temple for him in Jerusalem, which is in Judah. Anyone of his people among you may go up there, and may the LORD his God be with him.'"[5]

While some of the Jews in Babylon had been longing for a chance to escape their bondage from their alien patron, most in the community of exiles were generally unready for such an abrupt announcement. This was a different generation of Jews, children and grandchildren of the survivors of the attack on Jerusalem. They had grown up in exile and become accustomed to Babylonian life. They spoke Accadian and Aramaic and were deeply invested in their local holdings and livelihoods. For them to move back to Canaan would entail leaving behind the world they had grown up in, packing up their goods, abandoning the lands that their parents and grandparents had brought under cultivation, selling their properties (at a loss), embarking with their families and their livestock on a journey of a few months through unknown and possibly hazardous territory, to reach a place about which many of them knew little. And once on the ground in Judah, they would have to find and claim their respective ancestral lands. They would, of course, have to construct dwellings for their families as well as break up the soils for cultivation, some of which may have (as they later reported) lain fallow for years.[6] They could expect to be involved in strenuous work to get established. All this could involve meeting unknown relatives, defining boundaries, agreeing on communal issues such as the layout of roads and the management of common lands, the maintenance of irrigation canals and sewage lines—projects that required cooperation, organization, and leadership. And there was also the question of dealing with the people already living in the area: How would they respond to the golah's attempts to reclaim their ancestral lands?[7] So Cyrus's invitation, exhilarating as it seemed, was in reality less than exciting for many of the Jews

---

5. 2 Chr 36:23 NET; Ezra 1:2–4.

6. Lipschits, *Fall*, 113. On Judah as a wasteland, this notion is questioned by some scholars, who regard the biblical references as deliberate attempts by the authors to justify the co-optation of lands in Judah by the returning exiles (cf. Lipschits, *Fall*, 102–7). Cf. 108n10.

7. Albertz, *Israel*, 127. Even if the new arrivals described the land as empty, other Israelites, distant relatives, had been allowed to stay in Judah to till the land. Some scholars believe that the authors of the descriptions of the situation in Judah masked the existence of these folks in the area, presenting them as intruders into the affairs of the newly forming community in Judah. See Lipschits, *Fall*, 112–22.

in Mesopotamia. To undertake this radical relocation of their families and wealth was daunting and the benefits uncertain.[8]

## A Mysterious Prophet

But a prophetic voice arose in this period to urge these timid Jews to act on the opportunity that was opening up to them. Early in Cyrus's reign over the Persian Empire, if not before, this new voice was speaking out in the name of Yahweh, announcing that he was rising to act on their behalf, and he urged them to undertake this radical move to the faraway land of their ancestors. This prophet regarded the appearance of Cyrus as a work of Yahweh. Through Cyrus Yahweh is opening the way for them to return, he said; this was an opportunity not to be missed, a new mode of public existence.

The problem we have with this prophet is that we don't know who he was. He spoke of Yahweh with the authority and conviction of the prophet Isaiah, who had lived in the time of King Hezekiah a century and a half earlier (c. 716–687 BCE).[9] Indeed, this prophet was so much in the tradition of the great prophet of Jerusalem that the utterances of this new voice were later appended to the writings accorded to Isaiah. A body of prophetic utterances, perhaps by more than one person speaking at different times, chapters 40–66, are now part of the book of Isaiah. The book comes down to us as a single work, as if written by a single author. And indeed, many readers take it for granted that the whole book came from the voice and pen of one person, the prophet Isaiah of Jerusalem. They read the later chapters—which have an uncanny connection to circumstances after 539 BCE, long after Isaiah's time in the eighth century BCE—as a work of divine inspiration.[10] But since the nineteenth century scholars have expressed doubts that these chapters were written by one person. Most now hold that chapters 40 through 66 were written long after the time of Isaiah of Jerusalem by one or more unknown authors, perhaps individuals connected to the great prophet through his former disciples; some scholars see in

---

8. Lipschits (*Fall*, 113) says that the city of Jerusalem would not become the lively urban center it had formerly been until the Greek period (after 334 BCE).

9. I draw from those scholars who believe these chapters were written more immediately in the context of the return and afterwards. Some scholars believe that the whole book of Isaiah has been edited to reflect the lessons of the destruction of Jerusalem: "the events which befell Jerusalem in 587 B.C. . . . exercised a formative role in giving to the book [Isaiah] its present structure" (Clements, *Prophecies of Isaiah*, 436).

10. Cf. Oswalt, *Book of Isaiah*.

their pronouncements traces of his influence, even though their prophetic authors were living in later times.[11] Not only do the issues of concern in the later chapters seem specifically addressed to circumstances in Persian times, but in the writings beginning with chapter 40 some scholars believe they can identify traces of the Babylonian language (Akkadian) which was familiar to the golah in exile.[12] In any case, these chapters (40–66) are manifestly different in tone and topic from those in the previous half of the book. The reader then wonders: Who wrote these chapters? And how did these prophecies get attached to the writings of Isaiah of Jerusalem?

Today most scholars believe that there are more then one author of these chapters. They assign chapters 40 to 55 to an author whom they call, "Second Isaiah" (or "Deutero-Isaiah"), distinguished by his emphases on comfort and the restoration of Israel after Cyrus's invitation. They assign chapters 56 to 66 to someone else, or even several individuals who were probably living in the vicinity of the newly re-established city of Jerusalem.[13] These final chapters are now called "Third Isaiah," as the author is—or the authors are—preoccupied with affairs within or around the city at a time when immigrant Jews were establishing a new community there.[14] I

---

11. Whoever wrote chapters 40 through 66 had been influenced by a number of scriptural authors, including Isaiah of Jerusalem and possibly even more by Jeremiah (cf. Paul, *Isaiah 40–66*, 50–57). Clifford (*Isaiah*, 85) says, "One reason why [the author of these chapters] can be called the legitimate successor of Isaiah of Jerusalem, is that he held the same view of the judgment process and regarded his commission as continuing the commission of First Isaiah. In my view, divine judgment was [from the prophet's perspective] an ongoing process continuing into his own day. . . . [A] new state had been reached. . . . [A] new phase was about to begin: restoration." It is now believed by many scholars that the whole text of Isaiah, which had several authors, has been edited to give the work a compositional unity. For instance, Williamson, *The Book Called Isaiah*; Berges, *The Book of Isaiah*. For guidance to the literature see, inter alia, Clifford, *Isaiah*; Oswalt, *Book*; Paul, *Isaiah 40–66*.

12. For discussions of these issues see, for instance, Abernethy et al., *Isaiah in Imperial Context*, 2013.

13. Rollston (*Rise of Monotheism*, 112n47): "Prophetic components of Judaean society copied and perpetuated the Oracles of Isaiah of the 8th century, and they carried on his tradition by augmenting and recontextualizing his oracles so as to fortify the faith of those that suffered the destruction of Jerusalem in 587 and the Babylonian Exile; Isa 40–55 is the sacred product of these labors."

14. Mark Smith (*Origins of Biblical Monotheism*, 154) doubts that the passages ascribed to "Second Isaiah" were ever intended to appear separate from those of "First Isaiah"; he believes that the book in its current form reflects the extensive editing of later generations. Shalom M. Paul (*Isaiah 40–66*) contends that chapters 40 to 66 constitute "a single coherent opus composed by a single prophet." Chapters 40 to 48, he says, were

here focus on the role that "Second Isaiah" had in encouraging the exiles to return to their homeland. And when I address the issues going on inside Judah after some of the golah had arrived I draw from the chapters ascribed to "Third Isaiah." (Not all of Third Isaiah's concerns bear on my topic.)

## Time to Move! (Isaiah 40–48)

The main message of this prophet to the exiles in Babylon was that the period of "punishment" was over, and Yahweh was moving to restore them to their homeland. So he urges them not to hold back. "Move out," he says, "and return to your homeland."[15] New possibilities lay before them; they can now form a new society in which Yahweh would be the single focus of their worship. Their redemption is at hand, he says, for Yahweh, having terminated his punishments for their sins, is eager to restore them. He uses the term "Jerusalem," the city then in ruins, as a metonym for the humiliated and dispersed Israelite peoples in their captivity. He calls to them: "'Comfort, comfort my people,' says your God. 'Speak kindly to Jerusalem and tell her that her time of warfare is over, that her punishment is completed. For the LORD has made her pay double for all her sins.'"[16] He comes as a victorious warrior, but like a shepherd "he tends his flock; he gathers up the lambs with his arm; he carries them close to his heart; he leads the ewes along."[17] Yahweh is no longer angry; his fury has been assuaged; "their punishment is completed." He wants to support them. He will carry them "close to his heart."

While the prophets before the Babylonian attack had foreseen Yahweh's hand in the catastrophe, this prophet considers Cyrus to be Yahweh's

---

produced by this prophet while living in Babylon at about the time that Cyrus appeared, whereas chapters 49 to 54 were written in Jerusalem after the author had returned with some of his compatriots, "where he continued his prophetic career." Paul does not refer to a "Third Isaiah." He also believes that chapters 34 and 35 of Isaiah were written by the author of chapters 40–66, possibly as introductory to the new section beginning with chapter 40 (cf. Blenkinsopp, *Isaiah 56–66*, 27–37).

15. In discussing the themes of these chapters I take chapters 40–48 to be the voice of "Second Isaiah" while he was living in Babylon; chapters 49–54 as written also by "Second Isaiah" after he had moved with other immigrants into Judah; and chapters 55–64 as written by one or more authors living in Jerusalem (called "Third Isaiah" by many scholars).

16. Isa 40:1, 2 NET.

17. Isa 40:10–12 NET.

chosen vehicle of deliverance. He is "the one I appointed as shepherd to carry out all my wishes and to decree concerning Jerusalem, 'She will be rebuilt,' and concerning the temple, 'It will be reconstructed.'"[18] This gentile conqueror was being called by Yahweh into his service. "For the sake of my servant Jacob, Israel, my chosen one, I call you by name and give you a title of respect, even though you do not submit to me. I am the LORD, I have no peer, there is no God but me. I arm you for battle, even though you do not recognize me. I do this so people will recognize from east to west that there is no God but me; I am the LORD, I have no peer."[19]

The prophet instructs Cyrus, along with the exiles in Babylon, that this god is unique, unlike any other. In Yahweh's name he says, "I am the LORD, I have no peer. I am the one who forms light and creates darkness; the one who brings about peace and creates calamity. I am the LORD, who accomplishes all these things."[20] This God, maker of heaven and earth, challenges them to find anyone like him. "Who has measured out the waters in the hollow of his hand, or carefully measured the sky, or carefully weighed the soil of the earth, or weighed the mountains in a balance, or the hills on scales?" No one can understand him. "Who comprehends the mind of the LORD, or gives him instruction as his counselor?" In fact, for him "the nations are like a drop in a bucket; they are regarded as dust on the scales.... To whom can you compare God? To what image can you liken him?" He is nothing like the idols made by a metalworker or a goldsmith.[21]

Here is the *real* one, the prophet says. The other gods are not gods. They are contemptible, and in the voice of Yahweh he pours derision upon them, the ones that some of the people, even then, were worshipping, despite the standard narrative that many in the community had adopted. He reminds them that he, Yahweh, alone had foretold these very developments through his prophets. None of these false gods had prophesied the things that had happened. Yahweh challenges them: "I am the first and I am the last, there is no God but me. Who is like me? Let him make his claim! Let him announce it and explain it to me—since I established an ancient people—let them announce future events." Indeed, he says, the Jews in exile are witnesses of Yahweh's magnificent acts among them. They could acknowledge it if they would. "You are my witnesses! Is there any God but me? There is no other

---

18. Isa 44:28 NET.
19. Isa 45:4–6 NET.
20. Isa 44:6b–7 NET.
21. Isa 40 (selections) NET.

sheltering rock." "Your idols don't compare with me," he says. In fact, they cannot even "see; they recognize nothing."[22] "No god was formed before me, and none will outlive me. I, I am the LORD, and there is no deliverer besides me.... 'You are my witnesses,' says the LORD, 'that I am God.... [N]o one can deliver from my power; I will act, and who can prevent it?'"[23]

## *Yahweh's Agenda*

Actually, this whole project of Yahweh is not even a response to the prayers of the exiles, says the prophet. Rather, they have done nothing to win Yahweh's goodwill. In fact, "You did not call for me, O Jacob; you did not long for me, O Israel." Instead, "you made me weary with your evil deeds." Yahweh was doing these things for them despite their sins—and for reasons of his own. "I, I am the one who blots out your rebellious deeds for my sake; your sins I do not remember."[24] He reminds them of what their people have been through: they were a people "looted and plundered, ... trapped in pits and held captive in prisons ... with no one to rescue them" because they had sinned against their god. It was because of their sins that Yahweh had handed them over to "the looters." But they had suffered enough, he says. Yahweh is now eager to show them mercy. He is protecting them because they belong to him. He is speaking warmly to them and affirming that they are precious to him.[25] You, "Israel, are my servant. I have made you, ... I will not forget you. I have swept away your offenses like a cloud, your sins like the morning mist. Return to me, for I have redeemed you."[26] Isn't this reason to rejoice? asks the prophet. "Sing for joy, you heavens, for the LORD has done this; shout aloud, you earth beneath. Burst into song, you mountains, you forests and all your trees, for the LORD has redeemed Jacob, he displays his glory in Israel."[27]

So, the prophet urges them to get going. "Yahweh will help you," he says. To the timid he offers special promises. "Do not be afraid, for I am with you." To the tremulous, tentative, and doubting, and those who feel abandoned and have complained, "My way is hidden [from] Yahweh, my

22. Isa 44:7–9 NET.
23. Isa 43:2–11 NET.
24. Isa 43:22–25 NET.
25. Isa 42:14—43:4 (selections) NET.
26. Isa 41:10.
27. Isa 44:21–23.

cause is ignored"—to them Yahweh replies, "You are my servant. I have chosen you and not rejected you. Don't be afraid, for I am with you! Don't be frightened, for I am your God! I will strengthen you—yes, I help you—yes, I uphold you with my saving right hand!"[28] So why would they pine as if they had been forgotten? Yahweh "gives strength to the weary ... and the weak ... [while] those who hope in the LORD will renew their strength."[29]

And to further encourage these families Yahweh points out that they will not be alone in their venture. Others will be coming from far and wide. "From the east I will bring your descendants; from the west I will gather you. I will say to the north, 'Hand them over!' and to the south, 'Don't hold any back!' Bring my sons from distant lands, and my daughters from the remote regions of the earth, everyone who belongs to me, whom I created for my glory."[30]

He will even curb the opposition: "Look, all who were angry at you will be ashamed and humiliated; your adversaries will be reduced to nothing and perish. When you will look for your opponents, you will not find them; your enemies will be reduced to absolutely nothing. For I am the LORD your God, the one who takes hold of your right hand, who says to you, 'Don't be afraid, I am helping you.'"[31]

Yahweh promises to protect them through the long journey over unknown lands and across hazardous rivers: "When you pass through the waters, I am with you; when you pass through the streams, they will not overwhelm you." Don't worry about wildfires on the way. "When you walk through the fire, you will not be burned; the flames will not harm you. For I am the LORD your God, the Holy One of Israel, your deliverer. ... Yes, I will make a road in the wilderness and paths in the wastelands. The wild animals honor me, the jackals and ostriches, because I put water in the wilderness and streams in the wastelands, to quench the thirst of my chosen people, the people whom I formed for myself, so they might praise me."[32]

To reassure them that things will go well when they get to Canaan Yahweh says, "I will make streams flow down the slopes and produce springs in the middle of the valleys. I will turn the wilderness into a pool of water and the arid land into springs. I will make cedars, acacias, myrtles,

---

28. Isa 40:27; 41:9; 49:14–15 NRSV. Cf. Blenkinsopp, *Isaiah 40–55*, 105.
29. Isa 40:29–31.
30. Isa 43:5–7 NET.
31. Isa 41:11–13 NET.
32. Isa 43:4–7, 19b–21 NET.

and olive trees grow in the wilderness; I will make evergreens, firs, and cypresses grow together in the arid rift valley. I will do this so people will observe and recognize, so they will pay attention and understand that the LORD's power has accomplished this, and that the Holy One of Israel has brought it into being."[33]

True, says the prophet, Yahweh has seemed to be inactive for a long time, but now he is eager to get things moving. He will lead them back. Even the blind he will lead. Even though they will be passing through unfamiliar territory, some of it hazardous and rough, he will not abandon them.[34] And he promises to protect the vulnerable: "Can a woman forget her baby who nurses at her breast? Can she withhold compassion from the child she has borne? Even if mothers were to forget, I could never forget you! Look, I have inscribed your name on my palms."[35]

## Hero of Promise

The prophet announces even more reason to rejoice. A heroic figure is coming who will fulfill Yahweh's will and complete the moral rehabilitation of their society, and even bless the nations.[36] He will be a redeemer of the weak and vulnerable;[37] he will suffer for his people, even for those who have gone astray;[38] he will have an ignominious burial but will eventually triumph.[39] From ancient times readers of these passages have wondered who these prophesies refer to. Who would this heroic figure be? And when would he appear? Is it the prophet himself? Or a royal figure? At one point the prophet uses the term "Cyrus" to refer to this heroic figure,[40] but

---

33. Isa 41:18–20 NET.
34. Isa 42:16 NET.
35. Isa 49:15–16a NET.
36. Isa 49–54.
37. Isa 50:4–8.
38. Isa 52:13—53:12. Christians read this passage as descriptive of the atoning work of Christ.
39. Isa 53:4–12. The verses Isa 42:1–9 seem to be about a single individual and therefore can be read as messianic, but they are situated within a discourse that is aimed at the exiled community (cf. 41:8–9), in which case they are read by most scholars as descriptive of the role that the Israelite community will have as a vehicle of God's grace to the nations. Chapters 49–54 seem to be more concerned with an individual and so can be read as messianic as well as descriptive of the redemptive services of the Israelite community to the world.
40. Isa 44:28b.

the conqueror was clearly a cypher for someone else, even greater. Many scholars have proposed that this was a reference to the nation of Israel itself.[41] Christians have seen messianic predictions in these passages.

The moral appeal of these promises is heightened by their ambiguity, which allows for various interpretations to be proposed, whether they refer to the renewed nation of Israel or to a messianic figure. Whatever these passages foretell they conform to the now-well-established story that the people of Israel had suffered Yahweh's wrath because of their refusal to remain true to him, to worship him and obey his commandments, but because of Yahweh's enduring commitment to them they can expect to have their relationship to their god renewed. He will show them kindness, for his commitment to them is unshakable. In fact, he regrets how much they have missed owing to their rebellion. "If only you had obeyed my commandments, prosperity would have flowed to you like a river, deliverance would have come to you like the waves of the sea."[42] Now, in any case, he was acting to bring them back to their land, and to himself.

## *Gathering in Canaan*

However much encouragement the exiles received from the prophet in their midst, many of the exiles were still skittish about the challenges of undertaking such an ambitious project. It was an act of faith to pack up and move out. The few who first made the trek to Judah showed courage and commitment to the prophet's hope of a new social world and the promise for their people that he was proclaiming.[43]

---

41. Isa 49:1–5. Blinkinsopp (Isaiah 40–55, 83–84) says "the passages . . . speak of rejection and suffering to Israel."

42. Isa 48:18 NET.

43. A generally accepted sequence of events is the following:

(1) Sheshbazzar in the time of Cyrus (538 BCE or later) returned with a group of exiles who set out to build a new temple, but their activities were interrupted by the complaints of the local inhabitants (Ezra 1:8, 11; 5:14).

(2) In the time of Darius (521–485 BCE) Zerubbabel and Joshua led another group of exiles to the Jerusalem site and obtained permission to resume construction on the temple, completing it in 515 BCE.

(3) Ezra, in the time of Artaxerxes I (465–424), arrived with a group and established the Torah as the sacred authority for Jewish religious practice.

(4) Nehemiah arrived in roughly 445 to rebuild the city walls. Ezra and Nehemiah were both in the neighborhood when the ritual of confession, repentance,

But the actual situation they found in Judah would have been enough to sober their vision. "Devastation was the spectacle that greeted" them, says Lipschits.[44] Before them lay the brute reality of what they had to do in order to establish the community that the prophet had envisioned. The burned-out ruins of the city were unsuitable for their families, so they situated themselves in the surrounding villages.[45] After the new immigrants would find their ancestral lands, they could begin construction on dwellings for their families. They would also be negotiating boundaries, setting up regulations for the occupants of the city. Families who scarcely knew each other, arriving from various parts of the greater Near East, formed relationships. A new society was taking shape. Communal relations, friendships, even marital bonds developed among them.

For at least some it must have been a heady time of excitement and joy. Second Isaiah rejoiced at the arrival of new immigrants to the community: "How delightful it is to see approaching over the mountains the feet of a messenger who announces peace, a messenger who brings good news, who announces deliverance, who says to Zion, 'Your God reigns!' Listen, your watchmen shout; in unison they shout for joy, for they see with their very own eyes the Lord's return to Zion."[46] Indeed, he could see in these developments that Yahweh himself was consoling "Zion," turning her wildernesses into an Eden, bringing joy, thanksgiving, and music to their local communities.[47] No need, then, to be distracted by the taunting and insults of your neighbors, the prophet said, for Yahweh's vindication is already appearing. Yes, you have suffered at Yahweh's hand, but prosperity awaits you. You have suffered famine and sword, he says, but Yahweh has taken the goblet of his anger from you; in fact, he will give it to your tormentors.[48] The sense of the moment was expressed by a psalmist: "When the Lord restored the well-being of Zion, we thought we were dreaming. At that time we laughed loudly and shouted for joy.... 'The Lord did indeed accomplish great things for us.'"[49]

---

and renewal was performed by the members of the community (Neh 8–10).

44. Lipschits, *Fall*, 113.

45. Neh 7:4; 11:1–4.

46. Isa 52:7–8 NET.

47. Isa 51:3.

48. Isa 51. Blenkinsopp, *Isaiah 40–55*, 82–92.

49. Ps 126:1–3a NET. Other psalms may have been composed during this period of resettlement in Judah, such as Pss 146–50. See Goulder, *Psalms of the Return*, 304.

# 15

# New Community
## Community in Formation

THE EARLIEST SETTLERS TO arrive in Judah came from families whose origins were from both kingdoms, Israel (notably from the tribes of Benjamin, Ephraim, Manasseh, and Levi),[1] and Judah. They were descendants of the generations who had endured the catastrophic termination of their respective kingdoms, Israel in 722 BCE, Judah in 587. Their coming signaled an acknowledgement of Yahweh's place in their lives, his right to their loyalty and worship. They saw their journey to Canaan as evidence that Yahweh was showing them kindness, manifest in Cyrus's appearance on the scene and his invitation. In this society, as some envisioned the new society, they would pay to Yahweh the deference that had not been granted to him by their predecessors. Their return, an event foretold by the prophets, meant more than a return to their ancestral homeland; it marked a decisive turn to Yahweh as their god, their only god. And with it they brought a heady sense of promise that Yahweh would prosper them in this place.

This whole affair—the destruction of the Israelite countries and their displacement into gentile lands—had been, as they could now see clearly, Yahweh's project all along. The Yahwist prophets had proclaimed that his agenda had been to convince their people to give him the honor that he deserved, to worship him alone and abide by his commandments. The tragedies that had marked their history—the violence, the destruction, the

---

1. 1 Chr 9:1–34.

humiliation, the exile—revealed to them that Yahweh had been involved in their affairs all along, essentially to show mercy and kindness to them once they repented. He, they now believed, had an inexorable commitment to them. He was bound to them, as Jeremiah said, by an everlasting love. His ambition had been to reshape their moral sensibility, as Ezekiel had said, to turn them into obedient and loyal worshippers of Yahweh who would be faithful to him from the heart. He had waited for them to respond to his overtures of love, they believed, for he wanted to bless them and honor them as he had promised their ancestors. His terrifying anger against them was, as theologian Louis Stulman puts it, a "wrath of love."[2]

They continued the sacred customs they had been practicing in Babylon. They recited the laments they had learned in exile, and in their solemn meetings they read and discussed the texts that had been edited and provided to them by the learned authorities who had worked among them in Babylon—the words of Moses, the books of the Deuteronomic history, and the sayings and writings of the prophets.[3] These works were now read with great respect, as authoritative sources on the relation of their people to their god. Together the writings contributed to the sense that Yahweh had been involved with their people from ancient times. They affirmed the narrative that had become standard among them, that their ancestors had suffered because of their offenses against Yahweh. But now after decades of living as aliens in a gentile country they were seeing Yahweh show his kindness to them as they formed a new community in Canaan. They were still subjugated to gentile rule, and their city and country were still a ruin, but now they could envision a time when their people would flourish, for they saw in this situation evidence of Yahweh's goodwill.

## Problems at the Site

Even so, the number of Jewish exiles that actually undertook the journey to Judah was relatively small. And the place to which they had come—the ruined city—was uninhabitable. So they set up their tents in the neighborhood. Even as late as Nehemiah's time (second half of the fifth century

---

2. Stulman, *Jeremiah*, 20–21.

3. It is traditional to suppose that the writings of the Pentateuch were produced by Moses during the exodus period, but that is not commonly accepted among scholars. The actual period when these texts came into being is much discussed. Some believe that the Pentateuch came into being as late as the exile period; cf. Albertz, *Open-Mindedness*.

## New Community

BCE), when he came to the city to organize the reconstruction of its walls, he discovered that the city "is desolate and its gates are burned."[4] He even had to coax some of the men to bed down within the charred grounds of the city in order to work on the wall and defend it. He arranged "to bring one out of every ten to live in Jerusalem" and those who volunteered to live there were given special commendation.[5] Their families and the rest of the immigrants settled in villages nearby.

Of course, these immigrants were busy. They were confronted with multiple complications of the sort to be expected in the kind of move that they had undertaken. Besides their work on dwellings for their families and in organizing their communities, very early they began to build the sacred places necessary for their religious activities. They completed an altar for the sacrifices to be offered to Yahweh, as stipulated in the law. Then they commenced work on a new temple.

But their temple project awakened the concern of local residents. The experts have discussed who those people were. They may have been Samaritans, that is, families who claimed descent from one of the tribes of Israel but insisted that the sacrifices to Yahweh should take place on mount Gerizim rather than in Jerusalem. Some of them may have simply been the descendants of the poor families enlisted by the Babylonians to work on the land after the city had been destroyed. The text in Ezra says that they were the people brought into Samaria by the Assyrian King Esarhaddon, which is to say they had no knowledge the Israelite traditions.[6] Whoever they were, they manifestly lacked the perspective of the newcomers on what the project of renewing the city and the temple was all about. They did not share a common sense of the past, a common understanding of what their activities meant, or the sense of promise that had brought these new immigrants back to Canaan.

Having little in common with the local communities, the newcomers distrusted them. They said that they would not allow these neighbors to join in the work on their new temple. The local residents were of course offended, and they began to oppose the project, seeking imperial intervention. In response to their petition to the Persian administration to disallow it, the officials looked into their claim and found that indeed Jerusalem was

---

4. Neh 2:17.
5. Neh 11:1-2; 2:13-17; 7:60. Cf. Lipschits, *Fall*, 267-71.
6. These people were known as "Cutheans." Ezra 4:2. Cf. 2 Kgs 24:14; Goodman, *History*, 12; Jonker, *Chronicles*, 310.

notorious for its rebellions, as the complainants had argued. So the Persians ordered all work on the temple to cease.[7]

## Two New Prophets

As these activities were going on, a new prophetic voice appeared among the immigrants in Judah. At least chapters 56–66 of Isaiah seem to have been written by someone else, or possibly "Second Isaiah" after he has arrived in Jerusalem—only now he is stunned and shocked by the situation he finds in the environs of the city. His initial enthusiasm has given way to heartache over what he sees. "Take a good look at your people," he says to Yahweh, "Your chosen cities have become a wilderness; Zion has become a wilderness, Jerusalem, a desolate ruin. Our holy temple, our pride and joy, the place where our ancestors praised you, has been burned with fire; all our prized possessions have been destroyed. In light of all this, how can you still hold back, LORD? How can you be silent and continue to humiliate us?"[8]

To the prophet's appeals Yahweh replies,

> I made myself available to those who did not ask for me; I appeared to those who did not look for me. I said, "Here I am! Here I am!" to a nation that did not invoke my name. I spread out my hands all day long to my rebellious people, who lived in a way that is morally unacceptable, and who did what they desired. These people continually and blatantly offend me as they sacrifice in their sacred orchards and burn incense on brick altars. . . . They eat pork, and broth from unclean sacrificial meat is in their pans. They say, "Keep to yourself! Don't get near me, for I am holier than you!" These people are like smoke in my nostrils.[9]

Along with the wretched state of the city there were the indecent, dishonest, unjust, and brutal ways the new immigrants were behaving among themselves.[10] The well-off were exploiting the manual laborers. Even fistfights were taking place in the streets. And all the while they were supposed to be celebrating a special fast to Yahweh. In fact, declared the prophet, their fasting was nothing more than ritual pretense, "bobbing heads" and

---

7. Ezra 4–6.
8. Isa 64:9b–12 NET.
9. Isa 64:8—65:3 (selections) NET.
10. Lipschits, *Fall*, 112–13. Cf. Isa 64:10–11; Zech 1:12; 2:5–9.

"wearing sackcloth," as if such behavior constituted repentance from sins.[11] "No," said the prophet in the name of Yahweh. "You need to be helping the folks who are in need among you."

> I want you to remove the sinful chains, . . . to set free the oppressed, and to break every burdensome yoke. I want you to share your food with the hungry and to provide shelter for homeless, oppressed people. When you see someone naked, clothe them! Don't turn your back on your own flesh and blood!

If you do those things, the prophet said, Yahweh will respond generously:

> Then your light will dispel the darkness, and your darkness will be transformed into noonday. The LORD will continually lead you; he will feed you even in parched regions. He will give you renewed strength, and you will be like a well-watered garden, like a spring that continually produces water.[12]

The other prophet who arose among the immigrants to Canaan during the time when work on a new temple was suspended was Zechariah, and he had similar objections to the superficiality of their religious performances. In the voice of Yahweh he questioned the immigrants: "Ask all the people of the land and the priests, 'When you fasted and mourned in the fifth and seventh months for the past seventy years, was it really for me that you fasted? And when you were eating and drinking, were you not just feasting for yourselves?'" What they should have been doing to please Yahweh, he said, was to "[a]dminister true justice; show mercy and compassion to one another. Do not oppress the widow or the fatherless, the foreigner or the poor. Do not plot evil against each other." In fact, says the prophet, they had "made their hearts as hard as flint and would not listen to the law or to the words that the LORD Almighty had sent by his Spirit through the earlier prophets." As a result, he says, "I scattered them with a whirlwind among all the nations, where they were strangers. The land they left behind them was so desolate that no one traveled through it. This is how they made the pleasant land desolate."[13] And now, said the prophet, the returnees from exile were falling into the same sins as those of their ancestors, who had suffered the demise of their societies.

---

11. Isa 58:3b–5 NET.
12. Isa 58:6–9 NET.
13. Zech 7:4–14 NET.

# Jerusalem Burning

## A Change in the Situation

As these prophets were addressing the misbehaviors of the new immigrants to Canaan, something significant was taking place in the top echelons of the empire. In 522 BCE Cambyses, the successor of Cyrus, was suddenly stricken and died by an accidental wound. Because Cambyses left no male issue the matter of succession was ambiguous, and for the next two years several notable contestants fought it out for the throne. By 520 BCE Darius, a man who had been the personal spear-carrier for Cambyses, prevailed, crushing all rivals. He triumphally declared himself "King of Kings of the Achaemenid Empire." In the same year in Judah a new prophetic voice emerged to challenge the immigrant Jews. This was Haggai. He and Zechariah together began to encourage the Jews to resume work on the temple. Their remonstrations persuaded the immigrants to appeal to the new king for permission to resume working on their new temple. By Darius's command Persian officials searched through the imperial archives and found that indeed, as the immigrants had claimed, Cyrus himself had commissioned the construction of the temple and even given back to leaders of the Jewish community some of the sacred utensils that Nebuchadnezzar had seized during the invasion of Judah.[14] The new temple, a modest building, nothing like the magnificent palace that it replaced, was completed in 515 BCE, and from then on became the center of worship for Jews everywhere, even those living far from Judah. The city itself, however, was still being built. According to Lipschits, Jerusalem would not become a thriving metropolis for nearly two hundred years.[15]

What is significant for my story is the explanation for what the new immigrants were doing that they gave to the Persian officials when they appealed for permission to begin the rebuilding of the temple:

> We are servants of the God of heaven and earth. We are rebuilding the temple which was previously built many years ago. A great king of Israel built it and completed it. But after our ancestors angered the God of heaven, he delivered them into the hands of King Nebuchadnezzar of Babylon, the Chaldean, who destroyed this temple and exiled the people to Babylon. But in the first year of King Cyrus of Babylon, King Cyrus enacted a decree to rebuild this temple of God. Even the gold and silver vessels of the temple of God that Nebuchadnezzar had taken from the temple in Jerusalem

---

14. This was Darius Hystaspes (r. 522–486 BCE).
15. Lipschits, *Fall*, 113.

and had brought to the palace of Babylon—even those things King Cyrus brought from the palace of Babylon and presented to a man by the name of Sheshbazzar whom he had appointed as governor. He said to him, "Take these vessels and go deposit them in the temple in Jerusalem and let the house of God be rebuilt in its proper location." Then this Sheshbazzar went and laid the foundations of the temple of God in Jerusalem. From that time to the present moment it has been in the process of being rebuilt, although it is not yet finished.[16]

This statement was a version of the standard narrative that had been broadly adopted by the Jewish community in exile in Babylon. The Israelites, as they said, had been in captivity "because our ancestors angered the God of heaven." That was why they had been brought into subjection to the Babylonians. These immigrant Jews in Canaan were saying that they had come back to their homeland to establish a proper relationship to this god and were rebuilding a temple to him on the site of the former one. Rebellion was not implied in their project.

## Ezra and the Dedication

About seven decades after the new temple was completed, when a number of Jewish immigrants had settled themselves in the Persian province of Yehud, the community again voiced the standard narrative about who they were and what they had experienced, only this time it was in a public ritual of dedication. Two notable individuals figured in this communal activity, Nehemiah, an official from the court of Artaxerxes I in Persepolis, and Ezra, a priest who had dedicated himself to the study of the Torah, the law given to Moses.[17] A curious detail in the way the story is told is that the members of the community themselves initiated this formal dedication to Yahweh. The book of Nehemiah says, "[A]ll the people gathered together in the plaza which was in front of the water gate. They asked Ezra the scribe to bring the book of the law of Moses which the LORD had commanded Israel. So Ezra the priest brought the law before the assembly which included men and women and all those able to understand what they heard. . . . So he read

---

16. Ezra 5:11–15 NET.

17. Ezra arrived in 458 BCE. Nehemiah came to Jerusalem in roughly the same period but the exact dates of their respective times in the city are debated (cf. 145n44 above). Nehemiah would come a second time to Judah in 445 BCE to be its governor. Cf Demsky, *Who Came First?*

it before the plaza in front of the Water Gate from dawn till noon before the men and women and those children who could understand. All the people were eager to hear the book of the law."[18] Several days of ritual observances followed, and on the twenty-fourth day of the month the members of the community gathered to recite together a formal confession and dedication of their community to Yahweh. For this occasion they had covered themselves in sackcloth and thrown ashes on their heads, and as Ezra ascended on a platform for the reading of the "book of the law," presumably the book of Deuteronomy, the congregation stood. Ezra, with assistance by the Levites, led the community in a series of confessional statements, entering "into a curse and an oath to adhere to the law of God which was given through Moses the servant of God, and to obey carefully all the commandments of the LORD our Lord, along with his ordinances and his statutes."[19] Together they confessed the following:

- That they and their ancestors had "become arrogant and stiff-necked, and they did not obey your commands. They refused to listen and failed to remember the miracles you performed among them."
- That "[t]hey became stiff-necked and in their rebellion appointed a leader in order to return to their slavery."
- That even after Yahweh had many times protected and led his people, "they were disobedient and rebelled against you; they turned their backs on your law."
- That they had "killed your prophets, who had warned them in order to turn them back to you."
- That, after Yahweh had again punished them, "as soon as they were at rest, they again did what was evil in your sight."
- That, yet again, after they had suffered and were warned, "they sinned against your ordinances."
- And that, even though they were still further warned, "they paid no attention."

The congregation concluded their confessions to Yahweh by affirming that, "Our kings, our leaders, our priests and our ancestors did not follow your law; they did not pay attention to your commands or the statutes

18. Neh 7:73b—8:8 NET.
19. Neh 10:28–29 NET.

# New Community

you warned them to keep. Even while they were in their kingdom, enjoying your great goodness to them in the spacious and fertile land you gave them, they did not serve you or turn from their evil ways." It was, they declared, "[b]ecause of our sins [that our] abundant harvest goes to the kings you have placed over us. They rule over our bodies and our cattle as they please." After reciting this confessional statement to Yahweh the members of the community formally inscribed their names, beginning with the most notable among them.[20]

Such a communal affirmation was a deliberate expression of the collective will. By performing this ritual of confession and dedication these immigrant Jews were formally establishing their society as a community committed to Yahweh. This time, they were saying, they would obey his laws. They would worship him and no other. Implicit in these exercises was the hope that by their confession and repentance Yahweh would be induced not only to forgive but to prosper their community. It was a ritual of hope. They looked forward to a time when, as their prophets had promised, their people would prosper in the land that Yahweh had given them. Their capital city, in the process of being rebuilt, would be, as the prophets had foreseen, a thriving metropolis admired by the nations, and the griefs and humiliations of the past would be forgotten.[21] Even so, as they admitted in their dedicatory statement to Yahweh, they were still servants of a gentile power. They were still in "exile." "So today we are slaves! In the very land you gave to our ancestors to eat its fruit and to enjoy its good things—we are slaves."[22]

---

20. Neh 9 (selections).
21. Middlemas, *Templeless*, 137.
22. Neh 9:36.

# 16

# Learned Authorities

SEVERAL GROUPS OF LEARNED authorities living through this time had worked to preserve in writing their sense that Yahweh had been a critical influence on the course of events in their time. By performing these acts of service to the community they were merely continuing the literary activities that had been the practice of the Israelites for many generations. Certain individuals during the reign of Hezekiah, possibly employed by the court, had kept records of the king's activities, writing down what they believed were significant in their time. The disciples of Hosea and Amos, having fled to Jerusalem after the fall of Samaria, may have been putting down in writing the messages that those two prophets had proclaimed in Israel. Likewise, the disciples of Isaiah and Micah, prophets who had spoken out in Judah at about the same time, may also have been writing down the teachings and remonstrations of those prophets during Hezekiah's reign. A century later, with Josiah on the throne, a cabal of literate individuals led by Hilkiah, the high priest, as we have seen, aggressively took over the affairs of state and they would have encouraged if not directly sponsored the several writing projects being undertaken in that time. (One, or several, of those folks may have been involved in the production of the scroll that Hilkiah found in the temple.) The Deuteronomic History project—the production of the books of Joshua, Judges, Samuel, and Kings—was probably initiated during this time, if not earlier. All these writings reveal that the Israelites during these early periods were writing down their understandings of what was going on in their times, including of course their sense that Yahweh had been involved in their affairs.

It was in this tradition of recording events that, after the destruction of Jerusalem, certain anonymous individuals worked to write down their accounts of how Yahweh had influenced the affairs of their people.[1] Those individuals worked on various texts considered authoritative at the time. They assembled and edited the book of Lamentations; updated the Deuteronomic History; and edited prophetic texts as well as those of Chronicles, Ezra, and Nehemiah.[2]

As for the five poems in the book of Lamentations, no one knows how they were produced or joined together into a book. I wonder if some individuals had drafted notes and descriptions of what they had witnessed, exposing their deep confusion and despair because of the attack. Later their notes would have been collected and polished into the stylized laments that now appear in the book. In any case, the intricate, crafted style of these poems reveals that those who wrote them were highly accomplished poets. The rhythm of the poems was paced to facilitate the reciting of griefs and laments as a community. The collection could be recited as a testimony of what the attack had been like for those who experienced it. Today it stands, like the ruins of the city that were abandoned for decades, as an emblem of a memorable tragedy in the history of their people. It has been a device for instructing later generations on what the attack had been like for those who were alive at the time. Those who continued to grieve over what they had seen and heard during the siege and afterwards were able through these laments to share with their heirs the deep wounds that they bore within them of the brutal and comprehensive wreckage of their world.

For generations the Jews have recited these laments in formal ritual observances. At some point, according to the book of Zechariah, the exile community was holding collective rituals of lament four times a year.[3] Jews situated near the city may have recited the laments on the site of its ruins, while others who lived too far away would have turned their faces toward them as they recited their laments and pronounced their prayers. The book

---

1. My conception of these scholarly groups is something like what Richard Fox calls the "intellectual writing groups" in India, whose debates early in the twentieth century shaped the Quit India Movement that would seek to force the British out of India (Fox, *Gandhian Utopia*).

2. This discussion is essentially based on the writings of Oded Lipschits (*Fall*), Jill Middlemas (*Templeless*), and Rainer Albertz (*History*; *Israel*).

3. Zech 7:2-7; 8:18-19.

of Lamentations is still read annually by observant Jews on the ninth day of the month of Av.[4]

Some of the learned authorities living in exile after the attack also worked on the texts of the Deuteronomic History. This historical series of books had been produced in Josiah's time, or earlier, and concluded with the destruction of Israel, which took place in 722 BCE (2 Kgs 17). The learned authorities living in Babylon 135 years later made a few changes in the text produced earlier in order to append their own report of the destruction of Judah. In the revised and augmented text of the book of Kings the authorities linked the explanation for Israel's demise, already produced by the earlier learned authorities, to that of Judah's violent termination. They revised the original statement of why Israel had been destroyed (2 Kgs 17) to say that both countries had suffered tragic and shameful ends because of their sins against Yahweh. They added the note that "Even Judah did not keep the commands of the LORD their God. They followed the practices Israel had introduced. Therefor the LORD rejected all the people of Israel."[5] The book of Kings, and in effect the history of the Children of Israel from the time of Joshua to the destruction of Judah's sacred city, thus concludes with both kingdoms of the Israelites expunged from the earth, their cities left in ruins, their populations scattered across the broad Near East. And the reason? The citizens of both countries had stubbornly refused to give Yahweh the respect he had been due.[6]

Another group of learned authorities worked on the materials available on the preachings and teachings of the prophets who had warned the peoples of Israel and Judah against their apostasies from Yahweh. In this case, the problem was that most of the messages of the prophets had originally been delivered verbally and may not have been preserved in writing. The prophets were commissioned by Yahweh to speak to their communities, to preach in public places, to demonstrate openly what Yahweh wanted these people to know. Their means of communication were speeches, sermons, public announcements, even, as in Jeremiah's case, a protest demonstration. To enhance the impact of their declarations they commonly phrased them in poetic form, or as pithy oracles, or as catchy sayings so

---

4. Besides the laments collected in a separate book, there were other laments preserved in the Psalms, for example, Pss 44, 60, 74.

5. 2 Kgs 17:18–19. This edition of the Deuteronomic history now became, in the parlance of contemporary scholars, "Dtr2," the previous version, produced during Josiah's time, being, of course, "Dtr1" (2 Kgs 25:21; Lipshits, *Fall*, 272–304).

6. 2 Kgs 17:7–17.

as to be easily remembered.[7] But were their prophetic declarations written down, at least as first? Many scholars believe that what they had said and done had to be retrieved from their disciples and other individuals close to them. It is unclear how many of their public messages were recorded soon after they were pronounced to the public; a notable exception, of course, was the sermon that Jeremiah dictated to his assistant Baruch, to be read aloud later on the temple grounds.

It is impossible to be sure, that is, when many of the utterances of the prophets of Yahweh were first reduced to writing. The warnings and criticisms of Hosea and Amos against the citizens of Israel are believed to have been written down in Jerusalem, as were the declarations of Isaiah and Micah. In any case, the sayings of these and other Yahwist prophets had to be collected and edited into accessible texts. Different individuals may have worked on the prophetic texts at different times, reflecting in each case their respective interests and perspectives. Scholars believe that some of those works were collected into "books" very early. The testimonies of "The Prophets of Judgment" (Hosea, Amos, Micah, Zephaniah), may have been published together as one work during the exile.[8] Another collection believed to have been produced in Babylon consisted of the "minor prophets" (Hosea, Joel, Amos, Obadiah, Jonah, Micah, Nahum, Habakkuk, Zephaniah, Haggai, Zechariah, Malachi).[9] The book of Jeremiah, as the text itself reveals, was produced by someone close to the prophet, presumably Baruch; the editor, in any case, included Jeremiah's oral and written declarations along with, in some cases, descriptions of the times and circumstances when they were made. The final work may have been produced in Egypt.[10] The prophetic material of Isaiah of Jerusalem may have been collected and edited during the exile period. More editorial activity may

---

7. Sweeney (*Introduction*, 961) says, "[T]he poetic materials in the prophetic books originated as oral pronouncements by the prophet to a public audience . . . [and were] subsequently written down."

8. Most scholars believe these writings were published together in the exile period. See Albertz, *Israel*, 208–37. Many of them explicitly note that the exile of Israel and Judah was perceived as a kind of purification.

9. Albertz (*Israel*, 237–45) says that Habakkuk was edited late in the exile period but provides no explanation for this claim. He allows that this prophet might have "appeared before or contemporaneously with Jeremiah" (240). The "redactor" of his book "drew on descriptions of disaster (1:6–11, 14–17) with which the prophet Habakkuk had graphically warned the Judeans . . ." (241).

10. Albertz (*Israel*, 312–45) believes that the book of Jeremiah was edited at different times by three different individuals.

have been done on it after the appearance of the other prophets whose utterances were saved and attached to the book. The book of Ezekiel was likewise preserved during the exile period, but it seems to have been only lightly touched by other hands; the book appears as if it was written by the prophet himself or by close associates as events transpired in his life.[11]

## *Texts of Confession*

Through their literary activities—producing the book of Lamentations, revising the Deuteronomic history, and editing the prophecies of the prophets into accessible form—these anonymous editors reflected their belief that the Children of Israel had been guilty of grievous sins, for which Yahweh that struck them down. Yahweh had been justified in his wrath, they were saying.[12] According to the writer of the second poem in Lamentations, "The LORD has done what he planned; he has fulfilled his word, which he decreed long ago."[13]

The deliberate flouting of Yahweh's commandments by the Israelites, practiced so casually in times past, now seemed keenly odious and consequential.[14] But as the prophets had declared, and the texts of the Lamentations and the Deuteronomic History implied, what the citizens of Israel and Judah had suffered was mere prologue to another time, when their people would enjoy Yahweh's favor. The authorities (to steal a phrase from Ewa Domańska) "organized the past in order to make a case for a particular future."[15] The disastrous loss of everything need not be cause for despair, the authorities were saying to their fellow exiles; there was reason for hope. What had happened to them could now be seen as a mere episode in the on-going history of Yahweh's dealings with his people. He had taken extreme measures in order to draw them to himself, to enable them to make a commitment to him as their god and to obey his commandments. His plan,

---

11. Albertz (*Israel*, 345–76) summarizes several analyses of the book of Ezekiel and comes to the conclusion that the text of the book was produced by the prophet himself, or, more probably, by his disciples.
12. Middlemas, *Templeless*, 138.
13. Lam 2:17.
14. Albertz, *Israel*, 282.
15. Domanska, *Philosophy and Introduction*, 11.

as the prophets had indicated, was to act again, the next time to encourage, heal, and restore.[16]

But this prospect was contingent: if they were to enjoy Yahweh's good will, they must renounce their idolatrous ways and commit to obeying his will for them.

As these writings—the Lamentations, the books of the Deuteronomic History, and the works of the prophets—became available to the Jewish exiles, they would have been read and discussed in their weekly convocations. They seem to have been accepted rather quickly by the community, possibly because of the recognized importance of the original authors and the respect enjoyed by those who developed them into written form. As they came to be read in their religious convocations the authority of these texts increased and came to be regarded as authoritative, even sacred, the word of God.

## *The Literary Record*

As the Jews in exile came to regard the events that had so drastically overturned their society to be the work of Yahweh they not only saw it as an act of wrath but also an act of commitment to them. He would not abandon them. Although they were helplessly locked into serving a gentile empire, they needed now to focus their attention on what he might do for them in the future. For the prophets had said that Yahweh would relent and bring them back to their homeland. The prophets Jeremiah and Ezekiel had drawn vivid pictures of a glorious future that Yahweh had planned for them. Their people will be brought back to Canaan, they said, and their country would be admired by the world.

The writings produced during the exilic period in Babylon, and later under the Persians who succeeded them, constitute documentary evidence of the radical change in moral understanding that took place among the exiles who had been scattered throughout Mesopotamia and Syria-Palestine after the destruction of Jerusalem. The importance of these writing projects for these individuals, the learned authorities who produced them, is evident in the "almost frenzied" zeal with which they undertook their projects. They "seized the political opportunity" of their dislocation from the world they had known, in order to make accessible the writings that

---

16. Middlemas, *Templeless*, 62.

would enable themselves and their fellow exiles to understand what had happened to them.[17]

## *The Literary Impact*

Manifestly, the totality of these literary works has become a priceless legacy. The editorial activity had been the work of individuals whom I have called "learned authorities," folks who may have lived at different times and even may have had rather different opinions on certain issues. But collectively they produced a series of works that informed their community on how critical the relationship to Yahweh had been for the wellbeing of their people—and even a legacy for the wider world of non-Israelites, one of the great legacies of the ancient world.[18] Zeitlin notes that these "perfected and polished writings" attest to the fact that those who produced them represented "literary traditions going back many centuries."[19] Ancient as they are, many of them are considered great works of literature. Kathleen O'Connor describes Lamentations as "a potent work of art."[20] Stephen McKenzie describes the book of Samuel as a literary "masterpiece."[21] Walter Brueggemann describes the books of Jeremiah, Ezekiel, and Hosea as a "remarkable literary achievement."[22] It is possible, says Oded Lipschits, to see a "meticulous organization of the material" in these writings, and a "thematic, structural, and linguistic uniformity of the entire work."[23] Moreover, the Deuteronomic History has been described as the oldest "history" of its kind, predating Herodotus by almost a century.[24] Some scholars have

---

17. The phrases here are taken from Albertz, *Israel*, 4, 436.

18. Evidence of an editorial touch on the book of Judges appears at 18:30. We are told that the family of a Levite named Jonathan were priests for the tribe of Dan *until the time of the captivity of the land*, that is, until 587 BCE. This comment, obviously by someone living in the exile period, suggests that at least some priestly services continued after the Assyrian devastations of 722 BCE.

19. Zeitlin, *Ancient*,19.

20. O'Connor, *Lamentations*, 4.

21. McKenzie, *1 Samuel*, 399.

22. Brueggemann, *Hopeful*, 1.

23. Lipschits, *Fall*,286.

24. Albertz (*Israel*, 273) made his remark with respect to the exile period, which is when he believed they were written, or were at least edited; in any case, he was quick to add that there are essential differences of these Israelite writings from the historical writing of Herodotus, who took a determinedly disinterested perspective on the events

suggested that these writings should not be considered history because of its didactic intent. But Baruch Halpern insists that the anonymous authorities who produced the History are rightly considered "the first historians."[25] Yes, he acknowledges, their writings are biased, but all historical writings, he reminds us, are animated by distinctive agendas.[26] This body of writings, a literary treasure trove of inestimable value, essentially completed so early, arose from one of the most terrible and destructive events in Israelite history. The Hebrew Bible exists, says theologian Jill Middlemas, because "creative and innovative thinkers" believed that the catastrophic event that had brought their society to ruin had been an act of God.[27]

Even today these texts resonate with believers of many sorts. People living in radically different times and circumstances have found in them exhortations and models for living that have inspired them in their own attempts to make sense of issues pressing in their own lives. We turn to these texts in search of insight for living productively, even joyfully, to face a world in which certainties elude, situations defy reason, and malice and envy animate public behavior.

But who were these "learned authorities"? One author suggests that those individuals were a "variety of informal groups of theologians of every stripe."[28] They may have come from "the two leading families of the exile community in Babylon, the royal family (such as Jehoiachin, Zerubbabel) and the pre-eminent priestly family (such as Jozadak, Joshua)."[29] The fact remains, however, that no one knows who the learned authorities who produced these works in their present form were or what elements of the population they came from.

---

he describes.

25. Halpern, *First Historians*.

26. White, *Metahistory*; Ankersmit et al., *Refiguring Haden White*; Waldron, *How Politics Are Haunted by the Past*; Taylor, *Sources of the Self*, 50–51.

27. Middlemas, *Templeless*, 7.

28. Albertz, *Israel*, 139.

29. Albertz, *Israel*, 284; cf. Friedman, *Who Wrote the Bible?*, 146–49. A recent discussion of how the texts under discussion became scriptures can be found in Schniedewind, *Scripturalization*.

# 17

# Moral Imagination in Social Practice

THIS STORY HAS BEEN about a people who saw an unseen and unseeable Presence in their worldly experience. The critical affair, the total destruction of Jerusalem, was an event that overturned many of their presumptions about themselves, their temple, their city, their history, and their sense of the unseen world. The temple that was supposed to be inviolate was plundered, torn down, and burned. The city whose site had been chosen by their god was a charred, barren waste. Their king, last in the line of David, was blind, helpless, shackled, and a prisoner of his enemies. The other survivors of the attack were scattered throughout the lands of the Babylonian empire.

The survivors, as they were trying to make sense of how all this had happened, had questions about how it happened. They knew, of course, what events had occurred to bring about the destruction of their society. King Zedekiah tried to evade Nebuchadnezzar's claims on his treasury and so earned Nebuchadnezzar's wrath and prompted his fateful attack on Judah. But what the survivors wondered about was whether any unseen power had been a force in the catastrophe. This was how they came to think about Yahweh. That notion, that Yahweh had willed it, came out of the repertoire of customs, memories, presumptions, and other conventions of thought and practice that were familiar among the Israelites. They knew about the prophets speaking in the name of Yahweh who had arisen among their people to warn them that their indifference to Yahweh's commandments were offensive to him and would induce a terrible time of reckoning for their peoples. They appealed to the Israelites to honor the Mosaic command "to love the LORD your god with your whole mind, your whole being, and all your strength." And they were well aware that the Israelites had often been indifferent to Yahweh's rules.

The attack of the Babylonians on Jerusalem in 587 BCE shocked the Judahites into confusion and doubt about all that they had taken for granted, and when they began to think about how this whole affair had taken place they suspected that this dramatic event may have been what the prophets Zephaniah, Isaiah, Micah, Joel, Ezekiel, and Jeremiah had predicted. It was natural to perceive the violence against their city as the act of an angry god, for what the prophets had foretold had actually taken place.

The conviction that Yahweh had in wrath brought about the demise of their societies affected their views on virtually everything else that they understood about their people. As they could now see it, Yahweh had been a vital influence on their affairs for generations. But besides reshaping their perceptions of the past, their new perception drew them to envision what it meant for the future. The prophets who had predicted that after the Israelites had lived through such a time of rejection by Yahweh he would relent and set them free from their bondage, and even bless them beyond measure. Ezekiel, Jeremiah, and Third Isaiah had predicted an eventual reconstitution of Jerusalem and a time when the nations would come and join the Jews in worshipping Yahweh. Indeed, this whole experience of chaos, defeat, and dispersion from their homeland had been Yahweh's plan, Ezekiel said, in order to produce in them a new and different attitude, even a visceral commitment to him. Yahweh, he said, will "give you a new heart and put a new spirit in you; ... [and would] remove from you your heart of stone and give you a heart of flesh."[1] This new perspective constituted a "new model of reality" that pervaded the way they would think about many things: about what had happened to them, about themselves as a people, and about what they could look forward to in the future.[2] The chaotic experience to which they had been subjected could now be seen as evidence that they had been chosen by Yahweh and were indeed bound inescapably to him by an ancient covenant.

---

1. Ezek 36:26.

2. The quoted phrase is a term used by Arnold Momigliano, quoted in Bellah, *Religion*, 283.

# Jerusalem Burning

## *A Plethora of Significances*

The attack on their city in 587 BCE, horrifying as it was, came to stand for many things in the moral sensibility of the Jewish community. It stood for the "reality" of an unshakable covenant with Yahweh; it implied the years of rebellious sinful practices in the past by their people in which they had angered Yahweh and so brought their own societies to ruin. It evoked memories of the remonstrations of prophets, many of whom had been spurned, and reminded them of the losses and defeats sustained, the wealth lost and opportunities squandered, because of their disobedience. It stood for the fury of Yahweh against them because of their apostasies. And it stood for the time when Yahweh would relent and show them mercy. Yahweh was now a substantive Presence in their affairs, and a decisive force in what they could expect in the future. He was a fearsome personality, a force, someone who could not be regarded with indifference, whose will and purposes would not be denied. Even if he was unseen and unseeable, his presence, his influence on them and their situation, was undeniable, inescapable. His existence and his claims on them were now unassailable truth. Every loss sustained in the past, every abuse they had suffered, constituted material evidence that Yahweh was real and his anger terrifying.

Yes, it was all an act of the imagination, a leap of faith, a linking of the prophets' warnings with the horrific event that ruined their lives. It was a transformative insight that endowed the worldly event with the "reality" of an active spiritual Presence that would not be denied.

How radically their perception of events had changed was evidenced in the debris left behind by several generations of citizens who had lived in Jerusalem in the sixth and fifth centuries. Modern archaeologists have discovered, in the ruins of the city, relics of the deities that its inhabitants had worshipped at various times. The most notable of the objects left behind by the folks who lived in the city before the Babylonian attack were feminine icons of the "Queen of Heaven"—the goddess whom the women fleeing to Egypt had insisted on venerating, despite Jeremiah's remonstrations. In contrast, in the debris left behind by the Jews who returned to the city after its destruction, the archaeologists found no such religious artifices, only those related to the veneration of Yahweh. The difference in what the two communities left behind in the debris of the city—those who had lived there before the attack versus those who lived in it afterwards—indicates how differently the later generations conceived of their religious circumstances.³ No other god than Yahweh seemed important to the later generations.

## The Grand Lesson

Just to be clear how distinctive this "new order of reality" was, let us take note of the story that the Jews who formed a new community in Canaan were telling themselves. It was not a story about how their people, the Children of Israel, had earned Yahweh's favor by their dedication or their faithful practice of required rituals. It wasn't about how their zeal for Yahweh, despite many hardships, had finally won him over. No, it was about how this god had relentlessly pursued their people even though, for their part, they had refused to give him the respect and reverence that he claimed as a right. Out of his passionate desire for a relationship with them—even though they had no interest in him or his agendas for them—this god had been willing to do horrific things in order to get their attention, their respect, their loyalty, and their worship.⁴ They were his chosen people, he insisted. Only in exasperation had he acted against them. He was, and had been from ancient times, committed to leading these people, guiding them, instructing them, and in the end prospering them according to the terms of the covenant. He had been eager to relate to them, to win them over. As the prophets said, he was a jilted lover. The total devastation of their society, as the exiles in Babylon came to see it, had been an act of love. This was the story that the exiles embraced.

## The Main Character

In truth, as the story developed, Yahweh himself turned out to be its main character. He made promises and fulfilled them. He warned and remonstrated with his people. He implored them, "Turn back, turn back from your evil deeds! Why should you die, O house of Israel?" When he finally carried out the punishing acts he had predicted, he announced that he took

---

3. Cf. Middlemas, *Templeless*, 120 note (no source provided). Ariel David (*Archaeological Mystery*) says that the crafted images of naked women that had been "continuously used in Judah during the late First Temple period, from the eighth century B.C.E." ceased to be found by archaeologists in the remains from the period after the city was destroyed.

4. Cf. O'Connor, *Jeremiah*, 137.

"no pleasure in the death of the wicked."[5] He himself grieved over what he had done: "I am filled with sorrow because of the disaster that I have brought on you."[6] Before the city was brought to ruin he had said, "If my people would only listen to me, if Israel would only follow my ways . . . !"[7] After the terrible act, he lamented, "If only you had paid attention to my commands. . . ."[8] According to the writer of the third lament in the book of Lamentations, "Though he brings grief, he will show compassion, so great is his unfailing love. For he does not willingly bring affliction or grief to anyone."[9]

Such, for the believing Jews in exile, was their God. He was, on the one hand, gracious and gentle, but on the other, unmanageable, insistent on their loyalty and obedience, and terrifying.[10] He would assume different poses according to the way his people responded to him. For those who spurned him he could be insistent. For the rebellious he could be obstinate. For the indifferent he could be persistent. For the repentant he could be forgiving. For the crushed, lonely, and despairing he could be gentle, supportive, and encouraging. In any case, he would engage with those who in truth earnestly sought him. He had wanted to bless his people, prosper them. Now that things have gone otherwise, he was disappointed but no less committed to bringing his people home, to fulfill all that he had envisioned for them. But compassionate and merciful as he was, he would not be manipulated. As the prophets said, this was a god like no other.

## What Yahweh Wanted

Moreover, as the Jews understood it, this was a god whose demands on his people were unlike those of any other god. It was usual for the gods to demand sacrifices, owing to the need of their priests to have a reasonable income, even to live well. But as the prophets of Yahweh made clear, it was not good enough for his people to offer sacrifices as tokens of their worship. Amos, who had prophesied in the name of Yahweh to the citizens of Israel, told them that Yahweh was revulsed by their religious performances:

5. Ezek 33:11.
6. Jer 42:11.
7. Ps 81:13.
8. Isa 48:18.
9. Lam 3:33.
10. Middlemas, *Templeless*, 50.

## Moral Imagination in Social Practice

"I hate, I despise your religious festivals; your assemblies are a stench to me. Even though you bring me burnt offerings and grain offerings, I will not accept them.... Away with the noise of your [sacred] songs! I will not listen to the music of your harps." What Yahweh wanted from them instead was justice, generosity, and mercy in their worldly behavior: "Let justice roll on like a river, righteousness like a never-failing stream!"[11] Yahweh was offended that instead of practicing justice "you have turned justice into poison and the fruit of righteousness into bitterness."[12] He was offended that the wealthy were taking advantage of the unfortunate: "They sell the innocent for silver, and the needy for a pair of sandals. They trample on the heads of the poor... and deny justice to the oppressed. Father and son use the same girl and so profane my holy name."[13] Isaiah of Jerusalem, speaking to the generation of Judahites in Hezekiah's time, had a similar objection to their rituals: "Stop bringing meaningless offerings! Your incense is detestable to me.... Your New Moon feasts and your appointed festivals I hate with all my being."[14] "Take your evil deeds out of my sight; stop doing wrong. Learn to do right; seek justice. Defend the oppressed. Take up the cause of the fatherless; plead the cause of the widow."[15] Micah even directly raised the question of what Yahweh wanted of him. Should he bring him burnt offerings? How many? Would thousands of rams be enough? What if, like the neighboring communities, he should offer his own firstborn as a sacrifice? Yahweh replied that his demands were more behavioral and social: "to act justly and to love mercy and to walk humbly with your God."[16]

Such a strange god this was! He rejected the ritualized sacrifices of his people but demanded that, as a way of life, they show mercy, generosity, justice, and deference to the human beings in their world.

The persistent refusal of the Israelites' two kingdoms, Israel and Judah, to live out these social commandments of Yahweh had brought them to ruin. This was Amos's point: Because of "those who turn justice into bitterness... [who] detest the one who tells the truth... [and] levy a straw tax on the poor and impose a tax on their grain, there will be wailing in

---

11. Amos 5:21–24.
12. Amos 6:12b.
13. Amos 2:6b–8. Cf. Amos 5:14–15; Hos 6:6.
14. Isa 1:13–14.
15. Isa 1:16b–17.
16. Mic 6:6–8.

all the streets and cries of anguish in every public square."[17] Hosea had similarly declared that because there was in Israel "no faithfulness, no love, no acknowledgment of God in the land, ... only cursing, lying and murder, stealing and adultery, their leaders would vanish like the morning mists."[18] Isaiah of Jerusalem warned, "Woe to those who make unjust laws, to those who issue oppressive decrees, to deprive the poor of their rights and withhold justice from the oppressed of my people, making widows their prey and robbing the fatherless."[19] Accordingly, he said, "The LORD enters into judgment against the elders and leaders of his people: ... What do you mean by crushing my people and grinding the faces of the poor?"[20] Micah noted that the leaders in Judah "despise justice ... [and] judge for a bribe, [and the priests] teach for a price, and her prophets tell fortunes for money." Accordingly, he says, "Because of you Zion will be plowed like a field, Jerusalem will become a heap of rubble, the temple hill a mound overgrown with thickets."[21] The judgment against Judah was not without cause, says Ezekiel, for "they have treated father and mother with contempt; ... they have oppressed the foreigner and mistreated the fatherless and the widow. ... [They are] slanderers who are bent on shedding blood; ... [they] commit lewd acts; ... [they] dishonor their father's bed; ... [they] violate women during their period. ... [Also] one man commits a detestable offense with his neighbor's wife, another shamefully defiles his daughter-in-law, and another violates his sister, his own father's daughter." Some of them "accept bribes to shed blood; ... [and] take interest and make a profit from the poor. You extort unjust gain from your neighbors. And you have forgotten me, declares the Sovereign LORD." So, predicted Yahweh through Ezekiel, "I will disperse you among the nations and scatter you through the countries; and I will put an end to your uncleanness."[22]

## *And Yet Yahweh Loved Them*

But the stroke of wrath that Yahweh had visited upon his people had arisen out of a deep and enduring commitment to them. Even as Jeremiah had

---

17. Amos 5:7–17.
18. Hos 8:14; 10:4; 13:7–8.
19. Isa 10:1–3.
20. Isa 3:14–16.
21. Mic 3:11; 6:11, 12; also 7:2–6; 4:10.
22. Ezek 22:6–16.

announced Yahweh's commitment to destroy Jerusalem, he declared to the city in Yahweh's voice, "I have loved you with an everlasting love; I have drawn you with unfailing kindness. I will build you up again. . . . Again you will take up your timbrels and go out to dance with the joyful."[23] According to Ezekiel, even though Yahweh had punished his people, "I will remember the covenant I made with you in the days of your youth, and I will establish an everlasting covenant with you. Then you will remember your ways and be ashamed. . . . Then, when I make atonement for you for all you have done, you will remember and be ashamed and never again open your mouth because of your humiliation, declares the Sovereign LORD."[24] Indeed, this had been Yahweh's agenda all along—to show his people mercy, to renew a relationship with them. Second Isaiah, calling upon his countrymen to act on Cyrus's invitation, had said, "'[Y]ou, Israel, are my servant. I have made you . . . ; I will not forget you. I have swept away your offenses like a cloud. . . . Return to me, for I have redeemed you.' Sing for joy, you heavens, for the LORD has done this; shout aloud, you earth beneath. Burst into song, you mountains, you forests and all your trees, for the LORD has redeemed Jacob, he displays his glory in Israel."[25]

## The Visitation

What drove the imaginative understanding of the people who came out of the tragedy of Jerusalem's destruction was the sense that this god, the God of history, had displayed himself to them. The most destructive, shocking moment in their lives had been, as they saw it, a literal visitation of God. It was a perspective promoted by the prophets. Zephaniah had said, "the Maker of all things, who stretches out the heavens, who spreads out the earth by myself" was the person who frustrates the plans of the foolish and deceitful; he "foils the signs of false prophets and makes fools of diviners, who overthrows the learning of the wise and turns it into nonsense, who carries out the words of his servants and fulfills the predictions of his messengers." This was the real God of all the earth.[26] Second Isaiah would, in the voice of Yahweh, ask, "Who has done this and carried it through, calling forth the generations from the beginning? I, the LORD—with the first of

23. Jer 31:3-6.
24. Ezek 16:59-63.
25. Isa 44:21-23.
26. Zeph 3:24-26.

them and with the last—I am he. . . . But you, Israel, my servant, Jacob, whom I have chosen, you descendants of Abraham my friend, I took you from the ends of the earth, from its farthest corners I called you. I said, 'You are my servant'; I have chosen you. . . . So do not fear, for I am with you; . . . I am your God. I will strengthen you and help you; I will uphold you with my righteous right hand."[27] The Children of Israel had been visited by God—the God of History, the Creator, the Unique Eternal God. And he had told them that he loved them; they were his chosen people.

And how did these people know all this? Because their god had punished them. In one brutal moment—the wrecking, burning, slaughter, rapine—Yahweh displayed both his wrath and his relentless love for them. In that moment love and wrath converged. Punishment for sin was bonded with forgiveness, mercy, and redemption. This conjunction of wrath and mercy exposed something mysterious, awesome, and frightening about this personality. Habakkuk, foreseeing a tragedy he could not avoid, begged Yahweh, "In wrath, remember mercy."[28]

The enormity of the perspective that informed the experience of these Israelites is distilled in one sentence: "You only have I chosen of all the families of the earth; therefore I will punish you for all your sins."[29] Let us pause to marvel at the creativity and rhetorical power of the imaginative ability of these Israelites to conceive of such a god, to take him to be real, significant, compelling, knowable, and comforting! That is, to apprehend the invisible God.

## Wider Implications

I began this project by proposing to examine how the survivors of the disaster came to the view that Yahweh had willed it. But it turns out that, taking another point of view, we can regard it as an example of how the creative and supple human imagination is capable of infusing even the most cruel and chaotic situations with a sense of significance, even transcendence. As it is human to cope with a manifestly palpable world by framing it with conceptions of value, exalted notions of what we presume to be truth, justice, and purity, the story of the Israelites' discovery of God in their material

---

27. Isa 41:4–10 (selections).
28. Hab 3:2b.
29. Amos 3:2.

experience was an instance in which a particular set of sublime meanings was imputed to a notably horrific moment in human history.

It is human to look for enduring verities by which to order one's life, to cope with the endless practical challenges of living in a broken world. It is human to conceptually frame our experiences within idealized notions of truth, fairness, and enduring value. The quest for anchorage for the inner self in an unstable and shifting world is universal, I believe. It is what the French philosopher Simone Weil calls the search for "rootedness." "To be rooted," she writes, "is perhaps the most important and least recognized need of the human soul. . . . A human being has roots by virtue of his real, active and natural participation in the life of a community which preserves in living shape certain particular treasures of the past and certain particular expectations for the future." In reflecting on this statement the philosophical anthropologist Michael D. Jackson notes that rootedness is "inextricably linked to a person's real, active and natural participation in the life of a community." To belong, he says, is "to believe that one's being is integrated with and integral to a wider field of Being, that one's own life merges with and touches the lives of others—predecessors, successors, contemporaries and consociates, as well as the overlapping worlds of nature, the cosmos, and the divine."[30]

The human imagination is a moral instrument. It imposes idealized conceptions of a sublime, enduring "truth" upon the discordant affairs of human existence, enveloping the urgent, fleeting, tangled, earthly happenings of life within a set of abstract conceptions of justice, purity, and permanence. It enables human beings to believe that existence in a shifting, evolving, dying universe is not only bearable but is significant. Even a devastating experience can be infused, as in this case, with a sense of divine purpose, making it memorable, instructive, even a revelation of the Infinite God.

---

30. Weil, *The Need for Roots*, 41. Weil's statement appears, along with Jackson's comment, in Jackson, *Politics*, 12.

# Appendix
## Topics for Discussion

### Chapter One

1. What is the central concern of this book?
2. How does the author plan to address this topic?
3. What problems are entailed in using the best sources for examining the topic?

### Chapter Two

1. What was the Axial Age?
2. Describe the broad geopolitical context of the Israelite lands.
3. As of 700 BCE, what empire dominated this geopolitical region, and how did its dominance influence the lesser principalities ("kingdoms") of the region?
4. Describe the conceptual "world" of the peoples living in this period? What was, in their conception, the influence of the "unseen world" on their lives? How did they try to of related to that world?
5. Among the religious beliefs of the Israelites, what was the belief about their ancestors' relation to the god Yahweh?
6. How was the technology of writing practiced in the eighth century BCE?

# Appendix

## Chapter Three

1. Contrast the relative geopolitical contexts of the kingdoms of Israel and Judah. How did their geographic location affect their political affairs?
2. Describe the difference between Hezekiah's perspective and Sennacherib's when he brought his army to the gates of Jerusalem.
3. How did the outcome of that affair influence the way many folks in Jerusalem regarded their temple and their city?
4. Explain how the opportunities differed for King Josiah from those available to his grandfather King Hezekiah.
5. Explain how the discovery of a scroll in the temple profoundly changed the course of affairs in Judah.

## Chapter Four

1. What was the Deuteronomist movement? Why is it called "Deuteronomist"?
2. What enduring contribution did the Deuteronomists make to the understanding of Yahweh's relationship to the Children of Israel?
3. Describe the influence of the prophets of Yahweh on the moral understanding of the people of Judah.

## Chapter Five

1. How did the trouble in the Assyrian homeland contribute to the death of Josiah?
2. As Judah was going through its own throes of change a young prophet received a call from Yahweh. What are the problems in working with the available texts on his life?
3. What was this prophet told that his prophesies would accomplish?

## Topics for Discussion

### Chapter Six

1. What were the major themes of Jeremiah's declarations to his fellow-citizens in Jerusalem and how were they generally received?
2. Jeremiah offended the leaders of his community by his critiques of the practices of his countrymen. Describe how he was nearly executed by one group and threatened by another.
3. As Jeremiah was facing danger in Jerusalem, in Syria two great armies were preparing for a battle that would affect the affairs of many peoples in the Near East. Explain what had led up to this moment and what was at stake in the conflict.

### Chapter Seven

1. What was Jehoiakim's problem in the latter half of 605 BCE?
2. How did Jeremiah complicate Jehoiakim's situation?
3. How did the notables in the court respond to Jeremiah's critique?
4. Jehoiakim made a fateful decision. How was it fateful and why did Jehoiakim think it was a good move?
5. The Babylonian response to the king's decision had significant consequences for the country of Judah. Describe the fateful response of the Babylonians and how it affected the country.
6. What was Jeremiah's advice to the folks who were carried off to Babylon?

### Chapter Eight

1. Describe Ezekiel's call by Yahweh, what he saw, how he was affected. How much chance did he have to refuse the call?
2. What was the major concern of Ezekiel's prophetic activity in this early period of his captivity?
3. How did the second appearance of the divine apparition to Ezekiel seem to portend something ominous ahead?

# Appendix

4. What did Ezekiel's story of the adulterous lover seem to say to the Children of Israel?

## Chapter Nine

1. How did Jeremiah respond to the conference of kings that had been called by Zedekiah, the new king of Judah?
2. What was the debate with Hananiah really about?
3. What brought about Jeremiah's emotional collapse?
4. What was the perverse behavior of the slave masters toward their slaves during the siege?
5. What was the difficulty Jeremiah had in trying to claim his property?
6. How many times has Jeremiah been abused so far in the story? Why were so many people opposed to him?
7. Describe the way Zedekiah related to Jeremiah.

## Chapter Ten

1. As life in the city became ever more unbearable under the siege, Jeremiah was told to do something that required courage. How was it an act of courage for him to obey?
2. How did the messages of the prophets, Ezekiel in Babylon and Jeremiah in Judah, compare as the city of Jerusalem came to the edge of total collapse?

## Chapter Eleven

1. Describe what the poems of the survivors reveal about what the siege of the city and its subsequent destruction had been like.
2. For the writers of these dirges, how had Yahweh figured in the destruction of their world?

Topics for Discussion

## *Chapter Twelve*

1. The supposition that a descendant of David should always be on the throne of Judah was still alive despite the collapse of the city and the blinding of the king. How did it play out among the refugees of the city who had gathered in Mizpah?

2. Why did many of the members of the community at Mizpah decide to flee to Egypt? How did Jeremiah respond to this plan?

## *Chapter Thirteen*

1. In the aftermath of the destruction of Jerusalem what kinds of issues did the refugees scattered throughout Babylon have to work out?

2. How did the explanation for the disaster that the refugees came to accept differ from what one might expect? What considerations seem to have influenced their explanation?

3. How did the critiques of the prophets of Yahweh give the refugees reason to hope for better times ahead?

## *Chapter Fourteen*

1. After several decades of exile in Babylon a great conqueror possessed the region. About the same time a new prophetic voice appeared offering encouragement. What are the problems in identifying who this person was?

2. How did the mysterious prophet's messages to the Israelite exiles relate to the policies of the new conqueror?

## *Chapter Fifteen*

1. How was the mindset of the new arrivals in Canaan different from that of those who had been forced out the city by the Babylonian attack several decades earlier?

2. How did the early arrivals to the region of the burned city put in motion their new vision of themselves and their relation to Yahweh? What were the problems that soon arose? Why did they have to suspend their building activities?

3. What happened that allowed the new community of Jews in Canaan to resume their building activities?

4. In this chapter there are two formulations of what became the standard narrative of the Jews who had established themselves in the environment of the burned city. One was expressed in their request for permission to return to work on a new temple. The other was expressed in the ritual of confession and dedication to Yahweh that was led by Ezra and Nehemiah. In brief, what was the standard narrative?

## *Chapter Sixteen*

1. Describe the literary activities of the anonymous religious authorities who produced a body of texts for the benefit of the Jewish community that formed in Canaan after 539 BCE.

2. How did the work of these anonymous scholars compare with the literary activities of other societies during this period?

## *Chapter Seventeen*

1. Describe the ways in which the perspective of the Jewish community that formed in and around Jerusalem differed from that of their ancestors.

2. How did Yahweh figure in their understanding of themselves, their history, and their hopes for the future?

3. Discuss the various meanings that came to be associated with the Babylonian attack on Jerusalem in 587 BCE.

4. In what sense could the unique experience of the Israelites exemplify the way human beings cope with the problems of living in a conflicted world?

# Bibliography

Abernethy, Andrew T., et al., eds. *Isaiah and Imperial Context: The Book of Isaiah in the Times of Empire*. Eugene, OR: Pickwick, 2013.

Abrahamowitz, Sharon A. "The Poor Have Become Rich, and the Rich Have Become Poor: Collective Trauma in the Guinean Languette." *Social Science & Medicine* 61.10 (2005) 2106–18.

Adey, John W. "Social and Historical Aspects of the Lachish Letters." Academia.com (2014). https://www.academia.edu/9690335/Social_and_Historical_Aspects_of_the_Lachish_Letters.

Ahmed, Sami Said. *Southern Mesopotamia in the Time of Ashurbanipal*. Boston: de Gruyter Mouton, 1968. https://doi.org/10.1515/9783111396170.

Albertz, Rainer. *A History of Israelite Religion in the Old Testament Period*. Vol. 1, *From the Beginnings to the End of the Monarchy*. Louisville, KY: Westminster John Knox, 1994.

———. *Israel in Exile: The History and Literature of the Sixth Century B.C.E.* Atlanta: Society of Biblical Literature, 2003.

———. "Open-Mindedness for Understanding the Formation of the Pentateuch: The Challenge of Exodus 19–20." In *Open-Mindedness in the Bible and Beyond: A Volume of Studies in Honour of Bob Becking*, edited by Marjo Korpel et al., 1–9. London: Bloomsbury, 2015.

Ankersmit, Frank, et al. *Refiguring Hayden White*. Palo Alto, CA: Stanford University Press, 2009.

Bailey, F. G. *Prevalence of Deceit*. Ithaca, NY: Cornell University Press, 1991.

Barstad, Hans M. "After the 'Myth of the Empty Land': Major Challenges in the Study of Neo-Babylonian Judah." In *Judah and the Judeans in the Neo-Babylonian Period*, edited by Oded Lipschits and Joseph Henkinsapp, 3–20. Winona Lake, IN: Eisenbrauns, 2003.

Baumard, Nicolas, et al. "What Changed during the Axial Age: Cognitive Styles or Reward Systems?" *Communicative & Integrative Biology* 8.5 (2015). https://www.tandfonline.com/action/showCitFormats?doi=10.1080/19420889.2015.1046657.

Bellah, Robert N. *Religion in Human Evolution: From the Paleolithic to the Axial Age*. Cambridge: Harvard University Press, 2011.

Berges, Ulrich. *The Book of Isaiah: Its Composition and Final Form*. Sheffield, UK: Phoenix, 2012.

Berlin, Isaiah. Introduction to *Four Essays on Liberty*, xxx–xxxi. Oxford: Oxford University Press, 1969.

# Bibliography

Blenkinsopp, Joseph. *Isaiah 40–55: A New Translation with Introduction and Commentary*. Anchor Bible. New York: Doubleday, 2002.

———. *Isaiah 56–66*. Anchor Bible. New York: Doubleday, 2003.

Bloch-Smith, Elizabeth. "Assyrians Abet Israelite Cultic Reforms: Sennacherib and the Centralization of the Israelite Cult." In *Exploring the Longue Durée: Essays in Honor of Lawrence E. Stager*, edited by J. David Schloen, 35–44. Winona Lake, IN: Eisenbrauns, 2009.

Block, Daniel I. *The Book of Ezekiel: Chapters 1–24*. Grand Rapids: Eerdmans, 1997.

Boase, Elizabeth, "Constructing Meaning in the Face of Suffering: Theodicy in Lamentations." *Vetus Testamentum* 58.4/5 (2008) 449–68. http://www.jstor.org/stable/20504424.

Borschel-Dan, Amanda. "Archaeologist Claims to Find Oldest Hebrew Text in Israel, Including the Name of God." *The Times of Israel*, March 24, 2022. https://www.timesofisrael.com/archaeologist-claims-to-find-oldest-hebrew-text-in-israel-including-the-name-of-god/.

Bourdieu, Pierre. *Outline of a Theory of Practice*. Cambridge: Cambridge University Press, 1977.

Bright, John. *A History of Israel*. 2nd ed. Philadelphia: Westminster, 1972.

———. *Jeremiah: A Commentary*. Anchor Bible. Garden City, NY: Doubleday, 1965.

Brueggemann, Walter. *Hopeful Imagination: Prophetic Forces in Exile*. Philadelphia: Fortress, 1986.

———. *An Introduction to the Old Testament: The Canon and Christian Imagination*. Louisville, KY: Westminster John Knox, 2003.

———. *Like Fire in the Bones: Listening for the Prophetic Word in Jeremiah*. Edited by Patrick D. Miller. Indianapolis: Fortress, 2006.

———. *Theology of the Old Testament: Testimony, Dispute, Advocacy*. Minneapolis: Fortress, 1997.

Canfield, Robert L. "Efficacy and Hierarchy: Examples from Afghanistan." In *Ethnicity, Authority, and Power in Central Asia: New Games Great and Small*, edited by Robert L. Canfield and Gabriele Paleczek, 196–247. London: Routledge, 2010.

Carley, Keith W. *The Book of the Prophet Ezekiel*. Cambridge: Cambridge University Press, 1974.

Carr, David M. *Holy Resilience: The Bible's Traumatic Origins*. New Haven, CT: Yale University Press, 2014.

Clements, R. E. "The Prophecies of Isaiah and the Fall of Jerusalem in 587 B.C." *Vetus Testamentum* 30.4 (1980) 421–36.

Clifford, Richard J., SJ. "Isaiah." In *New Interpreters Bible Dictionary*, vol. 3, edited by Katharine Doob Sakenfeld, 75–91. Nashville: Abingdon, 2009.

Collins, Frances. *The Language of God*. New York: Simon and Schuster, 2006.

Cook, Stephen L. *The Social Roots of Biblical Yahwism: Studies in Biblical Literature*. Atlanta: Society of Biblical Literature, 2004.

Cross, Andrew. "Child Sacrifice at the Tophet." *Arcalog*, August 22, 2012. http://www.arcalog.com/papers/the-tophet-child-sacrifice.

Cunningham, George C. *Decoding the Language of God: Can a Scientist Really Be a Believer?* Amherst, NY: Prometheus, 2010.

David, Ariel. "An Archaeological Mystery: Why Ancient Hebrews Made Figurines of Naked Women." *Haaritz*, December 2, 2020. https://www.haaretz.com/

# Bibliography

archaeology/2020-12-02/ty-article-magazine/.highlight/why-ancient-hebrews-made-figurines-of-naked-women/0000017f-e850-da9b-a1ff-ec7f57bd0000.

Demsky, Aaron. "Who Came First, Ezra or Nehemiah? The Synchronistic Approach." *Hebrew Union College Annual* 65 (1994) 1–19. https://www.jstor.org/stable/23508526.

Diamond, A. R. Pete, et al., eds. *Troubling Jeremiah*. Library of Hebrew Bible / Old Testament Studies 260. London: Bloomsbury Academic, 1999.

Domańska, Ewa. "Philosophy and Introduction." In *Refiguring Hayden White*, edited by Frank Ankersmit et al., 11–13. Palo Alto, CA: Stanford University Press, 2009.

Duguid, Iain M. *Ezekiel and the Leaders of Israel*. Leiden: Brill, 1994.

Dworkin, Ronald. *Religion without God*. Cambridge: Harvard University Press, 2013.

Easton, Matthew George. *Illustrated Bible Dictionary*. Bible Study Tools Study Library, 1823–94. https://www.biblestudytools.com/dictionaries/eastons-bible-dictionary/.

Fantalkin, Alexander. *Why Did Nebuchadnezzar II Destroy Ashkelon in Kislev 604 B.C.E.?* Winona Lake, IN: Eisenbrauns, 2011.

Fox, Richard G. *Gandhian Utopia: Experiments with Culture*. Boston: Beacon, 1989.

Fretheim, Terrence E. *Deuteronomic History*. Interpreting Biblical Texts. Nashville: Abingdon, 1983.

Friedman, Richard Elliott. *Who Wrote the Bible?* New York: Harper Collins, 1997.

Frye, Northrup. *The Great Code: The Bible and Literature*. New York: Harcourt Brace Jovanovich, 1982.

Geertz, Clifford. "Anti Anti-Relativism." *American Anthropologist* 86.2 (1984) 263–78.

———. "Deep Play: Notes on the Balinese Cockfight." In *The Interpretation of Cultures*, 412–53. New York: Basic, 1973.

Glass, Benjamin. "Judean Mindset throughout the Babylonian Exile: Literary Study of Jeremiah and Baruch in Historical Context." *Jewish Bible Quarterly* 43.1 (2015) 1–46. https://jbqnew.jewishbible.org/assets/Uploads/431/jbq_431_glassjeremiah.pdf.

Goodman, Martin. *A History of Judaism*. Princeton, NJ: Princeton University, 2018.

Gottwald, Norman K. *The Hebrew Bible: A Brief Socio-Literary Introduction*. Minneapolis: Fortress, 2008.

Goulder, M. D. *The Psalms of the Return. Book V, Psalms 107–50*. Studies in the Psalter 4. Library of Hebrew Bible / Old Testament Studies. London: Bloomsbury, 1998.

Green, Alberto R. "The Fate of Jehoiakim." *Andrews University Seminary Studies* 20.2 (1982) 103–9.

Hadjiev, Tevdar S. "Zephaniah and the 'Book of the Twelve' Hypothesis." In *Prophecy and the Prophets in Ancient Israel: Proceedings of the Oxford Old Testament Seminar*, edited by John Day, 325–28. Library of Hebrew Bible / Old Testament Studies 531. London: T. & T. Clark, 2012.

Halbwachs, Maurice. *On Collective Memory*. Chicago: University of Chicago Press, 1992.

Halpern, Baruch. *The First Historians: The Hebrew Bible and History*. San Francisco: Harper and Row, 1984.

Haupert, Raymond S. "The Lachish Letters." *Biblical Archaeologist* 1.4 (1938) 30–32. https://doi.org/10.2307/3209237.

Hirsch, Emil G., et al. "Nebuchadnezzar." In *Jewish Encyclopedia* (1904) 200–203. https://www.jewishencyclopedia.com/articles/11407-nebuchadnezzar.

Hodgson, Marshall. *The Venture of Islam: Conscience and History in a World Civilization*. Vol. 1, *The Classical Age of Islam*. Chicago: University of Chicago Press, 1974.

Hoffman, Joel. *In the Beginning: A Short History of the Hebrew Language*. New York: New York University Press, 2004.

# Bibliography

Hutton, Rodney H. "Jeremiah." In *The New Oxford Annotated Bible: New Revised Edition with the Apocrypha*. 5th ed. Oxford: Oxford University Press, 2010.

Irving, Andrew. "Towards an Anthropology of Interior Dialogue." *Medical Anthropology Quarterly* 25.1 (2011) 22–44.

Jackson, Michael D. *The Politics of Storytelling: Violence, Transgression, and Intersubjectivity*. Copenhagen: Museum Tusculanum, 2002.

James, Wendy. *The Listening Ebony: Moral Knowledge, Religion, and Power among the Uduk of Sudan*. Oxford: Clarendon, 1988.

Jaspers, Karl. *The Future of Mankind*. Chicago: University of Chicago Press, 1961.

Jonker, Louis C. *1 & 2 Chronicles*. Understanding the Bible Commentary Series. Grand Rapids: Baker, 2013.

Josephus. *The Works of Josephus: Complete and Unabridged*. Translated by William Whiston. Peabody, MA: Hendrickson, 1987.

Kaiser, Walter C., Jr. *Exodus*. Grand Rapids: Zondervan, 2017.

Keimer, Kyle Henry. "The Socioeconomic Impact of Hezekiah's Preparations for Rebellion." PhD diss., University of California, Berkeley, 2011.

Klein, Ralph H. "Ezekiel at the Dawn of the Twenty-First Century." Introduction to *The Book of Ezekiel: Theological and Anthropological Perspectives*, edited by Margaret S. Odell and John T. Strong, 1–11. Atlanta: Society of Biblical Literature, 2000.

Knight, Douglas A. "Deuteronomy and the Deuteronomists." In *Old Testament Interpretation: Essays in Honour of Gene M. Tucker*, edited by James Luther Mays et al., 61–79. London: T. & T. Clark, 1995.

Kołakowski, Leszek. "The Idolatry of Politics." In *Modernity on Endless Trial*, 146–61. Chicago: University of Chicago Press, 1990.

"Lachish Letters." InfoGalactic planetary knowledge core. Google, accessed October 5, 2023. https://infogalactic.com/info/Lachish_letters.

Langer, Suzanne. *Philosophy in a New Key*. Cambridge: Harvard University Press, 1942.

Lester, Rebecca. "Back from the Edge of Existence: A Critical Anthropology of Trauma." *Transcultural Psychiatry* 50.5 (2013) 753–62.

Levenson, Jon D. *The Hebrew Bible, the Old Testament, and Historical Criticism: Jews and Christians in Biblical Studies*. Louisville, KY: Westminster John Knox, 1993.

Levinson, Bernard M. "Deuteronomy." In *The New Oxford Annotated Bible: New Revised Edition with the Apocrypha*, 247–49. Oxford: Oxford University, 2010.

Lipschits, Oded. *The Fall and Rise of Jerusalem: Judah under Babylonian Rule*. Winona Lake, IN: Eisenbrauns, 2005.

Lipschits, Oded, and Joseph Blenkinsop, eds. *Judea and the Judeans in the Neo-Babylonian Period*. Winona Lake, IN: Eisenbrauns, 2003.

Lloyd, Alan B. "The Late Period." In *The Oxford History of Ancient Egypt*, edited by Ian Shaw, 369–94. Oxford: Oxford University Press, 2002.

Malamat, Abraham. "The Last Kings of Judah and the Fall of Jerusalem: An Historical-Chronological Study." *Israel Exploration Journal* 18.3 (1968) 137–56.

McKenzie, Stephen L. "1 Samuel." In *The New Oxford Annotated Bible*, 399–400. Oxford: Oxford University Press, 2001.

Middlemas, Jill. *The Templeless Age: An Introduction to the History, Literature, and Theology of the "Exile."* Louisville, KY: Westminster John Knox, 2007.

Midgley, Mary. *Heart and Mind: The Varieties of Moral Experience*. London: Methuen, 1981.

# Bibliography

Miller, J. Maxwell, and John H. Hayes. *A History of Ancient Israel and Judah*. Philadelphia: Westminster, 1986.
de Moor, Johannes Cornelis. *The Rise of Jahwism: The Roots of Israelite Monotheism*. 2nd ed. Bibliotheca Ephemeridum Theologicarum Lovaniensium, 91. Leuven: Peeters, 1997.
Montefiore, Simon Sebag. *Jerusalem: The Biography*. New York: Random House, 2012.
Murdoch, Iris. *Metaphysics as a Guide to Morals*. New York: Penguin, 1994.
———. *The Sovereignty of Good*. London: Routledge and Kegan Paul, 1970.
Neimeyer, Robert A., et al. "A Social Constructionist Account of Grief: Loss and the Narration of Meaning." *Death Studies* 38 (2021) 485–98.
*New Bible Dictionary*. 3rd ed. Edited by J. D. Douglas et al. Downers Grove, IL: InterVarsity, 1996.
*New English Translation of the Bible*. NET. Dallas: Biblical Studies.
Norman, Sonya B., and Shira Maguen. "Moral Injury." *National Center for PTSD*, July 26, 2021. https://www.ptsd.va.gov/professional/treat/cooccurring/moral_injury.asp.
Noth, Martin. *The Deuteronomistic History*. Journal of the Study of the Old Testament Supplement Series 15. Sheffield, UK: Sheffield Academic, 1981.
———. *History of Israel: Biblical History*. 2nd ed. London: Adam and Black, 1958.
O'Connor, Kathleen M. *Jeremiah: Pain and Promise*. Minneapolis: Fortress, 2011.
———. *Lamentations & the Tears of the World*. Maryknoll, NY: Orbis, 2002.
Ortner, Sherry. *High Religion: A Cultural and Political History of Sherpa Buddhism*. Princeton, NJ: Princeton University Press, 1989.
Oswalt, John N. *The Book of Isaiah: Chapters 40–66*. Grand Rapids: Eerdmans, 1998.
Paul, Shalom. *Isaiah 40–66: A Commentary*. Eerdmans Critical Commentary. Grand Rapids: Eerdmans, 2012.
Ritner, R. K. *The Mechanics of Ancient Egyptian Magical Practice*. Chicago: University of Chicago Press, 2008.
Rofé, Alexander. *Deuteronomy: Issues and Interpretation*. London: T. & T. Clark, 2002.
Rollston, Christopher A. "The Rise of Monotheism in Ancient Israel: Biblical and Epigraphic Evidence." *Stone-Campbell Journal* 6 (2003) 95–115.
Sahlins, Marshall. *Apologies to Thucydides: Understanding History as Culture and Vice Versa*. Chicago: University of Chicago, 2004.
———. *Historical Metaphors and Mythical Realities: Structure in the Early History of the Sandwich Islands Kingdom*. Association for Social Anthropology in Oceania, Special Publication No. 1. Ann Arbor: University of Michigan Press, 1981.
———. *Islands of History*. Chicago: University of Chicago Press, 1985.
Schniedewind, William M. *How the Bible Became a Book* Cambridge: Cambridge University Press, 2004.
———. "Scripturalization in Ancient Judah." In *Contextualizing Israel's Sacred Writings: Ancient Literacy, Orality, and Literary Production*, edited by Brian B. Schmidt, 305–21. Atlanta: SBL, 2015.
Sewell, William H. *Logics of History: Social Theory and Social Transformation*. Chicago: University of Chicago Press, 2005.
Shea, William H. "Sennacherib's Description of Lachish and of Its Conquest." *Andrews University Seminary Studies* 26.2 (1988) 171–80.
Smith, Mark S. *The Early History of God: Yahweh and the Other Deities in Ancient Israel*. Grand Rapids: Eerdmans, 2002.

# Bibliography

———. *The Origins of Biblical Monotheism: Israel's Polytheistic Background and the Ugaritic Texts*. Oxford: Oxford University Press, 2001.

Sperling, David S. "An Arslan Tash Incantation: Interpretations and Implications." *Hebrew Union College Annual* 53 (1982) 1–10.

Stein, Dina. "Collapsing Structures: Discourse and the Destruction of the Temple in the Babylonian Talmud." *Jewish Quarterly Review* 98.1 (2008) 1–28.

Steinman, Andrew E. "A Chronological Note: The Return of the Exiles under Sheshbazzar and Zerubbabel Ezra 1–2." *JETS Journal of the Evangelical Society* 51.3 (2008) 513–22.

Stern, Ephraim. "The Babylonian Gap: The Archaeological Reality." *Journal for the Study of the Old Testament* 28 (2004) 273–77.

Stuart-Glennie, John. *The Modern Revolution, Proemia 1: Pilgrim Memories*. London: Longmans, Green, 1876.

Stulman, Louis. *Jeremiah*. Abingdon Old Testament Commentaries. Nashville: Abingdon, 2005.

Sweeney, Marvin A. "Introduction to the Prophetic Books." In *The New Oxford Annotated Bible. New Revised Standard Version with the Apocrypha*, edited by Michael D. Coogan et al., 961–67. Oxford: Oxford University Press, 2010.

Taylor, Charles. *Sources of the Self: The Making of Modern Identity*. Cambridge: Harvard University Press, 1989.

Telban, Borut. *Dancing through Time: A Sepik Cosmology*. Oxford Studies in Social Anthropology. Oxford: Oxford University Press, 1999.

Torrey, C. C. "The Edomites in Southern Judah." *Journal of Biblical Literature* 17.1 (1898), 16–20. https://www.jstor.ohrg/stable/3268802.

Turner, Victor. *Schism and Continuity in an African Society: A Study of Ndembu Village Life*. Manchester: Manchester University Press, 1957.

Vaknin, Yoav, et al. "Reconstructing Biblical Military Campaigns Using Geomagnetic Field Data." *PNAS Proceedings of the National Academy of Sciences* 119.44 (2022) 1–7.

Waldron, Jeremy. "How Politics Are Haunted by the Past." *New York Review of Books*, February 13, 2013, 41.

Weil, Simone. *The Need for Roots: Prelude towards a Declaration of Duties towards Mankind*. London: Routledge, 1952.

Weir, Cecil J. Mullo. "Aspects of the Book of Ezekiel." *Vetus Testamentum* 2.2 (1952) 97–112.

White, Haden. *Metahistory: The Historical Imagination in Nineteenth-Century Europe*. Baltimore: Johns Hopkins University Press, 1973.

Williamson, H. G. M. *The Book Called Isaiah: Deutero-Isaiah's Role in Its Composition and Redaction*. Oxford: Clarendon, 1994.

Wilson, R. Dick. "Sheshbazzar." In *International Standard Bible Encyclopedia*, edited by James Orr. Bible Study Tools. Chicago: Howard-Severance, 1915. https://www.biblestudytools.com/encyclopedias/isbe/sheshbazzar.html.

Winkle, Ross E. "Jeremiah's Seventy Years for Babylon: A Re-assessment." *Andrews University Seminary Studies* 25.2 (1987) 201–14.

———. "Jeremiah's Seventy Years for Babylon: A Re-assessment. Part II." *Andrews University Seminary Studies* 25.3 (1987) 289–99.

Wiseman, D. J. "New Babylonian Chronicles." *British Museum Quarterly* 21.2 (1957) 48–50.

# Bibliography

Zeitlin, Irving M. *Ancient Judaism: Biblical Criticism from Max Weber to the Present.* Cambridge: Polity, 1984.

Zertal, Adam. *A Nation Born: The Altar on Mount Ebal and the Birth of Israel.* Ariel, Israel: Samaria and Jordan Rift Valley Survey Association, 2018.

# Biblical Citations Index

## Genesis
| | |
|---|---|
| 12:2–3 | 17 |
| 13:14–18 | 17 |
| 14:17–24 | 17 |
| 15:1–20 | 17 |

## Exodus
| | |
|---|---|
| 19:05 | 19 |
| 20:4–6 | 18 |
| 20:23 | 18 |
| 20:23—23:29 | 26 |
| 23:20 | 18 |

## Leviticus
| | |
|---|---|
| 26:14–26 | 31 |

## Deuteronomy
| | |
|---|---|
| 6:1–3 | 34 |
| 6:4–5 | 18 |
| 18:9 | 33 |
| 26:16–19 | 30 |
| 28:15–44 | 31 |

## Joshua
| | |
|---|---|
| 24:14–15 | 19 |

## Judges
| | |
|---|---|
| 5 | 17 |
| 17:5 | 20 |
| 18:14, 24, 30 | 20 |

## 1 Samuel
| | |
|---|---|
| 7:3 | 20 |
| 19:13 | 20 |

## 2 Samuel
| | |
|---|---|
| 5:21 | |
| 7:5 | 20 |

## 1 Kings
| | |
|---|---|
| 9:8–9 | 20 |
| 11:4–6 | 20 |
| 12:26–33 | 20 |
| 14:22–23 | 20 |
| 18:20–40 | 20 |
| 22:24–47 | 20 |

## 2 Kings
| | |
|---|---|
| 11:17–18 | 20 |
| 12:04 | 20 |
| 13:06 | 20 |
| 15:24 | 20 |
| 16 | 22 |
| 16:3, 10–19 | 20 |
| 17 | 158 |
| 17:1–6 | 23 |
| 17:7–13, 41 | 36 |
| 17:7–17 | 20, 158 |
| 17:18–19 | 158 |
| 17:23–24 | 23 |
| 17:30–41 | 20 |
| 17:36 | 36 |
| 18:4 | 20 |

## Biblical Citations Index

### 2 Kings *(continued)*

| | |
|---|---|
| 18:13–16 | 76 |
| 21:18, 21 | 20 |
| 21:24 | 35 |
| 22:3 | 29 |
| 22:8 | 30 |
| 22:11–13 | 30 |
| 22:16–17 | 21 |
| 22:16–19 | 31 |
| 22:17 | 19 |
| 23:2 | 30 |
| 23:5 27 | 19 |
| 23:4–16 | 19 |
| 23:4–24 | 20 |
| 23:31–36 | 46 |
| 23:35 | 52 |
| 24:2 | 65 |
| 24:6 | 66 |
| 24:9 | 66 |
| 24:12 | 66 |
| 24:13–14 | 67 |
| 24:14 | 149 |
| 24:17 | 85 |
| 25:1–2 | 89 |
| 25:3 | 99 |
| 25:7 | 106 |
| 25:21 | 158 |
| 25:27 | 85 |
| 25:22–26 | 118 |
| 25:26 | 119 |
| 25:27–30 | 135 |

### 1 Chronicles

| | |
|---|---|
| 9:1–34 | 147 |
| 13:15 | 46 |

### 2 Chronicles

| | |
|---|---|
| 13:9 | 19 |
| 34:1–3, 8 | 29 |
| 34:3–7 | 32 |
| 34:6–7 | 32 |
| 35:22 | 46 |
| 36:1 | 46 |
| 36:6 | 65 |
| 36:11–20 | 3 |
| 36:23 | 137 |

### Ezra

| | |
|---|---|
| 1:2–4 | 137 |
| 1:8, 11 | 145 |
| 4:2 | 149 |
| 4–6 | 150 |
| 5:11–15 | 153 |
| 5:14 | 145 |

### Nehemiah

| | |
|---|---|
| 2:13–17 | 149 |
| 2:17 | 149 |
| 7:4 | 146 |
| 7:60 | 149 |
| 7:73—8:8 | 154 |
| 9 (selections) | 155 |
| 9:36 | 155 |
| 11:1–4 | 146 |

### Psalms

| | |
|---|---|
| 8:13 | 168 |
| 16:11 | 7 |
| 44 | 111 |
| 66 | 158 |
| 74 | 158 |
| 74 (selections) | 115 |
| 74:4–8 | 113 |
| 78:58–62 | 19 |
| 79:1–8 | 113 |
| 80 | 111 |
| 126:1–3a | 146 |
| 137 (selections) | 114 |
| 146–50 | 146 |

### Isaiah

| | |
|---|---|
| 1:13–14 | 169 |
| 1:16b–17 | 169 |
| 3:14–16 | 170 |
| 10:1, 2 | 25 |
| 10:1–3 | 170 |
| 11:12 | 132 |
| 15:2, 3 | 14 |
| 30:8–14 | 138 |
| 30:18 | 128 |
| 36–37 | 24 |
| 36:5–10 | 25 |
| 40–55 | 139 |

## Biblical Citations Index

| | | | |
|---|---|---|---|
| 40 (selections) | 141 | 1:10 | 120 |
| 40:1–2 | 140 | 1:11–15 | 50 |
| 40:10–12 | 140 | 1:16 | 127 |
| 40:27 | 143 | 1:17–19 | 50 |
| 40:29–31 | 143 | 2:1–5 | 53 |
| 40:9 | 143 | 2:20–25 | 53 |
| 41:4–10 (selections) | 172 | 2:26–27 | 66 |
| 41:8–9 | 144 | 2:28 | 54 |
| 41:10 | 142 | 2:30 | 54 |
| 41:11–13 | 143 | 2:32 | 54 |
| 41:18–20 | 144 | 2:34 | 54 |
| 42:1–9 | 144 | 3:5 | 54 |
| 42:14—43:4 (selections) | 142 | 3:6–8 | 42 |
| 42 16 | 144 | 3:6–10 | 51 |
| 43:2–11 | 142 | 3:8 | 129 |
| 43:4–7, 19b–21 | 143 | 3:12 | 54 |
| 43:5–7 | 143 | 3:18 | 132 |
| 43:22–25 | 142 | 6:6b–7 | 127 |
| 44:6b–7 | 141 | 7:2–15 | 55 |
| 44:7–9 | 142 | 7:3–11 | 55 |
| 44:21–23 | 142, 171 | 7:15 | 127 |
| 44:27 | 135 | 7:6, 9, 18 | 127 |
| 44:28 | 141 | 7:27 | 56 |
| 44:28b | 144 | 7:30–33 | 56 |
| 45:4–6 | 141 | 8:9–13 | 56 |
| 48:18 | 168 | 11:19–22 | 58 |
| 48:18 | 145 | 11:10 | 127 |
| 49–54 | 144 | 11:21 | 58 |
| 49:1–5 | 145 | 13:10 | 127 |
| 49:14 | 135 | 16:11, 13 | 127 |
| 49:14–15 | 143 | 19 | 91 |
| 49:15–16a | 144 | 19:13 | 127 |
| 50:1 | 135 | 20:1–6 | 91 |
| 50:4–8 | 144 | 20:7–10 | 91 |
| 51 | 146 | 20:11–18 | 92 |
| 51:3 | 146 | 21:1–10 | 90 |
| 52:7–8 | 146 | 21:6–8 | 90 |
| 52:13—53:12 | 144 | 22:2–22 | 87 |
| 53:4–12 | 144 | 22:3 | 51 |
| 58:3b–5 | 151 | 22:9 | 127 |
| 58:6–9 | 151 | 22:10 | 51 |
| 64:8—65:3 | 150 | 22:15 | 52 |
| 64:9b–12 | 150 | 22:15–19 | 52 |
| 64:10–11 | 150 | 22:18–28 | 65 |
| | | 22:29 | 69 |

### Jeremiah

| | |
|---|---|
| 1:5–8 | 49 |

## Jeremiah (continued)

| | |
|---|---|
| 23:3–8 | 67 |
| 23:6 | 132 |
| 24:4–10 | 67 |
| 25:1–14 | 63 |
| 25:6 | 127 |
| 25:11 | 64 |
| 26:8–19 | 57 |
| 26:2–23 | 57 |
| 26:24 | 58 |
| 26:30 | 64 |
| 27 | 86 |
| 27:2–22 | 87 |
| 28:1–4 | 87 |
| 28:10–11 | 87 |
| 28:13–17 | 87 |
| 29:1–23 | 88 |
| 29:5–19 | 68, 69 |
| 29:10 | 121 |
| 29:10–14 | 68 |
| 29:14 | 131 |
| 30:3 | 132 |
| 30:10 | 68 |
| 31:3 | 130 |
| 31:3–6 | 171 |
| 31:3–17 | 69 |
| 31:31 | 132 |
| 3:31–34 | 131 |
| 32:3–4 | 93 |
| 32:15 | 130 |
| 32:16–44 | 100 |
| 32:29 | 127 |
| 32:32–35 | 33 |
| 33:5–26 | 101 |
| 33:7 | 130 |
| 33:14 | 132 |
| 34:7 | 92, 93 |
| 34:8–11 | 94 |
| 34:13b–22 | 94 |
| 35:11 | 65 |
| 35:15 | 127 |
| 36:2–3 | 62 |
| 36:1–26 | 63 |
| 36:16 | 63 |
| 36:30–32 | 65 |
| 37–38 | 95 |
| 37:7b–10 | 93 |
| 37:8 | 95 |
| 37:11–12 | 95 |
| 37:12–16 | 95 |
| 37:17–21 | 96 |
| 38 | 98 |
| 38:2–13 | 97 |
| 38:4–6 | 96 |
| 38:14–20 | 97 |
| 39:2–7 | 107 |
| 39:12—40:6 | 118 |
| 39:16b–18 | 98 |
| 39:17–18 | 95 |
| 40:7–8 | 117 |
| 40:12 | 118 |
| 40:13–16 | 118 |
| 41 | 118 |
| 41:5 | 108 |
| 42 | 119 |
| 42:11 | 168 |
| 43 | 119 |
| 44 | 120 |
| 44:3, 5, 8, 15 | 127 |
| 46:7–26 | 65 |
| 50:2–5 | 88 |
| 51:61–64 | 88 |
| 52:30 | 107, 121 |

## Lamentations

| | |
|---|---|
| 1:1 | 110 |
| 1:5b, 12b, 15 | 114 |
| 1:6, 7 | 112 |
| 1:8 | 115 |
| 1:10 | 113 |
| 1:11 | 111 |
| 1:11–13 | 113 |
| 1:12–15 | 129 |
| 1:14–17 | 114 |
| 1:18 | 115 |
| 2:1–2 | 114 |
| 2:12 | 111 |
| 2:15 | 113 |
| 2:17 | 160 |
| 2:19 | 112 |
| 2:20 | 111 |
| 2:21 | 112 |
| 3:22–26 | 115 |
| 3:31–32 (selections) | 115 |

# Biblical Citations Index

| | |
|---|---|
| 3:33 | 168 |
| 3:40–42 | 115, 134 |
| 4:4 | 112 |
| 4:5 | 112 |
| 4:8 | 112 |
| 4:9 | 112 |
| 4:10 | 112 |
| 4:11 | 114 |
| 4:12 | 113 |
| 5:11–13 | 112 |

## Ezekiel

| | |
|---|---|
| 1:1 | 171 |
| 2–3 | 72 |
| 3:5–9 | 73 |
| 4:1–8 | 73 |
| 5:7–17 | 74 |
| 6:3b–7 | 74 |
| 8 | 105 |
| 8:9–10 | 75 |
| 8:14–15 | 75 |
| 8:16, 17 | 75 |
| 9:3–11 | 76 |
| 10:1–20 | 76 |
| 11:5b–13 | 77 |
| 11:16 | 126 |
| 11:16–21 | 77 |
| 11:17–18 | 131 |
| 12:12–20 | 78 |
| 12:28 | 78 |
| 14:1–6 | 78 |
| 16 | 81 |
| 16:35–42 | 128 |
| 16:59–63 | 171 |
| 17:15 | 89 |
| 18:30–32 | 81 |
| 20:4–12 | 81 |
| 20:13–20 | 82 |
| 20:21–44 | 82 |
| 20:46 | 103 |
| 21:2b–7 | 83 |
| 21:25, 26 | 83 |
| 22:3b–4 | 83 |
| 22:6–12 | 83 |
| 22:15 | 83 |
| 22::6–16 | 170 |
| 24:1 | 102 |
| 24:13 | 102 |
| 24:15–27 | 103 |
| 28:24–25 | 83 |
| 33:11 | 168 |
| 33:21 | 116 |
| 34:2–5 | 117 |
| 34:11–13 | 117 |
| 36:8 | 131 |
| 36:25–28 | 131 |
| 36:22–23 | 133 |
| 36:26 | 165 |
| 36:26–27 | 133 |
| 37 | 132 |
| 37:19–26 | 132 |
| 37:24 | 132 |
| 37:26b–28 | 133 |
| 41:1–8 | 73 |

## Daniel

| | |
|---|---|
| 1:1–4 | 67 |
| 5 | 136 |
| 9 | 134 |

## Hosea

| | |
|---|---|
| 4:1b–2 | 24 |
| 6:6 | 169 |
| 8:4b–5, 11–12, 14b | 128 |
| 8:14 | 170 |
| 10:04 | 170 |
| 11:8–11 | 130 |
| 13:7–8 | 170 |

## Joel

| | |
|---|---|
| 2:1b–11 | 40 |
| 2:12–15 | 39 |
| 2:19–27 | 41 |
| 2:28–32a | 41 |
| 3:1–3 | 130 |

## Amos

| | |
|---|---|
| 2:7–8 | 24 |
| 2:7–8, 13–16 | 129 |
| 3:2 | 172 |
| 2:6b–8 | 169 |
| 5:7–17 | 170 |
| 5:14–15 | 169 |

# Biblical Citations Index

## Amos (continued)

| | |
|---|---|
| 5:21–24 | 169 |
| 6:12b | 169 |

## Micah

| | |
|---|---|
| 1:7 | 19, 20 |
| 2:1–2 | 25 |
| 2:1–5 | 128 |
| 3:8–12 | 128 |
| 3:11 | 170 |
| 4:1–7 | 130 |
| 4:10 | 170 |
| 5:1–15 | 20 |
| 5:13 | 19, 20 |
| 6:6–8 | 169 |
| 6:11, 12 | 170 |
| 6:16 | 19, 20 |
| 7:2–6 | 170 |

## Nahum

| | |
|---|---|
| 1:1 | 27 |
| 2:2 | 127 |
| 3:19 | 27 |

## Habakkuk

| | |
|---|---|
| 1:3–4 | 38 |
| 1:5–10 | 38 |
| 1:13–15 | 38 |
| 3:2 | 39 |
| 3:2b | 172 |
| 3:7–19a | 39 |

## Zephaniah

| | |
|---|---|
| 1:1 | 37 |
| 1:4 | 27 |
| 1:4–6 | 21, 37 |
| 1:4–9 | 128 |
| 1:9 | 37 |
| 3:3–4 | 37 |
| 3:7 | 37 |
| 3:9 | 37 |
| 3:4–26 | 171 |
| 3:11–12 | 37 |
| 3:14–20 | 37 |
| 3:11–17 | 130 |

## Zechariah

| | |
|---|---|
| 1:12 | 150 |
| 2:5–9 | 150 |
| 7:2–7 | 151 |
| 7:4–14 | 151 |
| 8:18–19 | 157 |

# General Index

(Dates are BCE)

Ahaz, 22, 62
Albertz, Rainer, 9
Amon, 28
Amos, 17, 24, 26, 31, 41, 128, 156, 159, 168
Apostasy from Yahweh, Disobedience of Commandments. *See Also, Gods, Foreign; Efficacy, Forbidden Devices of; Yahweh, Yahweh's Critique of Israelite Behavior*, 20, 31, 37, 105, 160
Archaeology
  of Arslan Tash, 15
  of Jerusalem, 104, 166
  of Ras Shamra, 16
Ashurbanipal, 44
Ashur-etil-ilani, 44
Assyria, 23, 25, 27, 28, 44, 54, 60, 130
Assyrians, 13, 23, 24, 26, 27, 28, 31, 35, 44, 45, 46, 54, 59, 80, 121, 124
Axial Age, 10

Babylon, 1, 2, 3, 4, 5, 28, 38, 44, 45, 50, 60, 62–72, 77, 84–99, 102, 104–8, 113–18, 121–24, 126, 128, 131, 133, 135–37, 140–41, 148, 152–53, 158–163, 167
Babylonian exile, exiles, golah, 3, 4, 5, 36, 38, 49, 51, 67–78, 102–4, 116, 124, 127–45, 148, 151–68
Babylonians, Babylonian army, 1, 3, 4, 62, 64–66, 71, 85–88, 90, 92, 93, 94–99, 104, 106, 114, 119, 121, 127, 135, 136

Bellah, Robert, 14
Berlin, Isaiah, 8
Bright, John, 30, 66
Brueggemann, Walter, 6, 7, 162

Canaan, 8, 28, 34, 35, 37, 137, 143, 145, 147, 148, 149, 151, 153, 161, 167
Carchemish, 45, 46, 54, 58, 59, 60, 61
Commandments of Yahweh, 2, 4, 18, 19, 24, 30, 31, 36, 38, 41, 70, 72, 95, 119, 129, 133, 134, 145, 147, 154, 160, 164, 169,
Covenant of Yahweh with people of Israel, 15, 16, 18, 30, 32–36, 38, 39, 41, 70, 72, 74, 79–82, 88–101, 115, 131, 132, 161, 165–67, 171
Cyrus, 135, 136–37, 138–41, 144, 152, 153

Deuteronomy, the book of, 30, 31, 34, 35, 41, 154,
Deuteronomic history (Books of Joshua, Judges, Samuel, and Kings), 35, 148, 156–58, 160–62
Deuteronomists, 35, 36, 37, 41

Edomites, 86, 114
Efficacy, Forbidden Devices of, 11, 14, 15, 19, 20, 32, 58, 86
Egypt, Egyptian forces, 12, 16, 17, 18, 19, 22, 25, 45, 48, 57, 60, 64, 65, 81, 84, 89, 93, 119, 120, 121, 130, 159, 166,
Egyptian Pharaohs, 17, 18

# General Index

Eissfeldt, Otto, 9
Euphrates River, 111, 19, 45, 58, 88
Ezekiel, 2, 67, 70–79, 81–84, 89, 102, 105, 116, 117, 125, 127, 128, 130–133, 148, 160–62, 165, 170, 171, 177

Geertz, Clifford, 7
Gods, foreign generally, 2, 3, 4, 14, 15, 18–21, 25–26, 31, 32, 36, 37, 42, 50, 51, 54, 55, 62, 76, 86, 90, 102, 104, 105, 109, 119, 123, 127–29, 141, 168
Gods, foreign, Identified
  Ammonite, 32
  Amorite, 19
  Assyrian Gods
    Ishtar, 26
    Queen of Heaven, 105, 120, 166
    Shamash, Sun god, 26, 32, 75, 105
  Canaanite Gods
    Asherah, 15, 20, 32, 105,
    Baal, 15, 21, 29, 32, 37, 55, 90, 128
    El of the Covenant., 15
    Marduk, 15
    Moloch/Molok, god of child sacrifice, 26
    Starry Host, 21
Gods, Israelite. See Yahweh
Golah. See also Babylonian Exile; Survivors of the Attack on Jerusalem in 587. 67, 69, 71, 72, 78, 84, 88, 89, 113, 125, 133, 139, 140
Goodman, Martin, 5
Grief and Lamenting, 48, 49, 76, 83, 102, 103, 110, 111, 113, 115, 130, 157, 168

Habakkuk, 38, 39, 41, 84, 159, 172
Haggai, 152, 159
Halpern, Baruch, 8, 163
Hezekiah, 17, 20, 23, 24, 25, 29, 30, 40, 57, 59, 76, 125, 138, 156
History, Historical Writing, 1, 6, 8, 9, 19, 27, 29, 39, 122, 126, 127, 147
Historical Criticism, 5, 6, 7
Hophra (Apries), 93, 104

Hosea, 17, 24, 26, 31, 41, 128, 130, 156, 159, 162, 170
Hoshea, 22, 23
Huldah, 21, 31, 37, 41, 84
Human sacrifice. *Also see: Topheth*, 26, 55, 83, 169

Isaiah of Jerusalem, 17, 26, 138, 139, 159, 169, 170
Israel (Ephraim, Samaria) [Northern Kingdom], 2, 11, 23–25, 31, 32, 35, 50, 51, 54, 55, 67, 68, 73, 101, 128, 130, 131–33, 147, 149, 158, 159, 160, 168, 170

James, Wendy, 7
Jaspers, Karl, 10
Jeconiah, (Jehoiachin), 65, 66, 85, 87, 102, 125, 135, 163, 165, 187
Jehoahaz, 46, 47, 51
Jehoiakim, 46, 52, 54, 57, 59, 61, 64, 65, 66, 85
Jeremiah, 2, 3, 42, 47–49, 50–53, 57, 6364, 67, 69, 87, 90–92, 95, 97, 100, 119, 120, 127, 158, 159, 165
Jeremiah, Book of, 47, 48
Jordan River, 12, 34
Josephus, 106, 121
Josiah, 21, 28–31, 33–37, 38, 40–42, 44–47, 49, 51, 58, 62, 156
Judah, 11, 19, 21–29, 31, 33, 35–47, 50, 51, 54, -58, 60–68, 71, 73, 78, 104, 108, 112, 114, 117–21, 127–34, 137, 140, 145, 148, 150, 152, 156, 158, 164, 169, 170
Lamentations, Book of, 109, 110, 111, 113, 114, 134, 157, 158, 160, 161, 162, 168

Learned Authorities of the Israelites, 36, 67, 148, 156–63
Levenson, Jon, 6, 18
Lipschits, Oded, 109, 146, 152, 162,

Manasseh, 26, 27, 28, 37
Meaning(s), Significance(s), 5, 6, 9, 10, 11, 35, 48, 49, 50, 63, 73, 76, 122, 132, 136, 152, 156, 166, 172, 173

# General Index

Mesopotamia, 12, 13, 23, 44, 45, 50, 109, 124, 135, 136, 138, 161
Micah, 17, 20, 25, 26, 41, 57, 128, 130, 156, 159, 165, 169, 170
Midgley, Mary, 8
Moral imagination, Moral Sensibility, Moral Understanding, 2, 7, 8, 10, 13, 42, 51, 122, 130, 133, 144, 145, 148, 161, 164, 166, 173
Moses, 16, 18, 20, 21, 29, 30, 34, 148, 153, 154

Nabonidus, 135
Nabopolassar, 28, 44, 59
Nahum, 27, 39, 129, 159
Nebuchadnezzar, 2, 3, 60–67, 70, 85–93, 106–7, 119, 121, 152
Nebuzaradan, 106, 107, 118
Necho II, 45, 46, 47, 51, 52, 58, 59, 60, 64, 65
Nile River, Nile Delta, 11, 12
Northern Kingdom, See Israel, Israelite Kings

Pekah, 22
Perceiving, Seeing (Realizing), 7, 8, 39, 75, 113, 129, 142, 146, 147, 148, 151, 161, 164, 165, 167, 171
Prophets of Yahweh. See Amos, Ezekiel, Habakkuk, Haggai, Hosea, Huldah, Isaiah of Jerusalem, Jeremiah, Micah, Nahum, Second Isaiah, Third Isaiah, Uriah, Zechariah, Zephaniah
Psammeticus II, 44, 89
Rehoboam, 19
Repentance and Dedication to Yahweh, Formal performance, 153, 154, 155, 167
Return after exile, 69, 72, 77, 88, 115, 134, 135, 136, 138, 140, 142, 146, 147, 171

Sargon II, 23, 24, 124
Schniedewind, William M., 16, 17
Isaiah, Second, 139, 140, 146, 150, 171

Sennacherib, 24, 2526, 28, 76, 125

Shalmaneser V, 23
Sieges
 of Haran, 45
 of Jerusalem In 597, 65, 66, 157
 of Jerusalem in 588–87, 1, 24, 83, 86, 89, 90, 92–97, 99, 100, 102, 104, 106, 109, 111, 116
 of Samaria, 23
Sinsharishkun, 44
Survivors of the Attack on Jerusalem in 587 BCE. *See Also Babylonian Exile*, 2, 21, 48, 56, 67, 74, 84, 109, 110, 111, 123, 124, 129, 137, 164, 172
Syria, 16, 50, 54
Syria-Palestine, 12, 13, 14, 22, 23, 24, 28, 44, 45, 47, 50, 58–61, 64, 65, 89, 121, 161

Temple of Solomon, 26, 29, 55, 88, 103
Third Isaiah, 139, 140, 165
Tiglath-Pileser III, 22, 23
Tigris River, 12, 44, 45, 136
Topheth, site of human sacrifice in Jerusalem. *Also See: Human sacrifice*, 32, 55, 56, 90
Transcendent values, 7, 8, 9

Uriah, 57, 58, 84

Writing, Witten Down, 8, 9, 10, 11, 16, 17, 36, 39, 49, 62, 63, 65, 84, 92, 93, 129, 136, 138, 150, 156–59, 161

Yahweh, God of the Israelite ancestors. *See also, Apostasy from Yahweh Worship*
Yahweh, Agendas for His People, 130, 133, 142, 165, 168
Yahweh, Apparition to Ezekiel, 71, 76, 132
Yahweh, God of History, 27, 29, 39, 50, 71, 72, 123, 125, 129, 148, 156, 157, 162, 165, 166, 171
Yahweh, God of the Israelite Ancestors, 15, 17, 18, 28, 53, 79

# General Index

Yahweh, His Critiques of Israelite Behavior. *See Also, Prophets of Yahweh*, 54, 55, 57, 62, 72, 74–78, 83, 89, 90, 102, 119, 120, 127, 129, 150, 151, 154, 158, 169, 170

Yahweh, His Love and Mercy. *See Also Prophets of Yahweh*, 79, 80, 82, 100, 115, 117, 130, 134, 140, 142, 148, 166, 167, 170, 171, 172

Yahweh, His Name, 15, 92

Yahweh, His Personality, 18, 141, 166, 167

Yahweh, His Promises and Encouragement, 27, 39, 50, 62, 67, 68, 77, 80, 84, 88, 98, 100, 101, 116, 130, 131, 132, 133, 140, 142, 143, 144, 146, 147, 147, 151, 161, 165

Yahweh, His Punishment(s), 2, 3, 4, 20, 21, 24, 31, 36, 37, 38, 56, 64, 68, 72, 73, 76, 77, 78, 83, 86, 90, 93, 94, 96, 97, 98, 100, 102, 103, 120, 126, 127, 134, 154, 160, 170, 172

Zedekiah (597–587), 2, 3, 63, 66, 67, 78, 83, 85, 86, 88, 88–90, 93, 94, 96, 99, 106, 107, 120, 164

Zechariah, 151, 152, 157, 159

Zephaniah, 21, 37, 41, 84, 128, 130, 159, 165, 171

Zeitlin, Irving, 8, 162

www.ingramcontent.com/pod-product-compliance
Lightning Source LLC
Chambersburg PA
CBHW031356230426
43670CB00006B/565